From Web (HTML, CSS, and JavaScript) to Flutter Widgets:
A Web Developer's Guide to Flutter Apps

This book may be purchased in bulk for educational, business, fundraising, or sales promotional use.

ISBN:

Published by: Ekesy In-Outdoor Company
10B, MufutauOpeifa Street, Oke-Odo,
Ile-Epo B/Stop, Alimosho,
Lagos, Nigeria

Email: care@israeljoshua.com.ng

Tel: +234 803 815 4459, +234 813 2228 534

For information, please contact us @
care@israeljoshua.com.ng

www.israeljoshua.com.ng

Call: +234 803 815 4459

Whatsapp: +234 813 2228 534

Table of Content

Dedication

To Almighty God,
I give all the glory, honor, and praise to the Creator of the universe. Your guidance, wisdom, and grace have been the foundation of every step I take, every idea I have, and every page written. It is because of You that I have the ability to share my knowledge with others. This book, like all my other works, is a testament to Your endless love and support. Thank You for being my source of strength, for lifting me when I felt weak, and for giving me the courage to keep moving forward in the pursuit of my passions.

To My Kids,
You are the light of my life, my greatest motivation, and the reason I strive to be better each day. Watching you grow and evolve fills my heart with joy and reminds me of the importance of sharing knowledge, not just with you, but with the world. This book is dedicated to you both, with the hope that it will one day inspire you to follow your own dreams and make a positive impact in whatever field you choose. May you always stay curious, stay humble, and never stop learning.

To My Mum,
Your unwavering support, love, and belief in me have been a constant source of strength. You have shown me the value of hard work, persistence, and integrity. Every word in this book reflects the lessons you instilled in me, and every chapter is a tribute to the sacrifices you made so that I could pursue my passions. Thank you for being the foundation of who I am today. This book is a symbol of the love and gratitude I have for you.

To My Readers,
This book is for you. Whether you are just starting your journey into Flutter or looking to refine your existing skills, I hope this guide provides value, insight, and encouragement. The transition from web development with HTML, CSS, and JavaScript to Flutter may seem daunting, but it is also a rewarding challenge. My intention is to bridge that gap and show you that with the right mindset and resources, you can excel in Flutter development as you have with web development. Your dedication to learning and growing inspires me every day, and I am grateful to be a part of your learning journey.

As you work through the content of this book, I want to encourage you to be patient with yourself, to take one step at a time, and to always remember that growth comes with both triumphs and challenges. Flutter, like any other technology, takes time to master. But with persistence, you will not only become proficient but will also develop the ability to build beautiful, powerful apps.

I want to thank each of you for taking the time to read this book and for trusting me as your guide. The world of mobile app development is vast, and it is a privilege to contribute a small part of it to you. My hope is that you will take the knowledge you gain here and apply it to create apps that have a meaningful impact on your life and the lives of others.

Remember that learning is a lifelong process. Never stop seeking new knowledge, honing your skills, and improving yourself. You are capable of achieving great things, and I believe in your ability to succeed. As you go forward, may you be filled with confidence, creativity, and a deep sense of fulfillment in all that you do.

Thank you for reading, and I hope this book serves you well in your Flutter development journey. I am excited for what lies ahead for you, and I look forward to hearing about all the amazing projects you will create.

Israel Joshua Chukwubueze

Preface

My name is **Israel Joshua Chukwubueze**, formerly known as **Christopher Ekene Okade**, and I have spent over 14 years working in the field of **web** and **mobile app design** and **development**. Through my journey, I have come to appreciate the incredible potential of both the **web** and **mobile** platforms, as well as the tools and frameworks that enable developers to bring their ideas to life. Along the way, I've seen firsthand how technology evolves and how crucial it is to stay updated with the latest trends and frameworks. My passion for **writing** and **sharing** knowledge has led me to put together this guide — a resource for developers transitioning from the world of **web development** (specifically **HTML**, **CSS**, and **JavaScript**) to **Flutter**, a powerful framework for building **mobile**, **web**, and **desktop apps**.

In this book, I focus on helping **web developers** make the shift to **Flutter** with ease and confidence. I understand that learning a new framework can seem daunting, especially when it involves not only mastering a new programming language but also understanding the different development environments and paradigms. However, with the experience I've gained over the years, I've come to believe that **Flutter** offers a unique opportunity for web developers to leverage their existing skills while learning new techniques to build modern, high-performing applications.

The goal of this book is to provide a clear, structured guide to help **web developers** (who are already familiar with **HTML**, **CSS**, and **JavaScript**) **transition smoothly** into the world of **Flutter development**. You may already be well-versed in web technologies, but Flutter operates under a different paradigm that focuses on building **cross-platform applications** with a single codebase. While it may seem like a shift in mindset, this book will provide you with the tools, examples, and best practices to adapt your existing knowledge into the Flutter framework.

Flutter is one of the most exciting tools in modern development, offering a high degree of flexibility and performance. With its **rich set of widgets**, **hot reload** feature, and **single codebase** approach for **iOS**, **Android**, **web**, and **desktop**, it is a game-changer for developers looking to create **cross-platform** applications. As a web developer, you'll find **Flutter** to be an incredibly **developer-friendly** environment, especially if you are already familiar with object-oriented programming and the concepts of styling and layout.

One of the key strengths of **Flutter** is its reliance on **widgets**. Everything in **Flutter** is a widget, from the **basic elements** like **buttons** and **text fields** to more complex layouts. For a **web developer**, this is a concept that feels very natural because we often use similar elements like **divs** and **spans** in HTML, **CSS** for styling, and **JavaScript** for interactivity. The transition from HTML, CSS, and JavaScript to Flutter's **widget-based** system should feel like an extension of what you already know. In the same way you use CSS to style HTML elements, in Flutter, you style **widgets** to create beautiful and interactive applications.

Throughout this book, I will show you how the familiar concepts from web development can be mapped to Flutter development. You will see how **HTML** tags correspond to **Flutter widgets**, how **CSS styling** translates to **Flutter's layout system**, and how you can use **JavaScript**-like logic in **Flutter** with **Dart**, the language Flutter is built with. I'll also take the time to break down the various aspects of Flutter, so you can appreciate how it fits into the **cross-platform** development ecosystem.

As you read through this book, you'll also find practical examples and code snippets that will help solidify your understanding of the concepts I discuss. The goal is not just to explain the syntax and features of Flutter but to show you how you can apply them to solve real-world problems and build applications that meet the needs of users across different platforms.

To anyone reading this book, whether you are just starting your **web development** career or you're an experienced developer looking to expand your skillset, I want to emphasize that the journey ahead will require patience, practice, and persistence. **Flutter** is a powerful tool, and while it may take time to fully master it, I am confident that the knowledge you gain from this book will serve as a strong foundation for building **beautiful, responsive**, and **high-performance apps**.

I also encourage you to stay engaged, experiment with the examples, and take full advantage of **Flutter's features**. The more you practice, the more confident you'll become in using Flutter to build complex, cross-platform applications. As you progress through this guide, I hope you gain not only the technical skills required for building apps but also the confidence to approach new challenges with a problem-solving mindset.

I am thrilled to be part of your development journey and look forward to seeing the amazing projects you will create using the knowledge you gain from this book.

Israel Joshua Chukwubueze

About the Author:
Israel Joshua Chukwubueze

You can find out more about the Author's Books on Amazon
Click here to
https://www.amazon.com/stores/Israel-Joshua-Chukwubueze/author/B0BHF5T1V7

The Author's Official Website
Learn more about the Passion, Talents and Skills

Click here to
https://israeljoshua.com.ng

I know you will Enjoy this Book and don't forget to leave a review for this book.
Click Here to Leave a Review!

Chapter 1: Introduction to Flutter for Web Developers

1.1 Overview of Flutter

Flutter is an open-source UI software development toolkit created by Google. It is designed to enable developers to craft natively compiled applications for mobile, web, and desktop from a single codebase. Flutter stands out by using the Dart programming language, an optimized language for UI, which offers features such as hot reload, customizable widgets, and high performance.

Unlike traditional frameworks, Flutter does not use native platform UI elements. Instead, it employs its own rendering engine, Skia, to draw UI elements directly to the screen. This eliminates inconsistencies caused by different platform versions, ensuring a uniform user experience across devices.

1.2 Comparing Flutter Widgets with HTML and CSS Elements

To transition from web development to Flutter, it is essential to understand the core building blocks of both paradigms.

- **HTML** provides the structure of a web page, defining elements like headers, paragraphs, buttons, and forms.
- **CSS** handles the styling, dictating how these elements look and interact with the user's actions.

In Flutter, these roles are unified under the concept of **widgets**. Widgets in Flutter are fundamental building blocks used to create user interfaces, combining functionality, structure, and styling.

Example: A Simple "Hello World" Layout

HTML/CSS Example: chapter_01/example_1_2_1.html

cha

```
<!-- html -->
<div class="container">
  <h1 class="header">Hello World</h1>
</div>

<style>
```

```
.container {
  display: flex;
  justify-content: center;
  align-items: center;
  height: 100vh;
  background-color: lightblue;
}

.header {
  font-size: 24px;
  color: white;
}
</style>
```

Flutter Example: chapter_01/example_1_2_1.dart

```
//dart
import 'package:flutter/material.dart';

void main() {
  runApp(MyApp());
}

class MyApp extends StatelessWidget {
  @override
  Widget build(BuildContext context) {
    return MaterialApp(
      home: Scaffold(
        body: Container(
          color: Colors.lightBlue,
          child: Center(
            child: Text(
              'Hello World',
              style: TextStyle(fontSize: 24, color:
Colors.white),
            ),
          ),
        ),
      ),
    );
  }
}
```

Key Comparisons:

1 **Structure vs. Widgets**:
HTML separates structure (`<div>`, `<h1>`) and style (`CSS`). Flutter uses widgets that encapsulate both the structure and styling.

2 **CSS Flexbox vs. Flutter's Center Widget**:
The HTML example uses `display: flex` for alignment, while Flutter simplifies this with the `Center` widget.

3 **Text Styling**:
CSS applies styling using classes like `.header`, whereas Flutter uses `TextStyle` within the widget's properties.

1.3 Why Flutter for Web Developers?

For web developers looking to expand their skillset or transition into mobile and multi-platform development, Flutter offers a powerful, versatile toolkit. The following points outline its advantages:

Single Codebase for Multiple Platforms

Flutter allows developers to write code once and deploy it on iOS, Android, web, Windows, macOS, and Linux. This dramatically reduces development time and ensures consistency across platforms.

Declarative UI Approach

Flutter's declarative style resembles modern JavaScript frameworks like React. Developers accustomed to React or similar libraries will find the transition smoother, as they are already familiar with concepts such as state management, component trees, and reactive programming.

Performance Benefits

Flutter applications are compiled into native machine code rather than relying on web views or interpreters. This results in faster load times, smoother animations, and better overall performance compared to many hybrid frameworks.

Extensive Widget Library

Flutter includes a vast library of customizable widgets that adhere to Material Design and Cupertino standards. These widgets eliminate the need for third-party styling libraries, as everything is built into the framework.

Hot Reload for Rapid Iteration

The "hot reload" feature allows developers to see changes instantly in the emulator or real device without restarting the application. This speeds up the design and testing process, making it particularly appealing to those who enjoy rapid prototyping.

Examples of Enhanced Productivity

- **No Platform-Specific UI Issues**:
  Unlike traditional mobile development where UI rendering can differ slightly between iOS and Android, Flutter guarantees pixel-perfect layouts across platforms.
- **Integration-Friendly**:
  Flutter works seamlessly with Firebase, REST APIs, and GraphQL, making it a versatile choice for web developers familiar with these tools.

1.4 Key Concepts: Declarative UI and Widgets

Understanding Flutter's declarative UI approach is vital for web developers transitioning from frameworks like React or Vue.js. Flutter represents the user interface as a tree of widgets. Widgets describe what the UI should look like at any given moment based on the current state.

Declarative vs. Imperative UI Programming

- **Imperative UI (Traditional Approach):**
  Developers manually update the DOM to reflect changes in the UI. For example, hiding or showing an element involves modifying its CSS properties directly.

- **Declarative UI (Flutter's Approach):**
  Developers define the "what" instead of the "how." The UI reacts automatically to changes in state.

React Native Example: chapter_01/example_1_4_1.js

```
//js
import React, { useState } from 'react';
import { View, Text, Button } from 'react-native';

export default function App() {
  const [count, setCount] = useState(0);

  return (
    <View style={{ flex: 1, justifyContent: 'center',
alignItems: 'center' }}>
      <Text style={{ fontSize: 24 }}>Count: {count}</Text>
      <Button title="Increment" onPress={() =>
setCount(count + 1)} />
    </View>
  );
}
```

Flutter Equivalent: chapter_01/example_1_4_1.dart

```
//dart
import 'package:flutter/material.dart';

void main() {
  runApp(MyApp());
}

class MyApp extends StatelessWidget {
  @override
  Widget build(BuildContext context) {
    return MaterialApp(
      home: Counter(),
    );
  }
}

class Counter extends StatefulWidget {
  @override
  _CounterState createState() => _CounterState();
}
```

```
class _CounterState extends State<Counter> {
  int count = 0;

  @override
  Widget build(BuildContext context) {
    return Scaffold(
      body: Center(
        child: Column(
          mainAxisAlignment: MainAxisAlignment.center,
          children: [
            Text('Count: $count', style:
TextStyle(fontSize: 24)),
            ElevatedButton(
              onPressed: () {
                setState(() {
                  count++;
                });
              },
              child: Text('Increment'),
            ),
          ],
        ),
      ),
    );
  }
}
```

Key Highlights:

- In React Native, `useState` manages state, whereas Flutter uses the `State` class in a `StatefulWidget`.
- Flutter handles state changes by calling `setState`, which triggers a rebuild of the affected widgets.

Widget Classification in Flutter

Widgets in Flutter can be broadly classified into three categories:

1 **Structural Widgets**

  ○ Example: `Container`, `Row`, `Column`, `Stack`.

   - These widgets define the layout and position of UI elements.

2. **Styling Widgets**

   - Example: `Padding`, `Align`, `Center`.
   - These widgets modify the appearance or placement of other widgets.

3. **Interactive Widgets**

   - Example: `GestureDetector`, `Button`, `Switch`.
   - These widgets capture user input and trigger events.

Sample Code for Layout and Style:

- **HTML Flexbox: chapter_01/example_1_4_1.html**

```
<!-- html -->
<div class="flex-container">
  <div class="item">1</div>
  <div class="item">2</div>
  <div class="item">3</div>
</div>

<style>
.flex-container {
  display: flex;
  justify-content: center;
  align-items: center;
  gap: 10px;
}

.item {
  background-color: lightblue;
  padding: 20px;
  border-radius: 5px;
}
</style>
```

Flutter Equivalent: chapter_01/example_1_4_2.dart

```
//dart
class FlexExample extends StatelessWidget {
  @override
  Widget build(BuildContext context) {
```

```
    return Scaffold(
      body: Center(
        child: Row(
          mainAxisAlignment: MainAxisAlignment.center,
          children: [
            Container(
              padding: EdgeInsets.all(20),
              color: Colors.lightBlue,
              child: Text('1'),
            ),
            SizedBox(width: 10),
            Container(
              padding: EdgeInsets.all(20),
              color: Colors.lightBlue,
              child: Text('2'),
            ),
            SizedBox(width: 10),
            Container(
              padding: EdgeInsets.all(20),
              color: Colors.lightBlue,
              child: Text('3'),
            ),
          ],
        ),
      ),
    );
  }
}
```

1.5 Tools Needed: Setting Up Flutter

Setting up Flutter for development requires specific tools that cater to various stages of the application lifecycle, from coding to testing and deployment. These tools ensure seamless integration with your preferred operating system and development environment.

Core Tools

1. **Flutter SDK**:
   The SDK contains the framework libraries, tools for compilation, and everything needed to build and run Flutter apps. It is available for Windows, macOS, and

Linux.

2 **Dart SDK**:
While the Dart SDK is included in the Flutter SDK, it plays a critical role in compiling Flutter code into native binaries for efficient execution.

3 **Code Editor or IDE**:
Flutter supports popular IDEs such as:

- Visual Studio Code (lightweight with excellent extensions).
- Android Studio (robust with debugging tools).
- IntelliJ IDEA (powerful for advanced projects).

4 **Emulators and Devices**:
Testing requires access to simulators and physical devices. For mobile apps, Android Virtual Devices (AVDs) and iOS simulators are widely used, while browsers handle web application testing.

5 **Version Control System**:
Git is an essential tool for managing code repositories, especially when collaborating with teams or deploying projects.

Preparing Your System

Before installing Flutter, ensure that your system meets the basic requirements:

- **Windows**:
  - Operating System: Windows 10 or later (64-bit).
  - Space: At least 1.64 GB (excluding disk space for IDE/tools).
  - Tools: Git for Windows.
- **macOS**:
  - Operating System: macOS 10.14 or later.
  - Space: At least 2.8 GB.
  - Tools: Xcode for iOS development.
- **Linux**:
  - Operating System: Any modern distribution.
  - Tools: Bash, curl, git, mkdir, rm, unzip, and which.

Key Flutter Installation Tools

1. **Flutter Installation Command Line**: On most systems, Flutter is downloaded as a compressed archive. After extraction, it needs to be added to the system's PATH.
2. **Installing Dependencies**:
   - **Windows**: Install Git and ensure it is in the PATH.
   - **macOS**: Install Xcode for iOS-related builds.
   - **Linux**: Use the appropriate package manager for dependencies.
3. **Flutter Doctor**: The `flutter doctor` command checks your environment for missing components or configuration issues.

Example Output:

```
Doctor summary (to see all details, run flutter doctor
-v):

1  [✓] Flutter (Channel stable, 2.10.4, on macOS 12.2.1
   21D62 darwin-x64, locale en-US)
2  [✓] Android toolchain - develop for Android devices
3  [✓] Xcode - develop for iOS and macOS
4  [✓] Chrome - develop for the web
5  [✓] Android Studio (version 2021.1)
6  [✓] VS Code (version 1.66.1)
7  [✓] Connected device (3 available)
```

1.6 Installing Flutter SDK and IDE Plugins

Installing the Flutter SDK

1. **Download Flutter SDK**:
   - Visit the Flutter website and download the appropriate SDK for your OS.
   - Extract the downloaded file into a folder (`C:\flutter` on Windows, `~/flutter` on Linux/macOS).
2. **Add Flutter to PATH**:
   - **Windows**:
     Update the `PATH` environment variable by adding the path to the

`flutter/bin` folder.
- **macOS/Linux**:
  Add the following line to your `.bashrc` or `.zshrc` file:bash

```
export PATH="$PATH:`pwd`/flutter/bin"
```

Setting Up IDE Plugins

Plugins streamline development by providing features such as syntax highlighting, debugging tools, and hot reload functionality.

1. **Visual Studio Code**:
   - Install the "Flutter" and "Dart" extensions from the Extensions Marketplace.
   - Configure the editor to use Flutter's SDK by specifying the path.
2. **Android Studio**:
   - Open the Preferences menu and navigate to `Plugins`.
   - Search for "Flutter" and install it. The Dart plugin will install automatically.
3. **IntelliJ IDEA**:
   - Similar to Android Studio, install the Flutter and Dart plugins via the Plugins Marketplace.

React Native Comparison

Installing React Native involves slightly different steps:

- Install Node.js and npm/yarn for dependency management.
- Install the React Native CLI:

```
npm install -g react-native-cli
```

- Initialize a project

```
npx react-native init MyApp
```

Flutter skips the dependency on Node.js, relying instead on its SDK and CLI, which simplifies the setup process.

Installing React Native with Expo:

- Install Expo CLI globally using npm:
- `npm install -g expo-cli`

Create a New React Native Project with Expo

- Open your terminal and run the following command to create a new project:
- `expo init MyReactNativeApp`

Choose a template:

- Select the **blank** template for a minimal setup or another template if you prefer additional features.

Navigate to your project directory:

- `cd MyReactNativeApp`

Please install:

- `npx expo install react-dom react-native-web @expo/metro-runtime`

Run the App on the Web

- Start the Expo development server:
- `yarn web`

1.7 First Look: Flutter's File Structure

A Flutter project has a defined structure designed to organize code and resources effectively. Upon creating a new project, you'll notice the following hierarchy:

```
project/
├── android/
├── build/
├── ios/
├── lib/
```

```
│   ├── main.dart
├── test/
├── web/
├── pubspec.yaml
```

Directory Breakdown

1. **`android/`** and **`ios/`**:
   Contain platform-specific files for Android and iOS. These are mostly auto-generated but can be customized for advanced configurations.

2. **`lib/`**:
   This is where most of the application code resides. The `main.dart` file serves as the entry point of the application.

3. **`web/`**:
   Contains files required for running the app in a browser, such as `index.html`.

4. **`pubspec.yaml`**:
   This configuration file manages project metadata, dependencies, and assets.

React Native Comparison

React Native projects have a different layout:

```
project/
├── android/
├── ios/
├── node_modules/
├── src/
│   ├── App.js
├── package.json
```

In React Native:

- The `node_modules` directory contains all dependencies.
- The `App.js` file is the primary entry point, akin to Flutter's `main.dart`.

1.8 Running Your First Flutter App

After setting up your environment, the first step is to run a sample Flutter application. Flutter provides a built-in counter app as a starting template.

Steps to Run a Flutter App

- **Create a New Flutter Project**: Run the following command to create a project:

```
flutter create my_first_app

cd my_first_app
```

- **Run the App**: Use the `flutter run` command:

```
flutter run
```

This launches the app on a connected device, emulator, or browser (if web support is enabled).

Sample Code Explanation

The default counter app in Flutter is a minimal example demonstrating stateful widgets:

Flutter Example: **chapter_01/example_1_8_2.dart**

```
//dart
import 'package:flutter/material.dart';

void main() {
  runApp(MyApp());
}

class MyApp extends StatelessWidget {
  @override
  Widget build(BuildContext context) {
    return MaterialApp(
      home: CounterApp(),
    );
  }
}

class CounterApp extends StatefulWidget {
  @override
  _CounterAppState createState() => _CounterAppState();
```

```
}

class _CounterAppState extends State<CounterApp> {
  int _counter = 0;

  void _incrementCounter() {
    setState(() {
      _counter++;
    });
  }

  @override
  Widget build(BuildContext context) {
    return Scaffold(
      appBar: AppBar(
        title: Text('Flutter Counter'),
      ),
      body: Center(
        child: Column(
          mainAxisAlignment: MainAxisAlignment.center,
          children: <Widget>[
            Text('You have pushed the button this many
times:'),
            Text('$_counter', style:
Theme.of(context).textTheme.headlineMedium
),
          ],
        ),
      ),
      floatingActionButton: FloatingActionButton(
        onPressed: _incrementCounter,
        tooltip: 'Increment',
        child: Icon(Icons.add),
      ),
    );
  }
}
```

React Native Equivalent: chapter_01/example_1_8_1.js

React Native provides a similar "Hello World" app:

```
//js
import React, { useState } from 'react';
import { View, Text, Button } from 'react-native';

export default function App() {
  const [count, setCount] = useState(0);

  return (
    <View style={{ flex: 1, justifyContent: 'center',
alignItems: 'center' }}>
      <Text>You have pressed the button {count} times</
Text>
      <Button title="Press me" onPress={() =>
setCount(count + 1)} />
    </View>
  );
}
```

Tips for Running Your Flutter App

- **Hot Reload**:
  Make changes to your Dart code and press `r` in the terminal to instantly see updates without restarting the app.
- **Hot Restart**:
  Use `Shift + R` in the terminal to reset the app's state and reinitialize.

This is the second part of the chapter. Let me know if you'd like further content to complete the chapter or need additional examples!

Examples

Comparing Buttons in Flutter and HTML/CSS

Html: chapter_01/example_1_8_1.html

```
<!-- html -->
```

```
<button class="btn">Click Me</button>


<style>
.btn {
  padding: 10px 20px;
  background-color: blue;
  color: white;
  border: none;
  border-radius: 5px;
  cursor: pointer;
}
</style>
```

Flutter: chapter_01/example_1_8_3.dart

```
//dart


ElevatedButton(
        onPressed: () {
          print('Button Pressed');
        },
        style: ElevatedButton.styleFrom(
          backgroundColor: Colors.blue,
          padding: EdgeInsets.symmetric(horizontal: 20, vertical:
10),
          shape: RoundedRectangleBorder(
            borderRadius: BorderRadius.circular(5),
          ),
        ),
        child: Text('Click Me', style: TextStyle(color:
Colors.white)),
      )),
```

Centering Content: Flexbox vs. Flutter's Center Widget

```
<!-- html -->


<div class="container">
```

```
  <p>Hello, World!</p>
</div>

<style>
.container {
  display: flex;
  justify-content: center;
  align-items: center;
  height: 100vh;
}
</style>
```

Flutter:

```
//dart


Center(
  child: Text('Hello, World!'),
);
```

Displaying Images: chapter_01/example_1_8_2.html

```
<!-- html -->

<img src="assets/images.png" alt="Sample" class="image" />


<style>
  .image {
    width: 100%;
    border-radius: 10px;
  }
  </style>
```

Flutter: chapter_01/example_1_8_4.dart

```
//dart
```

```
Image.asset(
  'assets/image.jpg',
  width: double.infinity,
  fit: BoxFit.cover,
);
```

Tips

- Add the assets folder to the root of your flutter project
- Then add:

```
assets:
  - assets/images.png
```

- to your pubspec.yaml file, save and run "flutter pub get" on your terminal to update and get any required `dependencies needed to load the image.`
- Always use Flutter's **hot reload** feature to test small UI changes immediately without restarting the app. It significantly speeds up the development process.
- Leverage the **Flutter DevTools** to analyze widget rebuilds, debug layout issues, and optimize performance. The inspector can pinpoint widget structure and hierarchy problems.
- Focus on understanding **Dart's async-await model**, especially for handling network requests and asynchronous operations, as this is central to Flutter development.

Actionable Strategies

- Create a comparison chart mapping HTML elements, CSS properties, and JavaScript methods to Flutter widgets, properties, and Dart methods. Use this chart during initial learning to bridge the knowledge gap.
- Start with a small Flutter project, such as a "To-Do List" app, to apply core concepts like widgets, state management, and navigation in a focused environment.
- Dedicate time to understanding **Flutter's widget tree** and practicing the layout system (Row, Column, Stack) to master UI composition quickly.
- Build reusable components by creating custom widgets, which reduces redundancy and simplifies complex layouts in larger applications.
- Regularly review and update the `pubspec.yaml` file to manage dependencies

effectively and avoid breaking changes in package versions.

Chapter 2: Basics of Dart for Web Developers

2.1 Introduction to Dart and Its Syntax

Dart is a modern programming language designed by Google and optimized for building UI-centric applications. It serves as the backbone of Flutter, offering features such as sound null safety, strong typing, and asynchronous programming. Dart compiles to native code for mobile and desktop platforms while also supporting JavaScript compilation for web apps.

Key Features of Dart

- **Object-Oriented**: Dart supports classes, inheritance, and polymorphism, similar to JavaScript or Java.
- **Statically Typed with Type Inference**: While you can declare variable types explicitly, Dart also infers types where possible, offering flexibility without sacrificing safety.
- **Asynchronous Programming**: Dart uses `Future` and `Stream` to handle asynchronous operations, akin to JavaScript's `Promise`.
- **Rich Built-in Libraries**: Dart includes libraries for handling collections, asynchronous tasks, and I/O operations.

Basic Syntax Overview

Dart programs are structured similarly to other C-style languages, with a `main` function serving as the entry point.

Example: A Basic Dart Program

```
//dart
void main() {
  print('Hello, Dart!');
```

```
}
```

Code Structure Comparison: JavaScript vs. Dart

JavaScript Example:

```
//javascript
function main() {
  console.log('Hello, JavaScript!');
}
main();
```

Dart Equivalent:

```
//dart
void main() {
  print('Hello, Dart!');
}
```

Key Observations:

- Dart uses `void` to indicate a function does not return a value.
- The `print` function in Dart is equivalent to `console.log` in JavaScript.

2.2 Comparing JavaScript and Dart: Key Differences

For web developers transitioning to Dart, understanding its differences from JavaScript is crucial.

Variable Declaration

Dart offers `var`, `final`, and `const` for declaring variables:

- `var`: Allows reassignment and infers the type.
- `final`: A variable that can only be set once.
- `const`: A compile-time constant.

JavaScript Example:

```
//javascript
let name = "Alice"; // Mutable
```

```
const pi = 3.14; // Immutable
```

Dart Equivalent:

```
//dart
var name = "Alice"; // Mutable
final age = 30; // Immutable
const pi = 3.14; // Compile-time constant
```

Type Safety

Dart is a statically typed language, meaning types are checked at compile time, reducing runtime errors. JavaScript, on the other hand, is dynamically typed.

JavaScript Example:

```
//javascript
let age = 25; // Type inferred as number
age = "twenty-five"; // No error
```

Dart Equivalent:

```
//dart
int age = 25; // Explicitly declared as an integer
age = "twenty-five"; // Compilation error
```

Null Safety

Dart enforces null safety, preventing variables from holding null values unless explicitly allowed.

Dart Example:

```
//dart
String? name; // Nullable
String name = "Alice"; // Non-nullable
```

In JavaScript, any variable can potentially be `null` or `undefined`, leading to runtime errors.

Classes and Objects

Both Dart and JavaScript are object-oriented, but Dart enforces stricter rules around class declarations.

JavaScript Example:

```
//javascript
class Person {
  constructor(name, age) {
    this.name = name;
    this.age = age;
  }
  greet() {
    console.log(`Hello, my name is ${this.name}`);
  }
}
const person = new Person('Alice', 25);
person.greet();
```

Dart Equivalent:

```
//dart
class Person {
  String name;
  int age;

  Person(this.name, this.age);

  void greet() {
    print('Hello, my name is $name');
  }
}

void main() {
  final person = Person('Alice', 25);
  person.greet();
}
```

2.3 Data Types and Variables in Dart

Dart supports a range of data types, from basic types like `int` and `double` to more complex types like `List` and `Map`.

Basic Data Types

Numbers:

1. `int` for integers.
2. `double` for floating-point numbers.

Example:

```
//dart

int age = 30;
double height = 5.9;
```

Strings:
Dart strings are UTF-16 encoded and support interpolation.

Example:

```
//dart

String greeting = 'Hello';

String name = 'Alice';
print('$greeting, $name!');
```

Booleans:
Represent true/false values.

Example:

```
//dart


bool isFlutterAwesome = true;
```

Lists (Arrays):
Dart lists are ordered collections.

Example:

```
//dart
```

```
List<String> fruits = ['Apple', 'Banana', 'Cherry'];
```

Maps (Dictionaries):
Key-value pairs for structured data.

Example:

```
//dart


Map<String, int> scores = {'Alice': 95, 'Bob': 88};
```

Variable Declaration Tips

- Use `final` for variables that won't change during runtime.
- Prefer `const` for compile-time constants, as they improve performance.

2.4 Functions and Methods

Functions in Dart are first-class citizens, meaning they can be assigned to variables, passed as arguments, or returned from other functions.

Defining Functions

Dart functions can have named, positional, and default parameters:

```
//dart
int add(int a, int b) {
  return a + b;
}
```

J

avaScript Comparison:

```
//javascript
function add(a, b) {
  return a + b;
}
```

Anonymous Functions

Anonymous functions or lambdas are commonly used in Dart:

```
//dart
var multiply = (int a, int b) => a * b;
print(multiply(2, 3)); // Output: 6
```

Optional Parameters

Dart supports optional named and positional parameters:

```
//dart
void greet(String name, {int age = 18}) {
  print('Hello $name, age $age');
}

void main() {
  greet('Alice'); // Output: Hello Alice, age 18
}
```

Functions in Classes

Functions inside classes are called methods. They operate on class-level data:

```
//dart
class Calculator {
  int add(int a, int b) {
    return a + b;
  }
}

void main() {
  Calculator calc = Calculator();
  print(calc.add(5, 7)); // Output: 12
}
```

Arrow Functions

Arrow syntax provides a concise way to define single-expression functions:

```
//dart
```

```
int square(int n) => n * n;
```

This chapter establishes a strong foundation for Dart, making it easier for web developers to transition from JavaScript. Let me know if you'd like further details!

2.5 Understanding Classes and Objects in Dart

Dart, like other object-oriented programming languages, heavily relies on classes and objects to structure code. Classes define the blueprint for objects, encapsulating data (fields) and behaviors (methods). Objects are instances of classes that hold specific values.

Defining Classes

A class in Dart is defined using the `class` keyword. Properties and methods are encapsulated within the class.

Example: A Basic Class

```
//dart
class Person {
  String name;
  int age;

  // Constructor
  Person(this.name, this.age);

  // Method
  void greet() {
    print('Hello, my name is $name and I am $age years
old.');
  }
}

void main() {
  // Creating an instance
  Person person = Person('Alice', 30);
  person.greet(); // Output: Hello, my name is Alice and I
am 30 years old.
}
```

Key Features

1 **Constructors**:

- Dart allows parameterized constructors to initialize class fields.
- Named constructors can also be defined for specific initialization.

2

Example:

```
//dart


class Car {

  String brand;
  int year;

  // Named Constructor
  Car.honda(this.year) : brand = 'Honda';
}

void main() {
  Car car = Car.honda(2022);
  print('${car.brand} - ${car.year}'); // Output: Honda -
2022
}
```

Getters and Setters: Dart provides custom getters and setters to encapsulate field access and modification.

```
//dart

class BankAccount {

  double _balance = 0;

  // Getter
  double get balance => _balance;

  // Setter
```

```
  set deposit(double amount) {
    if (amount > 0) {
      _balance += amount;
    }
  }
}

void main() {
  BankAccount account = BankAccount();
  account.deposit = 100;
  print('Balance: \$${account.balance}'); // Output:
Balance: $100
}
```

Comparison with JavaScript

In JavaScript, constructors are defined inside the class using the `constructor` keyword, and there's no explicit syntax for getters or setters.

JavaScript Example:

```
//javascript
class Person {
  constructor(name, age) {
    this.name = name;
    this.age = age;
  }

  greet() {
    console.log(`Hello, my name is ${this.name} and I am $
{this.age} years old.`);
  }
}

const person = new Person('Alice', 30);
person.greet(); // Output: Hello, my name is Alice and I
am 30 years old.
```

Comparison Highlights:

- Dart uses the `this` keyword for parameter assignment in constructors, while

JavaScript uses `this` inside `constructor`.

- Dart supports optional named constructors for class flexibility.

2.6 Async Programming in Dart vs JavaScript

Dart's asynchronous programming model revolves around `Future` and `Stream`. These abstractions allow efficient handling of asynchronous tasks such as network calls or file I/O operations.

Future in Dart

A `Future` represents a value that will be available at some point in the future. Dart provides keywords like `async`, `await`, and `then` to work with `Future`.

Example: Future and Async-Await in Dart

```
//dart
Future<String> fetchData() async {
  return Future.delayed(Duration(seconds: 2), () => 'Data
loaded');
}

void main() async {
  print('Fetching...');
  String data = await fetchData();
  print(data); // Output: Fetching... Data loaded
}
```

Stream in Dart

A `Stream` is used to handle a sequence of asynchronous data. Streams are particularly useful for real-time data like user inputs or server events.

Example: Using a Stream

```
//dart
Stream<int> counter() async* {
  for (int i = 1; i <= 5; i++) {
    await Future.delayed(Duration(seconds: 1));
    yield i;
  }
```

```
}

void main() async {
  await for (int count in counter()) {
    print(count); // Outputs numbers 1 to 5, one per
second
  }
}
```

JavaScript Comparison

JavaScript's asynchronous programming model uses `Promise` and `async/await`.

JavaScript Example:

```
//javascript
function fetchData() {
  return new Promise((resolve) => {
    setTimeout(() => resolve('Data loaded'), 2000);
  });
}

async function main() {
  console.log('Fetching...');
  const data = await fetchData();
  console.log(data); // Output: Fetching... Data loaded
}

main();
```

Comparison Highlights:

- Dart's `Future` and `Stream` are similar to JavaScript's `Promise` and event-driven programming but provide more features like chaining and generators.
- Dart has built-in support for `await for` with streams, simplifying real-time data processing.

2.7 Exploring Dart Packages and Dependencies

Dart's package manager, **pub**, is essential for adding external libraries and managing dependencies. Flutter uses `pubspec.yaml` to define package configurations and dependencies.

Structure of pubspec.yaml

The `pubspec.yaml` file is located in the root directory of a Dart project. It defines:

- Project name, description, and version.
- Dependencies and development dependencies.
- Assets and fonts.

Example: Basic pubspec.yaml

```
//yaml
name: my_first_app
description: A sample Flutter project.
version: 1.0.0

dependencies:
  flutter:
    sdk: flutter
  http: ^0.15.0

dev_dependencies:
  flutter_test:
    sdk: flutter
```

Adding Packages

To add a package, use the `pub add` command or update the `pubspec.yaml` file manually, followed by running `flutter pub get`.

Example: Adding the `http` Package

```
# bash
flutter pub add http
```

Usage Example:

```
//dart
import 'package:http/http.dart' as http;
```

```
void fetchData() async {
  var url = Uri.parse('https://
jsonplaceholder.typicode.com/posts/1');
  var response = await http.get(url);
  print('Response: ${response.body}');
}
```

Best Practices for Managing Dependencies

- Always pin package versions to avoid unexpected changes.
- Regularly run `flutter pub outdated` to check for updates.
- Use development dependencies for testing libraries or tools.

2.8 Writing Your First Dart Program

The first Dart program typically involves understanding the structure and basics of a Dart file. All Dart programs begin execution from the `main` function.

Example: A Simple "Hello, World" Program

```
//dart
void main() {
  print('Hello, World!');
}
```

Using Variables

```
//dart
void main() {
  String name = 'Alice';
  int age = 30;
  print('My name is $name and I am $age years old.');
}
```

Control Flow Statements

Dart supports standard control flow statements like `if-else`, `for`, and `while`.

Example: Looping Through a List

```
//dart
void main() {
  List<String> fruits = ['Apple', 'Banana', 'Cherry'];
  for (String fruit in fruits) {
    print(fruit);
  }
}
```

React Native Comparison

In React Native, the entry point typically resides in a file like `App.js`, and logic is implemented using JavaScript.

Example: A React Native Program

```
//javascript
import React from 'react';
import { Text, View } from 'react-native';

export default function App() {
  const name = 'Alice';
  const age = 30;

  return (
    <View>
      <Text>My name is {name} and I am {age} years old.</
Text>
    </View>
  );
}
```

Key Takeaways:

- Dart programs use the `main` function, while React Native apps use `App.js`.
- Dart relies on widgets for UI, whereas React Native depends on components like `View` and `Text`.

Let me know if you'd like additional expansions, more examples, or further elaboration!

Examples

Defining Classes with Methods in Dart and JavaScript

```
//dart

class Animal {

  String name;
  Animal(this.name);

  void speak() {
    print('$name makes a sound.');
  }
}

void main() {
  var dog = Animal('Dog');
  dog.speak(); // Output: Dog makes a sound.
}


//javascript

class Animal {
  constructor(name) {
    this.name = name;
  }
  speak() {
    console.log(`${this.name} makes a sound.`);
  }
}

const dog = new Animal('Dog');
dog.speak(); // Output: Dog makes a sound.
```

Asynchronous Programming in Dart vs JavaScript

Dart (Future):

```
//dart


Future<String> fetchData() async {

  return Future.delayed(Duration(seconds: 2), () => 'Data
loaded');
}

void main() async {
  print('Fetching...');
  String data = await fetchData();
  print(data); // Output: Fetching... Data loaded
}
```

JavaScript (Promise):

```
//javascript

function fetchData() {
  return new Promise(resolve => {
    setTimeout(() => resolve('Data loaded'), 2000);
  });
}

async function main() {
  console.log('Fetching...');
  const data = await fetchData();
  console.log(data); // Output: Fetching... Data loaded
}

main();
```

Using Dart's Stream to Handle Real-Time Data

```
//dart
```

```
Stream<int> counter() async* {
  for (int i = 1; i <= 5; i++) {
    await Future.delayed(Duration(seconds: 1));
    yield i;
  }
}

void main() async {
  await for (int count in counter()) {
    print(count); // Output: 1 2 3 4 5, one per second
  }
}
```

Tips

- Leverage Dart's **null safety** to eliminate runtime errors caused by null values. Use nullable types (`?`) only when absolutely necessary and prefer initializing variables with default values.
- Take advantage of Dart's **collection methods** like `map`, `where`, and `forEach` for concise and expressive operations on lists and maps.
- When working with asynchronous tasks, always handle errors using `try-catch` for `Future` and `await for` streams to prevent crashes and unexpected behavior.

Actionable Strategies

- **Learn Dart Fundamentals Thoroughly**:
  Focus on core concepts like classes, objects, and inheritance before diving into advanced topics. A strong foundation simplifies transitioning to Flutter development.

- **Use DartPad for Practice**:
  DartPad is a browser-based editor for trying out Dart code without needing a full development environment. Utilize it to test and learn new concepts quickly.

- **Master the Use of Async-Await**:
  Dart's asynchronous programming model is critical for Flutter apps. Create small, focused projects to practice handling `Future` and `Stream`, such as fetching data from APIs or simulating real-time event streams.

- **Organize Code Using Packages**:

Structure your Dart applications with reusable packages and modules. Use the `pubspec.yaml` file to manage dependencies and maintain a clean, modular architecture.

- **Write Unit Tests for Dart Code**:
  Implement tests for your Dart functions and classes to ensure their reliability. Use packages like `test` to write and automate test cases, improving code quality and maintainability.

Chapter 3: Understanding Flutter Widgets

3.1 What Are Widgets?

Widgets are the fundamental building blocks of a Flutter application. They represent everything you see and interact with on the screen, from simple elements like text and buttons to complex layouts and animations. Unlike traditional UI frameworks where views and controls are distinct, Flutter unifies the concept under widgets.

Key Characteristics of Widgets

- **Declarative Nature**: Widgets describe the structure and appearance of the UI. When the state changes, Flutter rebuilds only the affected widgets.
- **Immutable**: Once a widget is created, it cannot be modified. Instead, a new widget is built to reflect any changes, which is more efficient and prevents unexpected side effects.
- **Composable**: Widgets can be nested within other widgets, creating a tree-like structure that defines the entire UI.

Example: A Simple Widget

```
//dart
import 'package:flutter/material.dart';

void main() {
  runApp(MyApp());
}

class MyApp extends StatelessWidget {
  @override
  Widget build(BuildContext context) {
    return MaterialApp(
      home: Scaffold(
        appBar: AppBar(title: Text('Hello, Widgets!')),
        body: Center(
          child: Text(
            'Welcome to Flutter',
            style: TextStyle(fontSize: 24, color:
Colors.blue),
```

```
            ),
          ),
        ),
      );
    }
  }
```

3.2 Stateless vs Stateful Widgets

Widgets in Flutter are categorized into two main types: **Stateless Widgets** and **Stateful Widgets**.

Stateless Widgets

Stateless widgets are immutable. Their appearance and behavior do not change once rendered. These widgets are ideal for static content, such as headers, images, or labels.

Example: Stateless Widget

```
//dart
class GreetingWidget extends StatelessWidget {
  final String message;

  GreetingWidget(this.message);

  @override
  Widget build(BuildContext context) {
    return Text(
      message,
      style: TextStyle(fontSize: 20),
    );
  }
}

void main() {
  runApp(MaterialApp(home: Scaffold(body:
GreetingWidget('Hello, Flutter!'))));
}
```

Stateful Widgets

Stateful widgets hold mutable state, which means they can rebuild their UI in response to changes. They are typically used for interactive elements such as forms, counters, or animations.

Example: Stateful Widget

```
//dart
class CounterWidget extends StatefulWidget {
  @override
  _CounterWidgetState createState() =>
_CounterWidgetState();
}

class _CounterWidgetState extends State<CounterWidget> {
  int _counter = 0;

  void _increment() {
    setState(() {
      _counter++;
    });
  }

  @override
  Widget build(BuildContext context) {
    return Column(
      mainAxisAlignment: MainAxisAlignment.center,
      children: [
        Text('Count: $_counter', style:
TextStyle(fontSize: 24)),
        ElevatedButton(onPressed: _increment, child:
Text('Increment')),
      ],
    );
  }
}

void main() {
  runApp(MaterialApp(home: Scaffold(body:
CounterWidget())));
}
```

Comparison with React Native

React Native also distinguishes components into stateless (functional) and stateful (class-based or hooks-based).

React Native Example:

```
//javascript
import React, { useState } from 'react';
import { View, Text, Button } from 'react-native';

const Counter = () => {
  const [count, setCount] = useState(0);

  return (
    <View style={{ justifyContent: 'center', alignItems:
'center' }}>
      <Text style={{ fontSize: 24 }}>Count: {count}</Text>
      <Button title="Increment" onPress={() =>
setCount(count + 1)} />
    </View>
  );
};

export default Counter;
```

Key Differences:

- Flutter uses `setState()` explicitly, whereas React Native utilizes hooks like `useState`.
- Flutter rebuilds the widget tree selectively based on state, ensuring high performance.

3.3 The Widget Tree Explained

Flutter applications are built using a **widget tree**. This tree represents the hierarchy of widgets, where each widget can have one or more child widgets. The widget tree defines both the layout and the appearance of the application.

Types of Widget Trees

1. **Single-Child Layout**: Widgets like `Container` or `Center` hold only one child.
2. **Multi-Child Layout**: Widgets like `Column`, `Row`, or `Stack` can hold multiple children.
3. **Dynamic Trees**: Widgets can dynamically generate children using builders, such as `ListView.builder`.

Example: A Nested Widget Tree

```
//dart
class NestedTree extends StatelessWidget {
  @override
  Widget build(BuildContext context) {
    return Scaffold(
      appBar: AppBar(title: Text('Nested Widget Tree')),
      body: Column(
        children: [
          Container(
            color: Colors.blue,
            padding: EdgeInsets.all(10),
            child: Text('Child 1', style: TextStyle(color:
Colors.white)),
          ),
          Container(
            color: Colors.green,
            padding: EdgeInsets.all(10),
            child: Text('Child 2', style: TextStyle(color:
Colors.white)),
          ),
        ],
      ),
    );
  }
}

void main() {
  runApp(MaterialApp(home: NestedTree()));
}
```

Debugging the Widget Tree

Use Flutter's **Widget Inspector** to visualize the widget tree and debug layout issues.

Tips for Widget Tree Management:

- Keep the tree shallow by extracting widgets into smaller, reusable components.
- Use `Expanded` or `Flexible` widgets to handle dynamic resizing within a tree.

3.4 Parent-Child Relationships in Widgets

The relationship between parent and child widgets is central to Flutter's layout system. Parent widgets control how child widgets are positioned, sized, and displayed. Each child widget inherits constraints from its parent.

Single-Child Relationship

Widgets like `Container` or `Padding` have a single child and modify its properties or position.

Example: Single-Child Relationship

```
//dart
Container(
  padding: EdgeInsets.all(16),
  color: Colors.blue,
  child: Text('Single Child'),
)
```

Multi-Child Relationship

Widgets like `Column` or `Row` accept multiple children and align them based on properties like `mainAxisAlignment` and `crossAxisAlignment`.

Example: Multi-Child Relationship

```
//dart
Column(
  children: [
    Text('Child 1'),
    Text('Child 2'),
```

```
  ],
)
```

Stack for Overlapping Children

The `Stack` widget positions children relative to each other, often overlapping them.

Example: Using Stack

```
//dart
Stack(
  children: [
    Container(color: Colors.blue, height: 100, width:
100),
    Positioned(
      top: 20,
      left: 20,
      child: Container(color: Colors.red, height: 50,
width: 50),
    ),
  ],
)
```

React Native Comparison

In React Native, parent-child relationships are defined similarly, with components nested inside others. However, CSS-like styles control positioning, whereas Flutter relies on layout widgets.

React Native Example:

```
//javascript
import React from 'react';
import { View, Text, StyleSheet } from 'react-native';

const App = () => (
  <View style={styles.parent}>
    <Text style={styles.child}>Child 1</Text>
    <Text style={styles.child}>Child 2</Text>
  </View>
```

```
);

const styles = StyleSheet.create({
  parent: {
    flex: 1,
    justifyContent: 'center',
    alignItems: 'center',
  },
  child: {
    margin: 10,
  },
});

export default App;
```

Key Takeaways:

- Flutter uses layout widgets like `Row`, `Column`, and `Stack` to manage child positioning.
- React Native depends on `View` components and CSS-style properties.

This chapter lays a solid foundation for understanding widgets in Flutter, their roles, and how they interact to build complex UIs. Let me know if you'd like further elaboration or additional examples.

3.5 Mapping HTML Tags to Flutter Widgets

For web developers transitioning to Flutter, mapping common HTML tags to their equivalent Flutter widgets is a vital first step. While HTML tags and Flutter widgets serve similar purposes in structuring and presenting the UI, their syntax and underlying behavior differ significantly.

Basic Mappings

HTML Tag	Flutter Widget	Description
`<div>`	`Container`	A versatile widget for layouts and styling.
`<p>` or `<h1>`	`Text`	Displays text with customizable styles.
`<img>`	`Image`	Displays images from assets, network, or

`<button>`	`ElevatedButton`	A button widget with styling and onClick functionality.
`<ul>`/ `<ol>`	`ListView`	Displays a scrollable list of items.
`<a>`	`InkWell` or `GestureDetector`	A tappable widget for links or gestures.
`<form>`	`Form`	Provides form handling and validation.
`<input>`	`TextField`	A widget for capturing user input.

Example 1: `<div>` vs. `Container`

HTML Example:

```
<!-- html -->
<div style="width: 200px; height: 100px; background-color:
blue;"></div>
```

Flutter Equivalent:

```
//dart
Container(
  width: 200,
  height: 100,
  color: Colors.blue,
)
```

Key Comparison:

- The `Container` widget combines size, padding, margin, and background color in a single widget, whereas HTML separates these properties into styles.

Example 2: `<p>` vs. `Text`

HTML Example:

```
<!-- html -->
<p style="font-size: 16px; color: gray;">This is a
paragraph.</p>
```

Flutter Equivalent:

```
//dart
Text(
  'This is a paragraph.',
  style: TextStyle(fontSize: 16, color: Colors.grey),
)
```

Example 3: `<img>` vs. `Image`

HTML Example:

```
<!-- html -->
<img src="image.jpg" alt="Sample Image" style="width:
100px; height: 100px;" />
```

Flutter Equivalent:

```
//dart
Image.asset(
  'assets/image.jpg',
  width: 100,
  height: 100,
)
```

3.6 Understanding Properties in Widgets

Every Flutter widget comes with a set of properties that determine its behavior, appearance, and layout. These properties are analogous to HTML attributes or CSS styles.

Common Properties in Widgets

1. **`key`**: Uniquely identifies a widget in the widget tree. Useful for maintaining state during updates.
2. **`color`**: Sets the background or foreground color.
3. **`padding` and `margin`**: Define the spacing inside or outside a widget.
4. **`alignment`**: Controls the positioning of child widgets within the parent.
5. **`child` and `children`**: Specify nested widgets.

Example: Customizing a Container with Properties

```
//dart
Container(
  width: 150,
  height: 150,
  color: Colors.blue,
  alignment: Alignment.center,
  child: Text(
    'Hello',
    style: TextStyle(color: Colors.white, fontSize: 20),
  ),
)
```

In this example:

- `width` and `height` define the container size.
- `color` sets the background color.
- `alignment` centers the child `Text` widget.

React Native Comparison

In React Native, properties are applied through styles.

React Native Example:

```
//javascript
import React from 'react';
import { View, Text, StyleSheet } from 'react-native';

const App = () => (
  <View style={styles.container}>
    <Text style={styles.text}>Hello</Text>
  </View>
);

const styles = StyleSheet.create({
  container: {
    width: 150,
    height: 150,
    backgroundColor: 'blue',
    justifyContent: 'center',
    alignItems: 'center',
```

```
  },
  text: {
    color: 'white',
    fontSize: 20,
  },
});

export default App;
```

3.7 Rendering Widgets Dynamically

Dynamic rendering refers to creating widgets at runtime based on data or user interaction. This is common for building lists, grids, and dynamic forms.

Example: Building a List Dynamically

```
//dart
List<String> items = ['Item 1', 'Item 2', 'Item 3'];

Widget build(BuildContext context) {
  return ListView.builder(
    itemCount: items.length,
    itemBuilder: (context, index) {
      return ListTile(title: Text(items[index]));
    },
  );
}
```

In this example:

- `ListView.builder` dynamically creates `ListTile` widgets for each item in the `items` list.

React Native Comparison

In React Native, a similar dynamic rendering approach is achieved using `FlatList`.

React Native Example:

```
//javascript
import React from 'react';
import { FlatList, Text, View } from 'react-native';
```

```
const App = () => {
  const items = ['Item 1', 'Item 2', 'Item 3'];

  return (
    <FlatList
      data={items}
      keyExtractor={(item, index) => index.toString()}
      renderItem={({ item }) => <Text>{item}</Text>}
    />
  );
};

export default App;
```

3.8 Debugging Widget Errors

Debugging is an essential skill for resolving layout and runtime issues in Flutter applications.

Common Errors

1. **`RenderFlex overflow`**: Indicates that a widget exceeds its parent's bounds.
2. **`NullPointerException`**: Arises when accessing null values in non-nullable variables.
3. **Widget Misalignment**: Caused by incorrect `alignment` or `padding` properties.

Debugging Tools

1. **Flutter Inspector**: Visualizes the widget tree and highlights layout issues.
2. **Error Messages**: Flutter provides detailed error messages to help locate and fix problems.
3. **`print()` Statements**: Useful for logging variable states and debugging logic.

Example: Fixing a RenderFlex Overflow

Error Scenario:

```
//dart
Row(
```

```
  children: [
    Container(width: 200, color: Colors.red),
    Container(width: 200, color: Colors.green),
  ],
)
```

Fix:

```
//dart
SingleChildScrollView(
  scrollDirection: Axis.horizontal,
  child: Row(
    children: [
      Container(width: 200, color: Colors.red),
      Container(width: 200, color: Colors.green),
    ],
  ),
)
```

Adding a `SingleChildScrollView` resolves the overflow by enabling horizontal scrolling.

Key Takeaways:

- Use tools like Flutter Inspector to pinpoint layout issues.
- Test your application on devices of various sizes to ensure responsiveness.
- Always initialize variables properly to avoid null-related errors.

Examples

Creating a Stateless and Stateful Widget
Stateless Widget:

```
//dart
class GreetingWidget extends StatelessWidget {

  final String message;

  GreetingWidget(this.message);
```

```
  @override
  Widget build(BuildContext context) {
    return Text(message, style: TextStyle(fontSize: 20));
  }
}
```

Stateful Widget:

```
//dart
class CounterWidget extends StatefulWidget {
  @override
  _CounterWidgetState createState() =>
_CounterWidgetState();
}

class _CounterWidgetState extends State<CounterWidget> {
  int _counter = 0;

  void _incrementCounter() {
    setState(() {
      _counter++;
    });
  }

  @override
  Widget build(BuildContext context) {
    return Column(
      children: [
        Text('Counter: $_counter', style:
TextStyle(fontSize: 24)),
        ElevatedButton(onPressed: _incrementCounter,
child: Text('Increment')),
      ],
    );
  }
}
```

Mapping HTML Tags to Flutter Widgets

HTML Example:

```
<!-- html -->
```

```
<div style="width: 200px; height: 100px; background-color: blue;">

  <p style="color: white;">Hello</p>
</div>
```

Flutter Equivalent:

```
//dart

Container(
  width: 200,
  height: 100,
  color: Colors.blue,
  child: Center(
    child: Text('Hello', style: TextStyle(color: Colors.white)),
  ),
)
```

Using ListView to Dynamically Render Widgets

```
//dart


List<String> items = ['Item 1', 'Item 2', 'Item 3'];


Widget build(BuildContext context) {
  return ListView.builder(
    itemCount: items.length,
    itemBuilder: (context, index) {
      return ListTile(title: Text(items[index]));
    },
  );
}
```

Tips

- When building a complex widget tree, break it into smaller, reusable widgets to improve readability and maintainability.

- Use Flutter's `hot reload` feature frequently during development to see changes instantly without restarting the app.
- Utilize `Expanded` and `Flexible` widgets to manage dynamic spacing and handle screen size variations effectively.

Actionable Strategies

- **Create a Mapping Table for Common HTML Tags**:
  Develop a personal cheat sheet that maps frequently used HTML tags and CSS styles to their Flutter equivalents to accelerate learning and application.

- **Practice Building Stateless and Stateful Widgets**:
  Create small projects like counters, toggle switches, and static screens to differentiate when to use stateless vs. stateful widgets.

- **Leverage Debugging Tools Like Flutter Inspector**:
  Use the inspector to visualize the widget tree and resolve layout issues effectively, especially when working with nested widgets.

- **Experiment with Dynamic Rendering**:
  Build dynamic widgets using `ListView.builder` or `GridView.builder` to master rendering items based on runtime data.

- **Understand Parent-Child Relationships Through Layout Exercises**:
  Practice creating complex layouts using `Column`, `Row`, and `Stack` to understand widget constraints and positioning rules.

Chapter 4: Styling and Aligning Text

4.1 Styling Text in HTML vs Flutter

Styling text is a fundamental part of any application. In web development, HTML provides semantic tags such as `<p>`, `<h1>`, and `<span>`, with CSS used for styling. In Flutter, the `Text` widget is the primary way to display and style text. While HTML separates structure (HTML) and styling (CSS), Flutter combines both into the widget's properties.

HTML and CSS Example: Styling Text

```
<!-- html -->
<p style="font-size: 20px; color: blue; font-weight:
bold;">Hello, World!</p>
```

Explanation:

- The `<p>` tag represents the paragraph.
- The `style` attribute defines the font size, color, and weight.

Flutter Equivalent: Using the Text Widget

```
//dart
Text(
  'Hello, World!',
  style: TextStyle(
    fontSize: 20,
    color: Colors.blue,
    fontWeight: FontWeight.bold,
  ),
)
```

- **Explanation**:
  - The `Text` widget is used to display text.
  - The `TextStyle` object allows customization of font properties directly within the widget.

Key Comparison Between HTML and Flutter

1 **Separation vs Combination**:

- HTML separates structure (`<p>`) and styles (`style` or CSS classes).
- Flutter integrates structure and style within the `Text` widget.

2 **Text Styling Syntax**:

- In HTML: `font-size`, `font-weight`, and `color` are CSS properties.
- In Flutter: `fontSize`, `fontWeight`, and `color` are properties of the `TextStyle` class.

3 **Reusability**:

- HTML uses classes and external stylesheets for reuse.
- Flutter can achieve reusability by defining `TextStyle` objects and using them across multiple `Text` widgets.

4.2 Using the Text Widget

The `Text` widget in Flutter is the simplest way to display text on the screen. It supports a wide range of properties for customization and behavior.

Basic Text Widget

```
//dart
Text('Hello, Flutter!');
```

This creates a basic text element without any additional styling.

Text Widget with Basic Properties

```
//dart
Text(
  'Welcome to Flutter!',
  textAlign: TextAlign.center,
  style: TextStyle(
    fontSize: 24,
    color: Colors.green,
  ),
)
```

- **Key Properties**:
  - **`textAlign`**: Aligns the text (e.g., left, right, center, justify).
  - **`style`**: Accepts a `TextStyle` object for further customization.

Multi-Line Text

Flutter automatically wraps text that exceeds the screen width. However, you can customize the behavior using the `softWrap` and `overflow` properties.

```
//dart
Text(
  'This is a long sentence that will wrap to the next line if it exceeds the screen width.',
  softWrap: true,
  overflow: TextOverflow.ellipsis,
)
```

- **`softWrap`**: Enables or disables text wrapping.
- **`overflow`**: Defines how overflowing text should be handled (e.g., ellipsis, fade).

4.3 Customizing TextStyle

The `TextStyle` class in Flutter provides a wide range of options for styling text, such as font size, weight, color, and decoration.

Font Properties

```
//dart
Text(
  'Custom Font Properties',
  style: TextStyle(
    fontSize: 18,
    fontWeight: FontWeight.w600,
    fontStyle: FontStyle.italic,
  ),
)
```

- **`fontSize`**: Sets the size of the text.
- **`fontWeight`**: Defines the thickness (e.g., `FontWeight.w400` for normal, `FontWeight.bold` for bold).
- **`fontStyle`**: Specifies whether the text is normal or italic.

Color and Decoration

```
//dart
Text(
  'Underlined and Colored Text',
  style: TextStyle(
    color: Colors.red,
    decoration: TextDecoration.underline,
    decorationColor: Colors.blue,
    decorationStyle: TextDecorationStyle.dotted,
  ),
)
```

- **`color`**: Sets the text color.
- **`decoration`**: Applies underlines, overlines, or strike-through effects.
- **`decorationColor`**: Defines the color of the decoration.
- **`decorationStyle`**: Changes the decoration style (e.g., dotted, dashed).

Google Fonts Integration

Flutter supports Google Fonts for custom typography.

```
//dart
import 'package:google_fonts/google_fonts.dart';

Text(
  'Styled with Google Fonts',
  style: GoogleFonts.lobster(fontSize: 24, color:
Colors.purple),
)
```

- Install the `google_fonts` package using `flutter pub add google_fonts`.
- Use the `GoogleFonts` class to apply various font styles.

4.4 Centering Text: Aligning in Flutter vs CSS

Text alignment ensures that text is positioned correctly within its parent container. In HTML, CSS properties such as `text-align` and `vertical-align` handle alignment, while Flutter uses widgets and alignment properties.

Horizontal Alignment

HTML Example:

```
<!-- html -->
<p style="text-align: center;">Centered Text</p>
```

Flutter Equivalent:

```
//dart
Text(
  'Centered Text',
  textAlign: TextAlign.center,
)
```

Vertical and Horizontal Alignment

HTML Example:

```
<!-- html -->
<div style="display: flex; justify-content: center; align-items: center; height: 100vh;">
  <p>Centered Text</p>
</div>
```

Flutter Equivalent:

```
//dart
Center(
  child: Text('Centered Text'),
)
```

Using Alignment in Parent Widgets

The alignment of text within a parent widget is controlled by widgets like `Align`, `Center`, or layout-specific widgets such as `Row` and `Column`.

```
//dart
Align(
  alignment: Alignment.bottomRight,
  child: Text('Aligned Text'),
)
```

- **`alignment`**: Accepts values such as `Alignment.center`, `Alignment.topLeft`, or custom offsets.

Tips and Key Points

Reusability: Define a reusable `TextStyle` constant for consistent styling across your app.

```
//dart
const TextStyle headlineStyle = TextStyle(fontSize: 24,
fontWeight: FontWeight.bold);
```

Avoid Hardcoding: Use `MediaQuery` to make text sizes responsive to different screen sizes.

```
//dart
Text(

  'Responsive Text',
  style: TextStyle(fontSize:
MediaQuery.of(context).size.width * 0.05),
)
```

Custom Fonts: Always include fallback fonts in your design for compatibility.

```
//dart
Text(

  'Fallback Font Example',
  style: TextStyle(fontFamily: 'CustomFont, Arial'),
)
```

4.5 Dynamic Font Sizes: Flexibility with Flutter

Dynamic font sizing is a key feature when building apps that adjust across multiple screen sizes and orientations. The ability to dynamically scale text ensures that your app provides a consistent and accessible experience, especially on devices with varying resolutions.

In traditional web development using HTML and CSS, dynamic text size is often achieved using relative units like percentages, `em`, `rem`, or viewport units (`vw`, `vh`). This allows the font size to scale based on the container's dimensions or the user's screen size.

In Flutter, managing dynamic font sizes is a natural fit, as it provides several ways to make text responsive, such as by using `MediaQuery`, `LayoutBuilder`, or simply calculating the font size based on the screen's width or height.

For example, the `MediaQuery` class allows you to retrieve screen properties like width, height, and text scale factor, enabling you to adjust font sizes dynamically according to these properties.

Example: Dynamic Font Size in Flutter

```
//dart
import 'package:flutter/material.dart';

class DynamicText extends StatelessWidget {
  @override
  Widget build(BuildContext context) {
    // Get the screen width and calculate the font size
    double screenWidth =
MediaQuery.of(context).size.width;
    double fontSize = screenWidth / 15;  // Font size is
relative to screen width

    return Scaffold(
      appBar: AppBar(title: Text('Dynamic Font Size')),
      body: Center(
        child: Text(
          'Responsive Text',
          style: TextStyle(fontSize: fontSize), // Adjust
font size dynamically
        ),
      ),
    );
  }
}

void main() {
  runApp(MaterialApp(home: DynamicText()));
}
```

In this example, the font size adjusts relative to the screen width. As the device's screen width increases, the text size will grow proportionally, ensuring readability across all devices.

In HTML, this would look something like this:

Example: Dynamic Font Size in HTML & CSS

```
<!-- html -->
<!DOCTYPE html>
<html lang="en">
<head>
  <meta charset="UTF-8">
  <meta name="viewport" content="width=device-width,
initial-scale=1.0">
  <title>Dynamic Font Size</title>
  <style>
    body {
      font-size: 5vw; /* Adjust font size relative to
viewport width */
    }
  </style>
</head>
<body>
  <h1>Responsive Text</h1>
</body>
</html>
```

Here, the `5vw` unit dynamically scales the text relative to the viewport width. As the browser window resizes, the font size will automatically adjust.

Both Flutter and HTML provide flexible solutions for making text responsive to screen size. While HTML uses viewport-based units or percentages, Flutter allows you to leverage built-in widgets like `MediaQuery` and `LayoutBuilder` to ensure text adapts based on the device's specifications.

4.6 Adding Shadows and Decorations to Text

Shadows and text decorations are effective tools for enhancing the visual appeal and readability of text in both Flutter and traditional web development. Text shadows can create a 3D effect, improve contrast, and make text stand out against complex backgrounds.

In Flutter, the `TextStyle` class provides the `shadows` property to apply shadow effects to text. This property takes a list of `Shadow` objects, where each shadow is defined by properties such as color, offset, and blur radius.

Example: Adding Shadows to Text in Flutter

```
//dart
import 'package:flutter/material.dart';

class ShadowText extends StatelessWidget {
  @override
  Widget build(BuildContext context) {
    return Scaffold(
      appBar: AppBar(title: Text('Text Shadows')),
      body: Center(
        child: Text(
          'Shadowed Text',
          style: TextStyle(
            fontSize: 40,
            fontWeight: FontWeight.bold,
            shadows: [
              Shadow(
                offset: Offset(3, 3),
                blurRadius: 5,
                color: Colors.black.withOpacity(0.3),
              ),
            ],
          ),
        ),
      ),
    );
  }
}

void main() {
  runApp(MaterialApp(home: ShadowText()));
}
```

In this example, the shadow is applied with an offset, blur radius, and a semi-transparent black color to give the text a floating appearance.

For comparison, here's how you can add shadows to text using HTML and CSS:

Example: Adding Shadows to Text in HTML & CSS

```
<!-- html -->
<!DOCTYPE html>
<html lang="en">
<head>
  <meta charset="UTF-8">
  <meta name="viewport" content="width=device-width,
initial-scale=1.0">
  <title>Text Shadows</title>
  <style>
    h1 {
      font-size: 40px;
      font-weight: bold;
      text-shadow: 3px 3px 5px rgba(0, 0, 0, 0.3); /*
Shadow with offset and blur */
    }
  </style>
</head>
<body>
  <h1>Shadowed Text</h1>
</body>
</html>
```

In this HTML example, the `text-shadow` property applies a shadow with an offset of `3px`, a blur radius of `5px`, and a semi-transparent black color. The result is similar to the Flutter implementation but done in CSS.

Additionally, Flutter allows you to apply other text decorations such as underlines, strikethroughs, and overlines. These can be achieved using the `decoration` property of `TextStyle`.

Example: Adding Text Decorations in Flutter

```
//dart
import 'package:flutter/material.dart';

class DecoratedText extends StatelessWidget {
  @override
  Widget build(BuildContext context) {
    return Scaffold(
```

```
        appBar: AppBar(title: Text('Text Decorations')),
        body: Center(
          child: Text(
            'Decorated Text',
            style: TextStyle(
              fontSize: 40,
              fontWeight: FontWeight.bold,
              decoration: TextDecoration.underline, //
Underline text
              decorationColor: Colors.blue,
              decorationThickness: 2,
            ),
          ),
        ),
      );
  }
}

void main() {
  runApp(MaterialApp(home: DecoratedText()));
}
```

This Flutter example demonstrates how to apply underlines, customize the color and thickness of the underline, and use other decorations like `lineThrough` or `overline` for additional styling.

4.7 Google Fonts in Flutter

Flutter's `google_fonts` package provides an easy way to integrate Google Fonts into your app. Google Fonts offers a wide range of free, high-quality fonts that can be accessed directly in Flutter, improving the design and readability of your app's text content.

To use Google Fonts in Flutter, follow these steps:

- Add the `google_fonts` package to your `pubspec.yaml` file.

```
//yaml
dependencies:
  google_fonts: ^2.1.0
```

Use the fonts in your Flutter app.

Example: Using Google Fonts in Flutter

```
//dart
import 'package:flutter/material.dart';
import 'package:google_fonts/google_fonts.dart';

class GoogleFontText extends StatelessWidget {
  @override
  Widget build(BuildContext context) {
    return Scaffold(
      appBar: AppBar(title: Text('Google Fonts')),
      body: Center(
        child: Text(
          'Styled with Google Fonts',
          style: GoogleFonts.lato(
            fontSize: 30,
            fontWeight: FontWeight.w700,
            color: Colors.purple,
          ),
        ),
      ),
    );
  }
}

void main() {
  runApp(MaterialApp(home: GoogleFontText()));
}
```

In this example, the `GoogleFonts.lato()` function is used to style the text with the "Lato" font, which is one of the popular Google Fonts. You can replace `lato()` with any font available in the Google Fonts library, such as `roboto()`, `openSans()`, or `poppins()`.

For comparison, here's how you would integrate Google Fonts in a web page using HTML and CSS:

Example: Using Google Fonts in HTML & CSS

```
<!-- html -->
<!DOCTYPE html>
<html lang="en">
<head>
  <meta charset="UTF-8">
  <meta name="viewport" content="width=device-width,
initial-scale=1.0">
  <title>Google Fonts</title>
  <link href="https://fonts.googleapis.com/css2?
family=Lato:wght@700&display=swap" rel="stylesheet">
  <style>
    body {
      font-family: 'Lato', sans-serif;
      font-weight: 700;
      font-size: 30px;
      color: purple;
    }
  </style>
</head>
<body>
  <h1>Styled with Google Fonts</h1>
</body>
</html>
```

In this HTML example, the Google Fonts API is used to load the "Lato" font, which is then applied to the body content. The process in web development involves linking to the Google Fonts URL and specifying the desired font family in the CSS.

4.8 Sample Code: HTML Text Styling vs Flutter Text Widgets

Below is a comparison of styling text in HTML with CSS and Flutter. We will examine the application of font size, color, shadows, and Google Fonts in both frameworks.

HTML & CSS Example

```
<!-- html -->
<!DOCTYPE html>
<html lang="en">
<head>
```

```
  <meta charset="UTF-8">
  <meta name="viewport" content="width=device-width,
initial-scale=1.0">
  <title>Text Styling</title>
  <link href="https://fonts.googleapis.com/css2?
family=Lato:wght@700&display=swap" rel="stylesheet">
  <style>
    body {
      font-family: 'Lato', sans-serif;
      font-size: 30px;
      color: purple;
      text-shadow: 3px 3px 5px rgba(0, 0, 0, 0.3);
    }
    h1 {
      text-align: center;
    }
  </style>
</head>
<body>
  <h1>Styled Text in HTML</h1>
</body>
</html>
```

Flutter Example

```
//dart
import 'package:flutter/material.dart';
import 'package:google_fonts/google_fonts.dart';

class StyledText extends StatelessWidget {
  @override
  Widget build(BuildContext context) {
    return Scaffold(
      appBar: AppBar(title: Text('Styled Text in
Flutter')),
      body: Center(
        child: Text(
          'Styled Text in Flutter',
          style: GoogleFonts.lato(
            fontSize: 30,
            fontWeight: FontWeight.w700,
            color: Colors.purple,
```

```
                shadows: [
                  Shadow(
                    offset: Offset(3, 3),
                    blurRadius: 5,
                    color: Colors.black.withOpacity(0.3),
                  ),
                ],
              ),
            ),
          ),
        );
  }
}

void main() {
  runApp(MaterialApp(home: StyledText()));
}
```

Both examples achieve similar results: a large purple text with shadows and using the Lato font from Google Fonts. However, the HTML version requires linking to an external stylesheet, whereas Flutter requires adding a package to manage the font styling and shadow effects.

Examples:

Basic Text Styling In both Flutter and web development, text styling includes properties such as color, font size, weight, and style. Here is a simple comparison.

HTML/CSS:

```
<!-- html -->
<!DOCTYPE html>

<html lang="en">
<head>
  <meta charset="UTF-8">
  <meta name="viewport" content="width=device-width,
initial-scale=1.0">
  <title>Styled Text</title>
  <style>
```

```
    body {
      font-size: 24px;
      color: #ff6347;
      font-weight: bold;
      font-family: Arial, sans-serif;
    }
  </style>
</head>
<body>
  <h1>Welcome to Web Styling</h1>
</body>
</html>
```

This HTML/CSS code uses `font-size`, `color`, and `font-weight` to style the text.

Flutter:

```
//dart
import 'package:flutter/material.dart';

void main() {
  runApp(MaterialApp(
    home: Scaffold(
      body: Center(
        child: Text(
          'Welcome to Flutter Styling',
          style: TextStyle(
            fontSize: 24,
            color: Colors.deepOrange,
            fontWeight: FontWeight.bold,
            fontFamily: 'Arial',
          ),
        ),
      ),
    ),
  ));
}
```

In Flutter, `TextStyle` is used for styling the text, which is directly applied to a `Text` widget.

Text Alignment: Centering the Text Aligning text centrally is one of the most common tasks in both Flutter and web development.

HTML/CSS:

```
<!-- html -->
<!DOCTYPE html>

<html lang="en">
<head>
  <meta charset="UTF-8">
  <meta name="viewport" content="width=device-width,
initial-scale=1.0">
  <title>Centered Text</title>
  <style>
    body {
      display: flex;
      justify-content: center;
      align-items: center;
      height: 100vh;
      margin: 0;
      font-family: Arial, sans-serif;
    }
    h1 {
      font-size: 36px;
    }
  </style>
</head>
<body>
  <h1>Centered Text in HTML</h1>
</body>
</html>
```

This example uses Flexbox to center the text both horizontally and vertically on the page.

Flutter:

```
//dart
```

```dart
import 'package:flutter/material.dart';

void main() {
  runApp(MaterialApp(
    home: Scaffold(
      body: Center(
        child: Text(
          'Centered Text in Flutter',
          style: TextStyle(fontSize: 36),
        ),
      ),
    ),
  ));
}
```

In Flutter, the `Center` widget wraps around the `Text` widget, automatically aligning it in the center of the screen.

Dynamic Font Size Based on Screen Width For responsive design, adjusting text size based on screen width is critical.

HTML/CSS:

```html
<!-- html -->
<!DOCTYPE html>

<html lang="en">
<head>
  <meta charset="UTF-8">
  <meta name="viewport" content="width=device-width,
initial-scale=1.0">
  <title>Responsive Font Size</title>
  <style>
    body {
      font-size: 5vw;  /* Font size is 5% of the viewport
width */
    }
  </style>
</head>
<body>
  <h1>Responsive Text</h1>
```

```
</body>
</html>
```

The `vw` unit in CSS is a viewport-based unit that adjusts the font size relative to the width of the browser window.

Flutter:

```
//dart
import 'package:flutter/material.dart';

class ResponsiveText extends StatelessWidget {
  @override
  Widget build(BuildContext context) {
    double screenWidth =
MediaQuery.of(context).size.width;
    double fontSize = screenWidth / 10;  // Font size is
10% of screen width

    return Scaffold(
      appBar: AppBar(title: Text('Responsive Text in
Flutter')),
      body: Center(
        child: Text(
          'Responsive Text in Flutter',
          style: TextStyle(fontSize: fontSize),
        ),
      ),
    );
  }
}

void main() {
  runApp(MaterialApp(home: ResponsiveText()));
}
```

In Flutter, `MediaQuery` allows access to screen properties, and the font size can be dynamically adjusted based on the screen width.

Text Shadows Adding shadows to text makes it stand out more effectively, especially on complex backgrounds.

HTML/CSS:

```
<!-- html -->
<!DOCTYPE html>

<html lang="en">
<head>
  <meta charset="UTF-8">
  <meta name="viewport" content="width=device-width,
initial-scale=1.0">
  <title>Text Shadows</title>
  <style>
    h1 {
      font-size: 40px;
      font-weight: bold;
      text-shadow: 3px 3px 5px rgba(0, 0, 0, 0.3);
    }
  </style>
</head>
<body>
  <h1>Shadowed Text in HTML</h1>
</body>
</html>
```

This example in HTML applies a shadow with an offset of `3px`, a blur radius of `5px`, and a black color with some transparency.

Flutter:

```
//dart
import 'package:flutter/material.dart';

class ShadowText extends StatelessWidget {
  @override
  Widget build(BuildContext context) {
    return Scaffold(
      appBar: AppBar(title: Text('Text Shadows')),
      body: Center(
        child: Text(
          'Shadowed Text in Flutter',
          style: TextStyle(
            fontSize: 40,
            fontWeight: FontWeight.bold,
```

```
              shadows: [
                Shadow(
                  offset: Offset(3, 3),
                  blurRadius: 5,
                  color: Colors.black.withOpacity(0.3),
                ),
              ],
            ),
          ),
        ),
      );
    }
  }

void main() {
  runApp(MaterialApp(home: ShadowText()));
}
```

Flutter uses `TextStyle` with the `shadows` property, which takes a list of `Shadow` objects for customizable shadow effects.

Tips:

- **1: Utilize Relative Units for Text Responsiveness**
  In both CSS and Flutter, it's essential to use relative units like percentages, `em`, or viewport-based units (e.g., `vw`, `vh`) for font sizes to ensure that the text adjusts dynamically across various screen sizes. Avoid hardcoding fixed pixel values unless necessary for static designs.

- **2: Leverage Flexbox and Center Widgets for Alignment**
  Aligning text properly is a crucial aspect of layout. In web development, Flexbox is a powerful tool to center and align text within its container. In Flutter, the `Center` widget simplifies this task by automatically centering any child widget, including text.

- **3: Apply Shadows for Depth and Readability**
  Text shadows are effective in improving text visibility, especially against complex or dynamic backgrounds. Use subtle shadows (i.e., small offsets and low opacity) to prevent overpowering the text, ensuring the text remains the

focal point.

Actionable Strategies:

- **1: Implement Accessibility Features with Text**
  Use dynamic font sizes that adjust to users' preferred reading settings. For example, in Flutter, you can use `MediaQuery.textScaleFactor` to allow for text scaling, ensuring readability for users with vision impairments. Similarly, in HTML, use relative units like `em` or `rem` instead of `px` to support browser-based text scaling.

- **2: Maintain Consistency Across Platforms**
  When building applications for both web and mobile, it's important to keep your text styles consistent. Leverage global style sheets in CSS or centralized `TextStyle` management in Flutter to ensure uniformity in font sizes, weights, and colors across your application. You can even abstract your text styling into reusable components or classes.

- **3: Customize Text for Different Themes and Branding**
  Both Flutter and web development allow customization of fonts for unique branding. Choose fonts that align with your app or website's identity, and ensure they are legible across devices and screen sizes. Flutter's `GoogleFonts` package is an excellent resource for using popular fonts, while in HTML, you can link to Google Fonts or custom web fonts.

- **4: Optimize Performance by Limiting Text Shadows**
  While text shadows can add visual appeal, overusing them can negatively impact performance, especially in mobile apps. Limit the number of text shadows and avoid excessive blur effects or heavy offsets. Use shadows sparingly to improve performance without compromising aesthetics.

- **5: Apply Typography Hierarchy for Better Readability**
  Implement a clear typography hierarchy for effective communication. Differentiate between headers, sub-headers, body text, and other text elements by using varying font sizes, weights, and styles. This practice not only improves readability but also enhances user experience by guiding the user through the content seamlessly.

These examples, tips, and strategies highlight the different ways text styling and alignment can be handled in HTML/CSS/JavaScript compared to Flutter. While both platforms offer powerful text manipulation capabilities, the approaches and methods for achieving the same effects vary. By understanding these differences and applying best practices, you can ensure consistent, responsive, and visually appealing text styling in your applications.

Chapter 5: **Container and Layout Basics**

In both Flutter and web development, layout and container management is essential for controlling how elements are displayed and arranged on the screen. The core concept of using a container widget to manage dimensions, colors, borders, and alignment is common across both platforms, albeit with different syntax and practices. Understanding these core principles will enable developers to build responsive, visually appealing user interfaces whether on the web or mobile.

5.1 Introducing the Container Widget

In Flutter, the `Container` widget is one of the most commonly used elements for arranging and styling other widgets. It serves as a box that can contain other widgets, and its properties allow developers to manipulate the size, padding, alignment, and decoration of the widget. It acts as a flexible wrapper that offers immense customization and control over the layout.

Flutter Example:

```
//dart
Container(
  width: 200.0,
  height: 100.0,
  padding: EdgeInsets.all(10.0),
  color: Colors.blue,
  child: Center(
    child: Text(
      'Container Widget in Flutter',
      style: TextStyle(color: Colors.white, fontSize: 18),
    ),
  ),
)
```

In this Flutter example, the `Container` widget has several properties:

- `width` and `height`: These define the size of the container.
- `padding`: Adds space between the container's boundaries and the child widget inside.
- `color`: Sets the background color of the container.
- `child`: Contains another widget, in this case, a `Text` widget, which will be displayed inside the container.

HTML/CSS Equivalent:

In web development, HTML and CSS can also achieve similar container management with `div` elements styled through CSS. For example:

```
<!-- html -->
<!DOCTYPE html>
<html lang="en">
<head>
  <meta charset="UTF-8">
  <meta name="viewport" content="width=device-width,
initial-scale=1.0">
  <title>Container Example</title>
  <style>
    .container {
      width: 200px;
      height: 100px;
      padding: 10px;
      background-color: blue;
      color: white;
      display: flex;
      justify-content: center;
      align-items: center;
      font-size: 18px;
    }
  </style>
</head>
<body>
  <div class="container">
    Container Widget in HTML/CSS
  </div>
</body>
</html>
```

In this HTML/CSS example, the `div` element acts as the container:

- The `width` and `height` properties define the size of the container.
- `padding` creates space between the container's boundary and the text.
- `background-color` adds color to the container.
- The `display: flex`, `justify-content: center`, and `align-`

`items: center` properties center the text inside the container.
Both approaches create a box with text inside, but the main difference lies in how the properties are defined. In Flutter, you rely on Dart syntax for container management, while in HTML/CSS, you use styling properties in a separate style tag or external stylesheet.

5.2 Setting Widths and Heights: Flutter vs CSS

Setting dimensions such as width and height is crucial for layout control. Flutter provides flexible options to define dimensions, allowing precise control over widget sizes. On the web, CSS gives developers the same level of control, but with a variety of units (pixels, percentages, viewport units, etc.).

Setting Width and Height in Flutter

In Flutter, `Container` is used to define width and height explicitly. These properties ensure the widget is given a fixed size. The following example demonstrates setting the width and height of a container:

Flutter Example:

```
//dart
Container(
  width: 250.0,
  height: 150.0,
  color: Colors.green,
  child: Text(
    'Flutter Container with Fixed Size',
    style: TextStyle(fontSize: 20, color: Colors.white),
  ),
)
```

This example explicitly defines the width (`250.0`) and height (`150.0`) of the container. The `Text` widget inside will be displayed based on the size of the container, and the text is centered inside the container.

Flutter also offers `double.infinity` for width or height to allow the widget to expand to the available space. For example:

```
//dart
Container(
  width: double.infinity,
```

```
  height: 200.0,
  color: Colors.red,
  child: Center(
    child: Text('Full Width Container'),
  ),
)
```

Here, the container will expand to fill the width of the parent widget but keep the height fixed at `200.0`.

Setting Width and Height in CSS

In CSS, defining width and height is straightforward. You can use pixels (`px`), percentages (`%`), or viewport units (`vw` for width, `vh` for height). The following example demonstrates setting width and height using CSS:

HTML/CSS Example:

```
<!-- html -->
<!DOCTYPE html>
<html lang="en">
<head>
  <meta charset="UTF-8">
  <meta name="viewport" content="width=device-width,
initial-scale=1.0">
  <title>Fixed Size Container</title>
  <style>
    .container {
      width: 250px;
      height: 150px;
      background-color: green;
      color: white;
      display: flex;
      justify-content: center;
      align-items: center;
    }
  </style>
</head>
<body>
  <div class="container">
    CSS Container with Fixed Size
  </div>
```

```
</body>
</html>
```

In this example, the `width` is set to `250px` and the `height` is set to `150px`. The `div` element takes up this space, and the text is centered within the container using Flexbox (`justify-content: center; align-items: center`).

For responsiveness, CSS allows using percentages or viewport units like `vw` and `vh`. For instance:

```
/* css */
.container {
  width: 100%;
  height: 50vh;
}
```

This makes the container take up the full width of the parent element and half the height of the viewport, adapting to different screen sizes.

5.3 Adding Background Colors

Both Flutter and web development offer the ability to set background colors to containers. However, the implementation syntax varies.

Setting Background Color in Flutter

In Flutter, you can set the background color of a container using the `color` property of the `Container` widget. The `Color` class can be used to define a variety of color options, including standard colors or custom ones.

Flutter Example:

```
//dart
Container(
  width: 250.0,
  height: 150.0,
  color: Colors.purple,
  child: Center(
    child: Text(
      'Purple Container in Flutter',
      style: TextStyle(color: Colors.white, fontSize: 20),
```

```
    ),
  ),
)
```

In this example, the `color` property is set to `Colors.purple`, which applies a purple background color to the container.

To create a custom color in Flutter, you can use the `Color` class and specify RGB or hexadecimal values:

```
//dart
Container(
  width: 250.0,
  height: 150.0,
  color: Color(0xFF42A5F5), // Custom color using
Hexadecimal value
  child: Center(
    child: Text(
      'Custom Color Container in Flutter',
      style: TextStyle(color: Colors.white, fontSize: 20),
    ),
  ),
)
```

Setting Background Color in CSS

In CSS, the `background-color` property is used to set the background color of an element. Colors can be specified using color names, hexadecimal values, RGB values, or even HSL.

HTML/CSS Example:

```
<!-- html -->
<!DOCTYPE html>
<html lang="en">
<head>
  <meta charset="UTF-8">
  <meta name="viewport" content="width=device-width,
initial-scale=1.0">
  <title>Background Color Example</title>
  <style>
    .container {
      width: 250px;
```

```
      height: 150px;
      background-color: purple;
      color: white;
      display: flex;
      justify-content: center;
      align-items: center;
    }
  </style>
</head>
<body>
  <div class="container">
    Purple Container in HTML/CSS
  </div>
</body>
</html>
```

In this example, the `background-color` property is set to `purple`, which colors the background of the `div` element. You can also use hexadecimal values like `#42A5F5` for custom colors.

5.4 Borders and Rounded Corners

Borders and rounded corners are an essential aspect of container styling, offering a way to differentiate elements visually. Both Flutter and web development provide options for customizing borders and corner radius.

Setting Borders and Rounded Corners in Flutter

In Flutter, the `decoration` property of the `Container` widget is used to apply borders, shadows, and rounded corners. The `BoxDecoration` class provides properties like `border` and `borderRadius`.

Flutter Example:

```
//dart
Container(
  width: 250.0,
  height: 150.0,
  decoration: BoxDecoration(
    color: Colors.green,
    border: Border.all(color: Colors.black, width: 3),
```

```
    borderRadius: BorderRadius.circular(20),
  ),
  child: Center(
    child: Text(
      'Container with Border and Rounded Corners',
      style: TextStyle(color: Colors.white, fontSize: 18),
    ),
  ),
)
```

In this example:

- `border`: Adds a black border with a width of `3`.
- `borderRadius`: Sets the radius of the corners to `20` pixels, creating rounded corners.

Setting Borders and Rounded Corners in CSS

In CSS, borders and rounded corners are applied using the `border` and `border-radius` properties.

HTML/CSS Example:

```
<!-- html -->
<!DOCTYPE html>
<html lang="en">
<head>
  <meta charset="UTF-8">
  <meta name="viewport" content="width=device-width,
initial-scale=1.0">
  <title>Border and Rounded Corners</title>
  <style>
    .container {
      width: 250px;
      height: 150px;
      background-color: green;
      color: white;
      display: flex;
      justify-content: center;
      align-items: center;
      border: 3px solid black;
```

```
      border-radius: 20px;
    }
  </style>
</head>
<body>
  <div class="container">
    Border and Rounded Corners in HTML/CSS
  </div>
</body>
</html>
```

In this example:

- `border`: Sets a `3px` solid black border around the container.
- `border-radius`: Rounds the corners with a `20px` radius.

CSS also allows for more complex border styling, such as using different border styles (`dotted`, `dashed`, etc.) and multiple borders around an element.

In conclusion, understanding how containers and layouts are handled in Flutter and web development is crucial for building responsive and visually engaging applications. While Flutter's `Container` widget provides a single, unified approach for layout and styling, web development offers greater flexibility in terms of HTML and CSS, allowing more diverse design patterns. Both approaches offer similar core concepts, but the syntax and specific implementation details differ, which is essential for developers to grasp for effective cross-platform development.

5.5 Shadows and Elevation Effects

Shadows and elevation effects are essential tools for creating visual depth and highlighting UI elements in both web and mobile applications. While the overall concepts of shadowing are similar across platforms, their implementation and fine-tuning differ, particularly between CSS for web and Flutter for mobile apps.

Shadows in Web Development with CSS

In web development, shadows are typically implemented using the `box-shadow` property. This property allows developers to create shadows around elements, offering a sense of depth and making UI components more prominent. A basic shadow is created by specifying horizontal and vertical offsets, blur radius, and color. Additionally, web developers can control the spread of the shadow and apply multiple shadows to the same element.

```
<!-- html -->
<!DOCTYPE html>
<html lang="en">
<head>
  <meta charset="UTF-8">
  <meta name="viewport" content="width=device-width,
initial-scale=1.0">
  <title>CSS Box Shadow Example</title>
  <style>
    .shadow-box {
      width: 300px;
      height: 200px;
      background-color: lightblue;
      box-shadow: 10px 10px 20px rgba(0, 0, 0, 0.3); /*
Horizontal offset, vertical offset, blur, and color */
      border-radius: 15px;
      margin: 50px;
    }
  </style>
</head>
<body>
  <div class="shadow-box"></div>
</body>
</html>
```

In the above code, the `box-shadow` property creates a shadow with a 10px horizontal and vertical offset, a 20px blur radius, and a black color with 30% opacity. Shadows can also be used with inset properties to create inner shadows, providing even more options for creative UI design.

Shadows in Flutter

Flutter, with its emphasis on a fluid and expressive design language, offers a more flexible and dynamic way of creating shadows using the `BoxShadow` widget. The `BoxShadow` class allows developers to customize the offset, blur radius, spread radius, and color of the shadow.

```
//dart
```

```
import 'package:flutter/material.dart';

class ShadowExample extends StatelessWidget {
  @override
  Widget build(BuildContext context) {
    return Scaffold(
      appBar: AppBar(title: Text('Flutter Shadow
Example')),
      body: Center(
        child: Container(
          width: 300,
          height: 200,
          decoration: BoxDecoration(
            color: Colors.lightBlue,
            borderRadius: BorderRadius.circular(15),
            boxShadow: [
              BoxShadow(
                color: Colors.black.withOpacity(0.3),
                offset: Offset(10, 10),
                blurRadius: 20,
              ),
            ],
          ),
        ),
      ),
    );
  }
}
```

In Flutter, the `BoxDecoration` widget is used to add shadows, borders, and rounded corners. The `boxShadow` parameter accepts a list of `BoxShadow` objects, allowing for multiple shadows to be applied to a single element. Here, the `offset` is specified as `(10, 10)`, creating a shadow with horizontal and vertical offsets. The `blurRadius` controls how soft the shadow appears, and the `color` allows transparency by using `withOpacity`.

Key Differences

- **CSS** uses the `box-shadow` property directly on the element, and shadows can be applied to a variety of element types, such as `div`, `button`, etc.
- **Flutter** uses the `BoxShadow` widget inside `BoxDecoration` and offers more

customization options, such as adding shadows to specific widget types (e.g., `Container`, `Card`, etc.).

Tips for Working with Shadows:

- **Soft Shadows for Elevated Components**: Shadows are particularly effective for creating a sense of elevation or layering in the UI. For example, cards or buttons that should appear elevated can have shadows applied with a larger blur radius.
- **Dynamic Shadows**: In Flutter, shadows can be modified dynamically, such as changing the shadow based on user interaction or scrolling, adding interactivity to the UI.
- **Use of Transparency**: By setting opacity on shadows, you can achieve more subtle and aesthetically pleasing effects.

5.6 Nested Containers for Complex Layouts

When building complex layouts, the ability to nest containers is fundamental in both web development and Flutter. By nesting containers, developers can create sophisticated layouts with multiple levels of hierarchy, each controlling specific aspects of the design such as positioning, styling, and alignment.

Nested Containers in Web Development

In web development, nested containers are created by embedding `div` elements within other `div` elements. This technique allows developers to structure content efficiently and control the layout using CSS. For example, a simple layout with a header, content area, and footer can be achieved by nesting `div` containers.

```
<!-- html -->
<!DOCTYPE html>
<html lang="en">
<head>
  <meta charset="UTF-8">
  <meta name="viewport" content="width=device-width,
initial-scale=1.0">
  <title>Nested Containers</title>
  <style>
    .container {
      width: 80%;
      margin: 0 auto;
```

```
    }
    .header, .footer {
      background-color: #333;
      color: white;
      padding: 10px;
    }
    .content {
      display: flex;
      justify-content: space-between;
    }
    .content .section {
      width: 48%;
      background-color: #f4f4f4;
      padding: 20px;
      box-shadow: 2px 2px 10px rgba(0, 0, 0, 0.1);
    }
  </style>
</head>
<body>
  <div class="container">
    <div class="header">Header Section</div>
    <div class="content">
      <div class="section">Left Section</div>
      <div class="section">Right Section</div>
    </div>
    <div class="footer">Footer Section</div>
  </div>
</body>
</html>
```

In this example, the `.container` div wraps all sections of the page, and inside it, the `.header`, `.content`, and `.footer` are defined. Within the `.content` section, two `.section` divs are nested side by side using Flexbox. The use of nested containers here provides flexibility in positioning and organizing content on the page.

Nested Containers in Flutter

Flutter also allows for nested containers using widgets like `Column`, `Row`, `Stack`, and `Container`. These widgets help manage complex layouts by allowing you to stack or arrange elements in various directions. For instance, a common pattern for creating a column layout with multiple sections can be implemented using the `Column` widget.

```
//dart
import 'package:flutter/material.dart';

class NestedContainersExample extends StatelessWidget {
  @override
  Widget build(BuildContext context) {
    return Scaffold(
      appBar: AppBar(title: Text('Nested Containers in
Flutter')),
      body: Container(
        width: double.infinity,
        padding: EdgeInsets.all(20),
        color: Colors.grey[200],
        child: Column(
          children: [
            Container(
              width: double.infinity,
              color: Colors.blue,
              padding: EdgeInsets.all(10),
              child: Text(
                'Header Section',
                style: TextStyle(color: Colors.white),
              ),
            ),
            Row(
              mainAxisAlignment:
MainAxisAlignment.spaceBetween,
              children: [
                Container(
                  width: 150,
                  color: Colors.orange,
                  padding: EdgeInsets.all(20),
                  child: Text('Left Section'),
                ),
                Container(
                  width: 150,
                  color: Colors.green,
                  padding: EdgeInsets.all(20),
                  child: Text('Right Section'),
                ),
              ],
            ),
```

```
                Container(
                  width: double.infinity,
                  color: Colors.blue,
                  padding: EdgeInsets.all(10),
                  child: Text(
                    'Footer Section',
                    style: TextStyle(color: Colors.white),
                  ),
                ),
              ],
            ),
          ),
        );
    }
}
```

In the Flutter code above, a `Container` wraps the entire layout, and inside it, there are nested `Container` widgets for the header, footer, and the row that holds the left and right sections. The use of the `Column` and `Row` widgets allows for vertical and horizontal arrangement of the elements, respectively.

Key Differences

- **CSS** requires `div` tags with specific classes for structure, and positioning/layout is handled with CSS properties like `display`, `flex`, and `grid`.
- **Flutter** uses widgets, with `Column` and `Row` for vertical and horizontal layouts. Containers in Flutter can be nested within each other to create complex UI structures.

Tips for Nested Containers:

- **Modular Approach**: When creating complex UIs, break down large containers into smaller reusable components. This approach enhances maintainability and readability.
- **Layering with Stacks**: In Flutter, the `Stack` widget allows for overlapping widgets, providing additional flexibility for complex layouts like floating buttons or cards.
- **Alignment and Spacing**: Proper alignment and spacing between nested elements improve the visual appeal. In Flutter, `Align`, `Padding`, and `SizedBox` can help control spacing effectively.

5.7 Debugging Layout Issues in Flutter

Layout issues in Flutter often arise from improper use of widgets or incorrect constraints. Flutter's rich set of debugging tools, such as the `Flutter Inspector`, can assist in identifying and resolving these issues. However, understanding common causes of layout issues and using the right debugging techniques is key to resolving problems efficiently.

Common Layout Issues in Flutter

1. **Overflowing Widgets**: This happens when the size of a widget exceeds the available space, causing it to overflow and display an error message like "A RenderFlex overflowed by X pixels."
    - **Solution**: Ensure that widgets are properly constrained, using `Expanded`, `Flexible`, or `SingleChildScrollView` to make sure widgets resize correctly based on the available space.
2. **Alignment Problems**: Misalignment occurs when widgets are not aligned according to the desired design.
    - **Solution**: Use alignment properties such as `Align`, `Center`, and `MainAxisAlignment` to adjust positioning.
3. **Unresponsive Layouts**: Sometimes, layouts may not behave as expected when the screen size changes, especially when designing for mobile devices with different screen sizes.
    - **Solution**: Use media queries, `LayoutBuilder`, or `FractionallySizedBox` to make layouts responsive to different screen sizes.

Debugging Layouts in Flutter

- **Flutter Inspector**: The Flutter Inspector is a powerful tool that helps visualize widget structures and constraints in your app. It shows widget hierarchies and provides information about the widget's size, position, and constraints.

1. Open it through Android Studio, VS Code, or Flutter DevTools.
2. Use the "Select Widget Mode" to inspect a widget and identify where problems occur.

- **Debugging with `debugPaintSizeEnabled`**: Enabling `debugPaintSizeEnabled` draws borders around widgets, helping to identify layout problems like widgets being off-screen or overlapping unexpectedly.

```
//dart
void main() {
  debugPaintSizeEnabled = true;
  runApp(MyApp());
}
```

- **Checking Render Errors**: Flutter logs often contain errors related to layout issues, such as constraint problems or widget overflow. Pay attention to warnings and errors in the console to identify and fix issues.

Tips for Debugging Layout Issues:

- **Check Constraints**: Always check constraints and ensure that widgets are not exceeding the available space.
- **Use Overflowing Widgets Wisely**: Avoid overflowing content. Use `SingleChildScrollView` or `ListView` when dealing with large amounts of content that might overflow.
- **Responsive Design**: Ensure that layouts adapt to various screen sizes by using responsive design techniques.

5.8 Sample Code: CSS Containers vs Flutter Containers

In this section, we compare the structure of HTML/CSS containers and Flutter containers, highlighting their similarities and differences.

HTML/CSS Example: Basic Layout with Containers

```
<!-- html -->
<!DOCTYPE html>
<html lang="en">
<head>
  <meta charset="UTF-8">
  <meta name="viewport" content="width=device-width,
```

```
initial-scale=1.0">
  <title>Basic Layout with Containers</title>
  <style>
    .container {
      width: 80%;
      margin: 0 auto;
      padding: 20px;
      background-color: #f4f4f4;
    }
    .header, .footer {
      background-color: #333;
      color: white;
      padding: 10px;
      text-align: center;
    }
    .content {
      display: flex;
      justify-content: space-between;
    }
    .content .section {
      width: 48%;
      background-color: #fff;
      padding: 20px;
      box-shadow: 0 0 10px rgba(0, 0, 0, 0.1);
    }
  </style>
</head>
<body>
  <div class="container">
    <div class="header">Header Section</div>
    <div class="content">
      <div class="section">Left Section</div>
      <div class="section">Right Section</div>
    </div>
    <div class="footer">Footer Section</div>
  </div>
</body>
</html>
```

Flutter Example: Similar Layout with Containers

```
//dart
```

```
import 'package:flutter/material.dart';

class BasicLayoutExample extends StatelessWidget {
  @override
  Widget build(BuildContext context) {
    return Scaffold(
      appBar: AppBar(title: Text('Basic Layout with
Containers')),
      body: Container(
        width: double.infinity,
        padding: EdgeInsets.all(20),
        color: Colors.grey[200],
        child: Column(
          children: [
            Container(
              width: double.infinity,
              color: Colors.blue,
              padding: EdgeInsets.all(10),
              child: Text(
                'Header Section',
                style: TextStyle(color: Colors.white),
              ),
            ),
            Row(
              mainAxisAlignment:
MainAxisAlignment.spaceBetween,
              children: [
                Container(
                  width: 150,
                  color: Colors.orange,
                  padding: EdgeInsets.all(20),
                  child: Text('Left Section'),
                ),
                Container(
                  width: 150,
                  color: Colors.green,
                  padding: EdgeInsets.all(20),
                  child: Text('Right Section'),
                ),
              ],
            ),
            Container(
```

```
                    width: double.infinity,
                    color: Colors.blue,
                    padding: EdgeInsets.all(10),
                    child: Text(
                      'Footer Section',
                      style: TextStyle(color: Colors.white),
                    ),
                  ),
                ],
              ),
            ),
          );
        }
      }
```

Key Differences in Layouts:

- **Structure**: Both CSS and Flutter use containers (`div` and `Container` widgets) to structure content, but Flutter uses a more declarative approach with widgets.
- **Flexbox vs Row/Column**: In CSS, Flexbox is used for responsive layouts, while Flutter uses `Row` and `Column` for horizontal and vertical layout management.
- **Styling**: CSS styles are applied using classes and stylesheets, while Flutter uses widget properties such as `decoration` to manage the appearance.

Through the comparison and detailed explanation of shadowing, nested containers, and debugging techniques, we understand that both web development (HTML/CSS) and Flutter offer similar concepts but have distinct implementations. Flutter's declarative UI and widget-based structure offer a more programmatic approach compared to the stylesheet-driven design of web applications. However, mastering both methods enables developers to create responsive, dynamic, and engaging UIs across multiple platforms.

Examples

- **Example 1: Centering Elements with Flexbox (HTML/CSS) vs Flutter**

In HTML and CSS, centering an element can be done using the `flexbox` layout. The `display: flex` property allows for easy alignment of elements in both horizontal and vertical directions.

HTML/CSS:

```
<!-- html -->
<div class="container">
  <div class="content">
    Centered Content
  </div>
</div>

<style>
  .container {
    display: flex;
    justify-content: center;
    align-items: center;
    height: 100vh;
    background-color: lightgray;
  }
  .content {
    padding: 20px;
    background-color: darkblue;
    color: white;
  }
</style>
```

In the Flutter framework, achieving the same effect involves using the `Center` widget, which automatically aligns its child both vertically and horizontally.

Flutter:

```
//dart
import 'package:flutter/material.dart';

void main() => runApp(MyApp());

class MyApp extends StatelessWidget {
  @override
  Widget build(BuildContext context) {
    return MaterialApp(
      home: Scaffold(
        body: Center(
          child: Container(
            padding: EdgeInsets.all(20),
            color: Colors.blue,
            child: Text(
```

```
                'Centered Content',
                style: TextStyle(color: Colors.white),
              ),
            ),
          ),
        ),
      );
  }
}
```

Example 2: Creating a Responsive Grid (HTML/CSS) vs Flutter
In CSS, you can create responsive grids using `grid` or `flexbox`. Here's an example using the `grid` layout:

HTML/CSS:

```
<!-- html -->
<div class="grid-container">
  <div class="item">Item 1</div>
  <div class="item">Item 2</div>
  <div class="item">Item 3</div>
  <div class="item">Item 4</div>
</div>

<style>
  .grid-container {
    display: grid;
    grid-template-columns: repeat(auto-fill, minmax(200px,
1fr));
    gap: 10px;
  }
  .item {
    background-color: lightcoral;
    padding: 20px;
    color: white;
    text-align: center;
  }
</style>
```

In Flutter, a similar grid can be created using the `GridView` widget, which allows you to define the grid structure and items dynamically.

Flutter:

```
//dart
import 'package:flutter/material.dart';

void main() => runApp(MyApp());

class MyApp extends StatelessWidget {
  @override
  Widget build(BuildContext context) {
    return MaterialApp(
      home: Scaffold(
        appBar: AppBar(title: Text('Flutter Grid
Example')),
        body: GridView.builder(
          gridDelegate:
SliverGridDelegateWithFixedCrossAxisCount(
            crossAxisCount: 2,
            crossAxisSpacing: 10.0,
            mainAxisSpacing: 10.0,
          ),
          itemCount: 4,
          itemBuilder: (context, index) {
            return Container(
              color: Colors.red,
              padding: EdgeInsets.all(20),
              alignment: Alignment.center,
              child: Text(
                'Item ${index + 1}',
                style: TextStyle(color: Colors.white),
              ),
            );
          },
        ),
      ),
    );
  }
}
```

Example 3: Stacking Elements on Top of Each Other (HTML/CSS) vs Flutter

In HTML/CSS, you can stack elements using the `position` property. By setting `position: absolute` and defining `top`, `left`, `right`, or `bottom` values, elements can overlap each other.

HTML/CSS:

```
<!-- html -->
<div class="container">
  <div class="background"></div>
  <div class="overlay">Overlay Content</div>
</div>

<style>
  .container {
    position: relative;
    width: 300px;
    height: 300px;
    background-color: lightblue;
  }
  .background {
    position: absolute;
    top: 0;
    left: 0;
    width: 100%;
    height: 100%;
    background-color: darkblue;
  }
  .overlay {
    position: absolute;
    top: 50%;
    left: 50%;
    transform: translate(-50%, -50%);
    color: white;
  }
</style>
```

In Flutter, the `Stack` widget serves the same purpose, allowing elements to be stacked on top of each other.

Flutter:

```
//dart
import 'package:flutter/material.dart';

void main() => runApp(MyApp());
```

```
class MyApp extends StatelessWidget {
  @override
  Widget build(BuildContext context) {
    return MaterialApp(
      home: Scaffold(
        body: Stack(
          children: [
            Container(
              width: 300,
              height: 300,
              color: Colors.blue,
            ),
            Center(
              child: Text(
                'Overlay Content',
                style: TextStyle(color: Colors.white),
              ),
            ),
          ],
        ),
      ),
    );
  }
}
```

Example 4: Creating a Card with Shadow (HTML/CSS) vs Flutter
In HTML/CSS, you can create a card-like component with a shadow effect using the `box-shadow` property.

HTML/CSS:

```
<!-- html -->
<div class="card">
  <h3>Card Title</h3>
  <p>This is a card with a shadow effect.</p>
</div>

<style>
  .card {
    background-color: white;
    padding: 20px;
```

```
    border-radius: 10px;
    box-shadow: 0 4px 8px rgba(0, 0, 0, 0.1);
  }
</style>
```

In Flutter, you can achieve the same result by using the `Card` widget, which comes with a built-in shadow effect.

Flutter:

```
//dart
import 'package:flutter/material.dart';

void main() => runApp(MyApp());

class MyApp extends StatelessWidget {
  @override
  Widget build(BuildContext context) {
    return MaterialApp(
      home: Scaffold(
        appBar: AppBar(title: Text('Card with Shadow')),
        body: Center(
          child: Card(
            elevation: 4.0,
            shape: RoundedRectangleBorder(
              borderRadius: BorderRadius.circular(10),
            ),
            child: Padding(
              padding: EdgeInsets.all(20),
              child: Column(
                children: [
                  Text(
                    'Card Title',
                    style: TextStyle(fontSize: 20,
fontWeight: FontWeight.bold),
                  ),
                  SizedBox(height: 10),
                  Text('This is a card with a shadow
effect.'),
                ],
              ),
            ),
```

```
            ),
          ),
        ),
      );
    }
  }
```

Tips

1: Use `Flex` and `Column/Row` Widgets to Mimic Flexbox Behavior

- While Flutter offers several ways to layout components, the `Column` and `Row` widgets work similarly to CSS's `flex` layout. For vertical or horizontal arrangements, use `Column` (vertical) or `Row` (horizontal), which automatically handles children alignment. The `MainAxisAlignment` and `CrossAxisAlignment` properties in Flutter map directly to the `justify-content` and `align-items` CSS properties.

2: Keep Flutter Layouts Efficient with `Expanded` and `Flexible`

- In Flutter, `Expanded` and `Flexible` widgets help distribute available space within a parent container in ways similar to CSS's `flex-grow` and `flex-shrink`. These widgets ensure that child elements take up appropriate space, especially when using `Row` or `Column` layouts.

3: Avoid Over-using Nested Containers for Performance

- Excessive nesting of `Container` widgets can negatively affect the performance of your Flutter application. If you're using containers for spacing or padding, consider whether other layout widgets like `Padding`, `Align`, or `Column/Row` can achieve the desired effect without additional layers of `Container`.

Actionable Strategies

1: Prioritize Flexbox or Grid for Adaptive Layouts

- Whether you're working in HTML/CSS or Flutter, always prioritize the use of flexbox or grid-like structures when building layouts that need to adapt to different screen sizes. In Flutter, `Column`, `Row`, and `GridView` provide powerful tools to handle adaptive layouts, while CSS's `display: flex` and `grid` offer similar flexibility for web design.

2: Optimize for Cross-Platform Performance

- When developing applications for both web (HTML/CSS) and mobile (Flutter), remember that the performance of layouts might vary across platforms. Always test your layout on multiple devices and browsers to ensure it renders as expected. For Flutter, test on both iOS and Android devices, considering different screen sizes and resolutions.

3: Make Use of Reusable Widgets

- In Flutter, creating custom widgets allows you to encapsulate and reuse layout structures, which makes code more maintainable and organized. Similarly, in web development, CSS classes and reusable components (e.g., buttons, cards, containers) help keep the design consistent and efficient.

4: Use `MediaQuery` and `LayoutBuilder` for Responsive Layouts in Flutter

- To create responsive layouts in Flutter, use `MediaQuery` to get information about the screen's size and orientation, and combine it with `LayoutBuilder` to make layout decisions based on the available space. This approach mimics the responsive design techniques used in web development with CSS media queries.

5: Utilize Debugging Tools for Layout Issues

- Both HTML/CSS and Flutter provide tools for debugging layout issues. In web development, you can use browser developer tools to inspect and manipulate the layout live. In Flutter, the `Flutter Inspector` and `flutter debugPaintSizeEnabled` help identify issues with widget sizes, alignment, and positioning during development.

Chapter 6: Flexbox vs Row and Column

In the world of web and mobile app development, layout management plays a crucial role in defining how user interfaces (UIs) are structured. Whether you are working with HTML and CSS for web development or with Flutter for mobile app development, understanding layout management tools like Flexbox, Row, and Column is fundamental for creating responsive, flexible designs. This chapter dives into these tools in detail and compares their usage in both HTML/CSS and Flutter, with a particular focus on how Flexbox is implemented in web development and how Row and Column widgets work in Flutter.

6.1 Understanding Flexbox in HTML

Flexbox is a layout model in CSS that allows developers to design complex layouts with simple, flexible containers. Flexbox is particularly useful when dealing with dynamic or unknown sizes of elements within a container. It provides a more efficient way to distribute space and align items, compared to traditional layout methods like floats or positioning.

What Flexbox Does

Flexbox works by setting a container as a flex container and defining its children as flex items. The key advantage of Flexbox is its ability to adjust and align these items inside the container, making it ideal for responsive layouts. Flexbox introduces several properties that control the alignment, order, and distribution of flex items. These properties are designed to make it easier to achieve complex layouts without needing to rely on floats or more complex grid systems.

The Basics of Flexbox

To enable Flexbox in a container, you use the `display: flex` property. This turns the container into a flex container, and its children become flex items. Flexbox enables the arrangement of these items in rows or columns and provides flexible ways to control their alignment.

Example: Basic Flexbox Layout in HTML/CSS

```
<!-- html -->
<div class="flex-container">
  <div class="flex-item">Item 1</div>
```

```
  <div class="flex-item">Item 2</div>
  <div class="flex-item">Item 3</div>
</div>

<style>
  .flex-container {
    display: flex;
    justify-content: space-between;
    align-items: center;
    height: 100vh;
    background-color: lightgray;
  }
  .flex-item {
    background-color: lightblue;
    padding: 20px;
    margin: 5px;
    text-align: center;
  }
</style>
```

In this example, the `flex-container` is defined with `display: flex`, turning it into a flex container. The `justify-content: space-between` property distributes the flex items with equal space between them. The `align-items: center` property centers the items vertically within the container.

Key Flexbox Properties

1. **`display: flex`** – Defines a flex container and applies Flexbox behavior to its child elements.
2. **`flex-direction`** – Controls the direction of the flex items (row, column, row-reverse, column-reverse).
3. **`justify-content`** – Aligns items along the main axis (horizontally, if `flex-direction` is row).
4. **`align-items`** – Aligns items along the cross axis (vertically, if `flex-direction` is row).
5. **`align-self`** – Allows individual flex items to override the alignment set by `align-items`.
6. **`flex-wrap`** – Defines whether the items should wrap onto multiple lines if necessary.

6.2 Row and Column Widgets in Flutter

In Flutter, the layout model takes a slightly different approach from Flexbox but shares similar principles. The `Row` and `Column` widgets in Flutter work as primary tools for creating flexible and responsive layouts. Just like Flexbox, they allow you to arrange children horizontally (`Row`) or vertically (`Column`).

While Flexbox is a CSS-based layout system, Flutter uses a widget tree, where every component is considered a widget. `Row` and `Column` widgets allow you to build flexible and responsive UIs by arranging child widgets.

The Row Widget in Flutter

The `Row` widget arranges its children in a horizontal direction, similar to the `flex-direction: row` in Flexbox. The children of a `Row` are laid out from left to right.

Example: Basic Row Layout in Flutter

```
//dart
import 'package:flutter/material.dart';

void main() {
  runApp(MyApp());
}

class MyApp extends StatelessWidget {
  @override
  Widget build(BuildContext context) {
    return MaterialApp(
      home: Scaffold(
        body: Row(
          mainAxisAlignment:
MainAxisAlignment.spaceEvenly,
          crossAxisAlignment: CrossAxisAlignment.center,
          children: <Widget>[
            Container(
              color: Colors.blue,
              padding: EdgeInsets.all(20),
              child: Text(
                'Item 1',
                style: TextStyle(color: Colors.white),
              ),
            ),
```

```
              Container(
                color: Colors.green,
                padding: EdgeInsets.all(20),
                child: Text(
                  'Item 2',
                  style: TextStyle(color: Colors.white),
                ),
              ),
              Container(
                color: Colors.red,
                padding: EdgeInsets.all(20),
                child: Text(
                  'Item 3',
                  style: TextStyle(color: Colors.white),
                ),
              ),
            ],
          ),
        ),
      );
    }
}
```

In this example, the `Row` widget arranges three `Container` widgets horizontally. The `mainAxisAlignment: MainAxisAlignment.spaceEvenly` property evenly distributes the items along the main axis (horizontally), while `crossAxisAlignment: CrossAxisAlignment.center` vertically centers the items within the row.

The Column Widget in Flutter

The `Column` widget works similarly to `Row`, but it arranges its children vertically, just like the `flex-direction: column` property in Flexbox.

Example: Basic Column Layout in Flutter

```
//dart
import 'package:flutter/material.dart';

void main() {
  runApp(MyApp());
}
```

```
class MyApp extends StatelessWidget {
  @override
  Widget build(BuildContext context) {
    return MaterialApp(
      home: Scaffold(
        body: Column(
          mainAxisAlignment: MainAxisAlignment.center,
          crossAxisAlignment: CrossAxisAlignment.start,
          children: <Widget>[
            Container(
              color: Colors.blue,
              padding: EdgeInsets.all(20),
              child: Text(
                'Item 1',
                style: TextStyle(color: Colors.white),
              ),
            ),
            Container(
              color: Colors.green,
              padding: EdgeInsets.all(20),
              child: Text(
                'Item 2',
                style: TextStyle(color: Colors.white),
              ),
            ),
            Container(
              color: Colors.red,
              padding: EdgeInsets.all(20),
              child: Text(
                'Item 3',
                style: TextStyle(color: Colors.white),
              ),
            ),
          ],
        ),
      ),
    );
  }
}
```

In this example, the `Column` widget arranges the three `Container` widgets vertically. The `mainAxisAlignment: MainAxisAlignment.center` property centers the items vertically, and the `crossAxisAlignment: CrossAxisAlignment.start` aligns them to the start of the horizontal axis.

6.3 Aligning Items Horizontally and Vertically

Aligning items horizontally and vertically is a core concept when working with layouts in both web and mobile development. Flexbox and Flutter's Row and Column widgets provide different ways to achieve this alignment. However, the goal remains the same: to control the positioning of elements within their parent container.

Aligning Items Horizontally

In HTML and CSS, horizontal alignment within a flex container is handled using the `justify-content` property. This property aligns items along the main axis, which is horizontal when using `flex-direction: row`.

Example: Horizontal Alignment in Flexbox

```
<!-- html -->
<div class="flex-container">
  <div class="flex-item">Item 1</div>
  <div class="flex-item">Item 2</div>
  <div class="flex-item">Item 3</div>
</div>

<style>
  .flex-container {
    display: flex;
    justify-content: center;
  }
  .flex-item {
    background-color: lightblue;
    padding: 20px;
    margin: 5px;
  }
</style>
```

In Flutter, horizontal alignment within a `Row` widget is managed through the `mainAxisAlignment` property. This property can take values like `MainAxisAlignment.start`, `MainAxisAlignment.center`, and

`MainAxisAlignment.end`.

Example: Horizontal Alignment in Flutter

```
//dart
Row(
  mainAxisAlignment: MainAxisAlignment.center,
  children: <Widget>[
    Container(
      color: Colors.blue,
      padding: EdgeInsets.all(20),
      child: Text('Item 1'),
    ),
    Container(
      color: Colors.green,
      padding: EdgeInsets.all(20),
      child: Text('Item 2'),
    ),
    Container(
      color: Colors.red,
      padding: EdgeInsets.all(20),
      child: Text('Item 3'),
    ),
  ],
);
```

Aligning Items Vertically

Vertical alignment is handled differently in HTML/CSS and Flutter. In Flexbox, vertical alignment within a flex container is controlled by the `align-items` property. This property defines how items are aligned along the cross axis, which is vertical when using `flex-direction: row`.

Example: Vertical Alignment in Flexbox

```
<!-- html -->
<div class="flex-container">
  <div class="flex-item">Item 1</div>
  <div class="flex-item">Item 2</div>
  <div class="flex-item">Item 3</div>
</div>

<style>
```

```
  .flex-container {
    display: flex;
    justify-content: center;
    align-items: center;
    height: 100vh;
  }
  .flex-item {
    background-color: lightblue;
    padding: 20px;
    margin: 5px;
  }
</style>
```

In Flutter, vertical alignment within a `Row` widget is achieved using the `crossAxisAlignment` property. Values like `CrossAxisAlignment.start`, `CrossAxisAlignment.center`, and `CrossAxisAlignment.end` help position the children widgets along the vertical axis.

Example: Vertical Alignment in Flutter

```
//dart
Row(
  crossAxisAlignment: CrossAxisAlignment.center,
  children: <Widget>[
    Container(
      color: Colors.blue,
      padding: EdgeInsets.all(20),
      child: Text('Item 1'),
    ),
    Container(
      color: Colors.green,
      padding: EdgeInsets.all(20),
      child: Text('Item 2'),
    ),
    Container(
      color: Colors.red,
      padding: EdgeInsets.all(20),
      child: Text('Item 3'),
    ),
  ],
);
```

6.4 MainAxisAlignment and CrossAxisAlignment Explained

The two key properties that help control alignment in both Flexbox and Flutter are `mainAxisAlignment` and `crossAxisAlignment`. These properties are essential when designing layouts, as they help you align items either along the main axis or the cross axis.

MainAxisAlignment

In Flexbox, `mainAxisAlignment` controls the alignment of items along the main axis (horizontal when `flex-direction: row` and vertical when `flex-direction: column`).

- **Example values for `mainAxisAlignment` in Flexbox**:
  - `flex-start` (aligns items at the start of the container)
  - `center` (aligns items in the center of the container)
  - `space-between` (distributes items with space between them)
  - `space-around` (distributes items with space around them)
  - `space-evenly` (distributes items with equal space between them)

Example: MainAxisAlignment in Flexbox

```
<!-- html -->
<div class="flex-container">
  <div class="flex-item">Item 1</div>
  <div class="flex-item">Item 2</div>
  <div class="flex-item">Item 3</div>
</div>

<style>
  .flex-container {
    display: flex;
    justify-content: space-evenly;
  }
  .flex-item {
    background-color: lightblue;
    padding: 20px;
    margin: 5px;
  }
</style>
```

In Flutter, `mainAxisAlignment` works in a similar manner within the `Row` and `Column` widgets, aligning children along the main axis.

Example: MainAxisAlignment in Flutter

```
//dart
Row(
  mainAxisAlignment: MainAxisAlignment.spaceEvenly,
  children: <Widget>[
    Container(
      color: Colors.blue,
      padding: EdgeInsets.all(20),
      child: Text('Item 1'),
    ),
    Container(
      color: Colors.green,
      padding: EdgeInsets.all(20),
      child: Text('Item 2'),
    ),
    Container(
      color: Colors.red,
      padding: EdgeInsets.all(20),
      child: Text('Item 3'),
    ),
  ],
);
```

CrossAxisAlignment

In Flexbox, `crossAxisAlignment` controls the alignment of items along the cross axis, which is vertical when the `flex-direction` is `row`. It is used to align the items perpendicularly to the main axis.

- **Example values for `crossAxisAlignment` in Flexbox**:
  - `stretch` (stretches items to fill the container along the cross axis)
  - `center` (centers items along the cross axis)
  - `flex-start` (aligns items to the start of the cross axis)
  - `flex-end` (aligns items to the end of the cross axis)

Example: CrossAxisAlignment in Flexbox

```
<!-- html -->
<div class="flex-container">
  <div class="flex-item">Item 1</div>
  <div class="flex-item">Item 2</div>
  <div class="flex-item">Item 3</div>
</div>

<style>
  .flex-container {
    display: flex;
    align-items: center;
    height: 100vh;
  }
  .flex-item {
    background-color: lightblue;
    padding: 20px;
    margin: 5px;
  }
</style>
```

In Flutter, `crossAxisAlignment` does the same job within a `Row` or `Column`, aligning the children widgets along the cross axis.

Example: CrossAxisAlignment in Flutter

```
//dart
Column(
  crossAxisAlignment: CrossAxisAlignment.start,
  children: <Widget>[
    Container(
      color: Colors.blue,
      padding: EdgeInsets.all(20),
      child: Text('Item 1'),
    ),
    Container(
      color: Colors.green,
      padding: EdgeInsets.all(20),
      child: Text('Item 2'),
    ),
    Container(
```

```
      color: Colors.red,
      padding: EdgeInsets.all(20),
      child: Text('Item 3'),
    ),
  ],
);
```

By comparing the Flexbox layout model in HTML/CSS with the Row and Column widgets in Flutter, you can see that the principles of layout management and item alignment are quite similar across both platforms. Flexbox offers a powerful set of tools for creating flexible layouts on the web, while Row and Column in Flutter provide an equivalent set of tools for mobile app development. Understanding these similarities and differences will enable you to work effectively across both web and mobile platforms, ensuring your designs are responsive and well-aligned, no matter the device.

6.5 Spacing Between Widgets

Spacing between widgets is a critical aspect of layout design. Proper spacing ensures that your UI appears clean, organized, and visually appealing. In both Flutter and Flexbox (HTML/CSS), managing space between elements is essential for creating a balanced and user-friendly interface. Let's dive into how spacing works in these environments and compare their approaches.

Flexbox Spacing

In Flexbox, spacing between items is controlled using a combination of properties such as `justify-content`, `align-items`, and `gap` (or `grid-gap` for CSS Grid layouts). The `gap` property is one of the simplest ways to manage space between flex items, adding consistent spacing between each item. Let's break down the options:

Justify-Content: Controls the space distribution along the main axis (horizontal or vertical). Common values include:

- `flex-start`: Items are packed at the start of the container.
- `flex-end`: Items are packed at the end of the container.
- `center`: Items are centered in the container.
- `space-between`: Items are spaced out with equal space between them.
- `space-around`: Items are spaced with equal space around them.
- `space-evenly`: Items are spaced out evenly with equal space between and around them.

Align-Items: Controls how items are aligned along the cross axis (vertical when `flex-direction: row`). Values include:

- `stretch`: Items stretch to fill the container's height (or width in the case of a column).
- `flex-start`, `flex-end`, `center`: Similar to `justify-content` but for the cross axis.

Gap: This property directly manages the space between flex items. It is used to provide consistent spacing between items in both rows and columns.

Example of Spacing in Flexbox

```
<!-- html -->
<div class="flex-container">
  <div class="flex-item">Item 1</div>
  <div class="flex-item">Item 2</div>
  <div class="flex-item">Item 3</div>
</div>

<style>
  .flex-container {
    display: flex;
    justify-content: space-between; /* Distribute space
between items */
    align-items: center; /* Align items vertically */
    gap: 10px; /* Consistent spacing between items */
  }
  .flex-item {
    background-color: lightblue;
    padding: 20px;
    margin: 5px;
  }
</style>
```

In this example:

- The `gap` property sets a consistent 10px space between the flex items.
- The `justify-content: space-between` ensures that the items are spaced with equal gaps between them along the main axis (horizontal).
- The `align-items: center` aligns the items vertically.

Spacing in Flutter

In Flutter, spacing between widgets can be controlled using several approaches:

1. **Padding**: The `Padding` widget adds space inside a widget, around its child widget.
2. **SizedBox**: The `SizedBox` widget is used for creating fixed spaces between widgets. It can have a defined width or height, depending on the axis.
3. **MainAxisAlignment and CrossAxisAlignment**: These properties control the distribution of space along the main and cross axes, respectively.

Using Padding

Padding allows you to insert space inside a widget. It's commonly used to add space between the widget's content and its boundary.

Example of Padding in Flutter

```
//dart
Row(
  children: <Widget>[
    Padding(
      padding: EdgeInsets.all(8.0),  // Add padding of 8
pixels
      child: Container(
        color: Colors.blue,
        padding: EdgeInsets.all(20),
        child: Text('Item 1'),
      ),
    ),
    Padding(
      padding: EdgeInsets.all(8.0),  // Add padding of 8
pixels
      child: Container(
        color: Colors.green,
        padding: EdgeInsets.all(20),
        child: Text('Item 2'),
      ),
    ),
    Padding(
      padding: EdgeInsets.all(8.0),  // Add padding of 8
```

```
pixels
      child: Container(
        color: Colors.red,
        padding: EdgeInsets.all(20),
        child: Text('Item 3'),
      ),
    ),
  ],
);
```

In this example, each `Container` widget is wrapped in a `Padding` widget that adds 8 pixels of space around the widget.

Using SizedBox

`SizedBox` is a versatile widget in Flutter that allows you to control space between widgets. You can specify the width or height, depending on the orientation.

Example of SizedBox for Horizontal Spacing in Flutter

```
//dart
Row(
  children: <Widget>[
    Container(
      color: Colors.blue,
      padding: EdgeInsets.all(20),
      child: Text('Item 1'),
    ),
    SizedBox(width: 20),  // Add 20px horizontal space
    Container(
      color: Colors.green,
      padding: EdgeInsets.all(20),
      child: Text('Item 2'),
    ),
    SizedBox(width: 20),  // Add 20px horizontal space
    Container(
      color: Colors.red,
      padding: EdgeInsets.all(20),
      child: Text('Item 3'),
    ),
  ],
);
```

Here, `SizedBox(width: 20)` creates 20 pixels of horizontal spacing between the containers. You can also use `SizedBox(height: 20)` for vertical spacing in a `Column`.

Using MainAxisAlignment and CrossAxisAlignment

These properties in `Row` and `Column` allow you to control the spacing between children along the main axis and cross axis.

Example with MainAxisAlignment in Flutter

```
//dart
Row(
  mainAxisAlignment: MainAxisAlignment.spaceBetween,  //
Space items evenly
  children: <Widget>[
    Container(
      color: Colors.blue,
      padding: EdgeInsets.all(20),
      child: Text('Item 1'),
    ),
    Container(
      color: Colors.green,
      padding: EdgeInsets.all(20),
      child: Text('Item 2'),
    ),
    Container(
      color: Colors.red,
      padding: EdgeInsets.all(20),
      child: Text('Item 3'),
    ),
  ],
);
```

In this Flutter example, `MainAxisAlignment.spaceBetween` ensures that the items are spaced evenly, with equal space between them along the row.

6.6 Responsive Design with Flex in Flutter

Responsive design is crucial when building applications that need to work across different screen sizes. Flutter offers multiple tools for creating responsive layouts, many of which are inspired by Flexbox concepts in HTML/CSS. In this section, we'll look at how to use Flex properties to ensure that your Flutter application is adaptable to different screen sizes and orientations.

Flex and Expanded Widgets

The `Flex` widget in Flutter, along with its `Row` and `Column` derivatives, helps in creating flexible layouts. The `Expanded` widget is used to fill available space within a flex container, which makes it responsive to different screen sizes.

Using Flex and Expanded for Responsiveness

Example of Flex in Flutter for Responsiveness

```
//dart
Row(
  children: <Widget>[
    Expanded(
      child: Container(
        color: Colors.blue,
        padding: EdgeInsets.all(20),
        child: Text('Item 1'),
      ),
    ),
    Expanded(
      child: Container(
        color: Colors.green,
        padding: EdgeInsets.all(20),
        child: Text('Item 2'),
      ),
    ),
    Expanded(
      child: Container(
        color: Colors.red,
        padding: EdgeInsets.all(20),
        child: Text('Item 3'),
      ),
    ),
  ],
);
```

In this example, the `Expanded` widget causes each `Container` to take equal space along the main axis (horizontal), which allows the layout to adapt to different screen sizes. If the screen width changes, the available space is distributed evenly among the children.

MediaQuery for Screen Size

In Flutter, `MediaQuery` is a powerful tool that helps to access screen size information, enabling the app to adjust its layout dynamically based on the screen dimensions.

Example of Using MediaQuery for Responsiveness

```
//dart
MediaQuery.of(context).size.width > 600
  ? Row(
      children: <Widget>[
        Expanded(child: Container(color: Colors.blue,
child: Text('Item 1'))),
        Expanded(child: Container(color: Colors.green,
child: Text('Item 2'))),
        Expanded(child: Container(color: Colors.red,
child: Text('Item 3'))),
      ],
    )
  : Column(
      children: <Widget>[
        Container(color: Colors.blue, child: Text('Item
1')),
        Container(color: Colors.green, child: Text('Item
2')),
        Container(color: Colors.red, child: Text('Item
3')),
      ],
    );
```

This code uses `MediaQuery` to check the screen width. If the width is greater than 600 pixels, the layout is displayed as a row (for large screens). For smaller screens (under 600 pixels), the layout switches to a column for better visibility and touch interactions.

LayoutBuilder for Responsiveness

Another useful tool for responsive layouts in Flutter is `LayoutBuilder`, which allows you to build widgets based on the parent widget's constraints. You can use it to determine the size of a widget and change the layout accordingly.

Example of Using LayoutBuilder

```
//dart
LayoutBuilder(
  builder: (context, constraints) {
    if (constraints.maxWidth > 600) {
      return Row(
        children: <Widget>[
          Expanded(child: Container(color: Colors.blue)),
          Expanded(child: Container(color: Colors.green)),
          Expanded(child: Container(color: Colors.red)),
        ],
      );
    } else {
      return Column(
        children: <Widget>[
          Container(color: Colors.blue),
          Container(color: Colors.green),
          Container(color: Colors.red),
        ],
      );
    }
  },
);
```

In this example, `LayoutBuilder` is used to adjust the layout based on the available screen width, switching between a row and a column dynamically.

6.7 Debugging Alignment Issues

Aligning widgets in Flutter and CSS can be tricky, especially when dealing with different screen sizes, padding, and margin. Let's go over common alignment issues and how to debug them effectively.

Common Alignment Issues

1. **Misalignment Due to Parent Container**: Often, misalignment occurs because the parent container is not given enough space or constraints. Ensure that the parent container is large enough to accommodate the children.
2. **Overriding Properties**: Overriding alignment properties in nested widgets can lead to unexpected results. Always check the alignment properties of parent and child widgets.
3. **Flexible Space Distribution**: When using `Expanded` or `Flexible` widgets, the layout can sometimes look off if the space distribution is not as expected. Ensure that the space is being distributed according to the intended proportions.

Debugging Tips

- **Use the Flutter Inspector**: Flutter's `Flutter Inspector` is a powerful tool to visually inspect widget layouts. You can inspect the hierarchy of widgets and see how each widget is laid out in real-time. This helps identify where the alignment issue occurs.
- **Use `SizedBox` for Debugging**: If widgets are overlapping, use `SizedBox` to add temporary spacing between them to identify where the problem lies.
- **Check for Constraints**: Sometimes, alignment issues arise when widgets are not constrained properly. Ensure that parent widgets have appropriate constraints for their children, and use `Expanded` or `Flexible` for dynamic resizing.

6.8 Sample Code: Flexbox vs Flutter Row and Column

Let's now compare how Flexbox and Flutter's `Row` and `Column` handle layout and alignment, using sample code.

Flexbox Example

```
<!-- html -->
<div class="flex-container">
  <div class="flex-item">Item 1</div>
  <div class="flex-item">Item 2</div>
  <div class="flex-item">Item 3</div>
</div>

<style>
  .flex-container {
```

```
    display: flex;
    justify-content: space-between;
    align-items: center;
    gap: 20px;
  }
  .flex-item {
    background-color: lightblue;
    padding: 20px;
  }
</style>
```

In this HTML/CSS example, a flex container holds three items with space evenly distributed between them, and vertical centering is done using `align-items: center`.

Flutter Example

```
//dart
Row(
  mainAxisAlignment: MainAxisAlignment.spaceBetween,
  crossAxisAlignment: CrossAxisAlignment.center,
  children: <Widget>[
    Container(
      color: Colors.blue,
      padding: EdgeInsets.all(20),
      child: Text('Item 1'),
    ),
    Container(
      color: Colors.green,
      padding: EdgeInsets.all(20),
      child: Text('Item 2'),
    ),
    Container(
      color: Colors.red,
      padding: EdgeInsets.all(20),
      child: Text('Item 3'),
    ),
  ],
);
```

In this Flutter example, the `Row` widget is used, and the properties `mainAxisAlignment` and `crossAxisAlignment` mirror Flexbox's `justify-`

`content` and `align-items` properties, respectively.

Examples

- **HTML/CSS Flexbox Example:**

```
<!-- html -->
<div style="display: flex; justify-content: space-between;
align-items: center;">
  <div>Item 1</div>
  <div>Item 2</div>
  <div>Item 3</div>
</div>
```

In this HTML example, we use a `div` with `display: flex` to apply the Flexbox layout. The `justify-content: space-between` ensures that the items are spaced equally across the main axis, and `align-items: center` vertically aligns the items in the container.

- **Flutter Row Example:**

```
//dart
Row(
  mainAxisAlignment: MainAxisAlignment.spaceBetween,
  crossAxisAlignment: CrossAxisAlignment.center,
  children: <Widget>[
    Text('Item 1'),
    Text('Item 2'),
    Text('Item 3'),
  ],
)
```

This Flutter `Row` widget is similar to the Flexbox layout in HTML. The `mainAxisAlignment: MainAxisAlignment.spaceBetween` achieves the same effect of spacing the items equally, and `crossAxisAlignment: CrossAxisAlignment.center` aligns them vertically.

- **HTML/CSS Flexbox with Wrap Example:**

```
<!-- html -->
```

```
<div style="display: flex; flex-wrap: wrap;">
  <div style="flex: 1 1 100px;">Item 1</div>
  <div style="flex: 1 1 100px;">Item 2</div>
  <div style="flex: 1 1 100px;">Item 3</div>
  <div style="flex: 1 1 100px;">Item 4</div>
</div>
```

This HTML/CSS example demonstrates a Flexbox layout with wrapping enabled. The `flex-wrap: wrap` ensures that items wrap onto new lines when there's insufficient space.

- **Flutter Wrap Example:**

```
//dart
Wrap(
  children: <Widget>[
    Text('Item 1'),
    Text('Item 2'),
    Text('Item 3'),
    Text('Item 4'),
  ],
)
```

In Flutter, the `Wrap` widget works similarly to `flex-wrap` in CSS. It allows the items to automatically wrap to the next line when the space is insufficient.

Tips

- **Consistent Alignment:** To maintain consistent alignment across different screen sizes, both Flexbox and Flutter's Row/Column can use alignment properties like `align-items`, `crossAxisAlignment`, and `mainAxisAlignment` to center or space out child elements. Aligning children properly ensures that layouts are responsive and visually balanced.

- **Flexibility with Space Distribution:** Flexbox's `flex-grow`, `flex-shrink`, and `flex-basis` offer great flexibility to distribute space dynamically. Similarly, Flutter's `Expanded` and `Flexible` widgets give you control over how much space a widget occupies, enabling you to design more adaptable UIs.

- **Managing Overflow Issues:** Both Flexbox and Flutter layouts may experience overflow if content exceeds container space. In HTML/CSS, `overflow: auto` or `overflow: hidden` can help manage this, while in Flutter, wrapping widgets like `SingleChildScrollView` can prevent overflow by enabling scrollable content.

Actionable Strategies

- **Use Flutter's `Expanded` Widget for Flexible Layouts:** Just like using Flexbox's `flex` property in CSS, Flutter offers the `Expanded` widget, which makes its child widget flexible to take up any remaining space within a `Row` or `Column`. This is helpful when you want a widget to occupy the space left after the other widgets have been sized. For example:

```
//dart
Row(

  children: <Widget>[
    Text('Item 1'),
    Expanded(child: Container(color: Colors.blue)),
    Text('Item 2'),
  ],
)
```

- **Leverage Flex Wrap for Mobile Responsiveness:** Use `Wrap` in Flutter to replicate the behavior of `flex-wrap` in CSS for handling mobile layouts. By doing so, your layout will adapt based on the available screen width, making it easier to manage responsive designs where items may need to shift to new rows.

```
//dart
Wrap(

  children: <Widget>[
    Text('Item 1'),
    Text('Item 2'),
    Text('Item 3'),
    Text('Item 4'),
  ],
)
```

- **Create Adaptive Layouts Using Flex and FlexDirection:** For both Flexbox and Flutter's Row/Column widgets, the `flex-direction` property (in CSS) or `mainAxisAlignment` and `crossAxisAlignment` properties (in Flutter) allow you to create layouts that adapt based on the direction of the layout. In Flutter, you can switch between a vertical (`Column`) or horizontal (`Row`) layout by adjusting the main axis. Use these to create adaptive designs based on screen sizes.

```
//dart
Column(

  mainAxisAlignment: MainAxisAlignment.center,
  children: <Widget>[
    Text('Item 1'),
    Text('Item 2'),
  ],
)
```

- **Keep Performance in Mind:** When designing with Flexbox or Flutter layouts, avoid excessive nesting of widgets or divs. Nested structures can impact performance, especially on mobile. Utilize Flutter's `ListView` or `GridView` for complex layouts that need to handle dynamic content efficiently. In CSS, minimize the use of deeply nested flex containers when possible to reduce layout recalculations and improve load times.

- **Consider Cross-Platform Consistency:** Whether you're working with Flexbox in web development or `Row/Column` in Flutter for mobile apps, it's crucial to keep the user experience consistent across platforms. Flutter's `Row` and `Column` allow you to write reusable code across both mobile and desktop versions of your app. Similarly, Flexbox offers adaptability for creating layouts that are consistent across desktop and mobile browsers. Always test your layouts across devices to ensure a seamless experience.

Chapter 7: Lists and Grids in Flutter

Creating lists and grids is one of the most fundamental tasks in mobile app development. Flutter provides powerful tools like `ListView` and `GridView` to efficiently display and manage large sets of data. These components allow developers to create responsive, scrollable, and interactive UI elements with ease. The process of creating lists in Flutter is similar to that in HTML, but Flutter provides more flexibility and optimization for mobile environments.

7.1 Creating Lists: From HTML to Flutter

In web development, lists are often created using HTML tags like `<ul>`, `<ol>`, and `<li>`. The list items inside these tags are typically styled with CSS, and dynamic content can be added using JavaScript. Flutter handles lists and collections of data more efficiently by using widgets that are optimized for mobile environments.

HTML/CSS Example (Simple List):

```
<!-- html -->
<ul>
  <li>Item 1</li>
  <li>Item 2</li>
  <li>Item 3</li>
</ul>
```

In this simple example, an unordered list (`<ul>`) is used, and list items (`<li>`) are added inside it. CSS can then be applied to style the list and its items, such as setting margins, padding, and font styles.

JavaScript Example (Dynamic List):

```
<!-- html -->
<ul id="myList"></ul>

<script>
  const items = ['Item 1', 'Item 2', 'Item 3'];
  const list = document.getElementById('myList');

  items.forEach(item => {
    const li = document.createElement('li');
    li.textContent = item;
```

```
    list.appendChild(li);
  });
</script>
```

In the JavaScript example, the `forEach()` method is used to iterate over an array of items. For each item, a new `<li>` element is created and appended to the `<ul>`. This demonstrates how dynamic lists can be generated in the web.

Flutter Example (Simple List):

```
//dart
ListView(
  children: <Widget>[
    ListTile(title: Text('Item 1')),
    ListTile(title: Text('Item 2')),
    ListTile(title: Text('Item 3')),
  ],
)
```

Flutter provides the `ListView` widget, which is used to create scrollable lists. In this example, each item in the list is represented by a `ListTile` widget, which is a predefined widget designed for lists. The `ListTile` contains a `Text` widget to display the text for each item. The `ListView` widget automatically handles scrolling when the list grows beyond the screen size.

The transition from HTML/CSS/JS to Flutter is smooth because Flutter's `ListView` offers many customizable features such as separators, scroll behaviors, and item customization, all within a native environment.

7.2 Using the ListView Widget

In Flutter, the `ListView` widget is a powerful and flexible tool for displaying lists. It is one of the most commonly used widgets for building scrollable lists of data. Flutter offers multiple ways to implement lists, and the `ListView` widget comes in various types, each suited for different use cases.

Basic ListView Example:

```
//dart
ListView(
  children: <Widget>[
    Text('Item 1'),
    Text('Item 2'),
```

```
    Text('Item 3'),
    Text('Item 4'),
  ],
)
```

In this example, a `ListView` is used to create a basic scrollable list. Each item in the list is a `Text` widget, and the list is automatically scrollable.

ListView.builder Example:

```
//dart
ListView.builder(
  itemCount: 100,
  itemBuilder: (context, index) {
    return ListTile(
      title: Text('Item $index'),
    );
  },
)
```

For dynamic data or large lists, it is more efficient to use the `ListView.builder` constructor. This constructor lazily builds the list items as they are scrolled into view, improving performance for long lists. The `itemCount` property defines the total number of items in the list, while the `itemBuilder` function generates each item based on the index.

ListView.separated Example:

```
//dart
ListView.separated(
  itemCount: 100,
  separatorBuilder: (context, index) {
    return Divider();
  },
  itemBuilder: (context, index) {
    return ListTile(title: Text('Item $index'));
  },
)
```

The `ListView.separated` constructor is similar to `ListView.builder`, but it allows you to add a separator between list items, such as a divider or custom widget. This is useful when you want to visually separate each item in the list with a custom divider.

Advantages of ListView in Flutter:

- **Performance Optimization:** ListView is highly optimized for performance, especially for large lists, as it only builds the widgets visible on the screen.
- **Customization:** ListView can be customized with separators, custom item builders, and scroll behavior settings.
- **Infinite Scrolling:** By using `ListView.builder`, you can implement infinite scrolling, loading more data as the user scrolls.

7.3 Customizing List Items

Customizing list items allows for more flexibility and creativity when building user interfaces in Flutter. You can customize individual list items by wrapping them in more complex widgets, such as `Container`, `Card`, or custom-built layouts.

Custom List Item Example:

```
//dart
ListView.builder(
  itemCount: 10,
  itemBuilder: (context, index) {
    return Card(
      margin: EdgeInsets.all(8.0),
      child: ListTile(
        leading: Icon(Icons.star),
        title: Text('Item $index'),
        subtitle: Text('Description for item $index'),
        trailing: Icon(Icons.arrow_forward),
      ),
    );
  },
)
```

In this example, each list item is wrapped in a `Card` widget, which gives it a material design elevation and shadow effect. The `ListTile` is customized with an icon (`leading`), a title (`title`), a subtitle (`subtitle`), and a trailing icon (`trailing`), making the list more interactive and visually appealing.

You can also add gesture detectors to list items, enabling actions such as tapping or swiping.

Custom List with GestureDetector:

```
//dart
ListView.builder(
  itemCount: 10,
  itemBuilder: (context, index) {
    return GestureDetector(
      onTap: () {
        print('Tapped on item $index');
      },
      child: ListTile(
        title: Text('Item $index'),
      ),
    );
  },
)
```

In this case, a `GestureDetector` is added to each list item, allowing the user to tap on items and trigger actions. The `onTap` callback is executed when the user taps on the list item.

Customizing with Complex Widgets:

```
//dart
ListView.builder(
  itemCount: 5,
  itemBuilder: (context, index) {
    return Container(
      color: index % 2 == 0 ? Colors.blue : Colors.green,
      padding: EdgeInsets.all(16.0),
      child: Row(
        mainAxisAlignment: MainAxisAlignment.spaceBetween,
        children: <Widget>[
          Icon(Icons.star, color: Colors.white),
          Text('Item $index', style: TextStyle(color:
Colors.white)),
          Icon(Icons.arrow_forward, color: Colors.white),
        ],
      ),
    );
  },
)
```

Here, a `Container` is used to customize each list item with padding and a background color. The list item is designed with a `Row` widget to arrange the icon and text horizontally.

7.4 Creating Horizontal Scrollable Lists

Horizontal lists are particularly useful when displaying items like images, categories, or cards that the user may scroll horizontally. Flutter's `ListView` widget can be used to create horizontal lists by setting the `scrollDirection` property to `Axis.horizontal`.

Horizontal ListView Example:

```
//dart
ListView(
  scrollDirection: Axis.horizontal,
  children: <Widget>[
    Container(color: Colors.red, width: 200),
    Container(color: Colors.green, width: 200),
    Container(color: Colors.blue, width: 200),
  ],
)
```

This example demonstrates a simple horizontal list of colored containers. The `scrollDirection` is set to `Axis.horizontal`, which ensures that the list is scrollable horizontally instead of vertically. Each container in the list has a fixed width of 200 pixels.

Horizontal ListView.builder Example:

```
//dart
ListView.builder(
  scrollDirection: Axis.horizontal,
  itemCount: 10,
  itemBuilder: (context, index) {
    return Card(
      child: Container(
        width: 150,
        margin: EdgeInsets.symmetric(horizontal: 8.0),
        color: index.isEven ? Colors.orange :
Colors.purple,
        child: Center(child: Text('Item $index')),
      ),
    );
```

```
  },
)
```

In this example, a horizontal `ListView.builder` is used to create a dynamic list of cards. The cards alternate between orange and purple based on the index, and each item is placed inside a `Container` with a fixed width.

Horizontal ListView with Images:

```
//dart
ListView.builder(
  scrollDirection: Axis.horizontal,
  itemCount: 5,
  itemBuilder: (context, index) {
    return Padding(
      padding: EdgeInsets.all(8.0),
      child: Image.network('https://via.placeholder.com/
150'),
    );
  },
)
```

This example shows how to create a horizontal list of images. Each image is fetched from a network URL, and the list is scrollable horizontally.

Final Thoughts

Lists and grids are integral to building any mobile application. Flutter's `ListView` and `GridView` widgets provide high-performance, customizable options for displaying large amounts of data. Whether you're building simple lists or complex, horizontally scrolling collections, Flutter offers flexibility and efficiency that allows for smooth user experiences.

7.5 Introducing GridView for Flutter

When building applications, displaying data in grid layouts is a common requirement, especially for image galleries, product listings, or complex forms. In Flutter, the `GridView` widget is an essential tool for implementing such layouts. This widget allows for the creation of scrollable grids, which can be fully customized to meet specific design requirements. It is especially useful when you need to display multiple items in both rows and columns.

The `GridView` widget works similarly to `ListView`, but instead of displaying items in a single column, `GridView` arranges the items in multiple columns and rows. The grid can be vertical or horizontal depending on the configuration.

The basic structure of `GridView` is composed of several constructors, including `GridView.builder`, `GridView.count`, and `GridView.extent`, which allow developers to choose the most efficient method depending on the number of items in the grid.

- **GridView.builder**: This constructor builds a grid lazily, which means it builds only the visible items and recycles them when they are scrolled off the screen. This approach is suitable for long lists of items.

Example:

```
//dart
GridView.builder(

  gridDelegate: SliverGridDelegateWithFixedCrossAxisCount(
    crossAxisCount: 3,  // Number of columns
    crossAxisSpacing: 10.0,  // Space between columns
    mainAxisSpacing: 10.0,  // Space between rows
  ),
  itemCount: 20,  // Total number of items
  itemBuilder: (context, index) {
    return Card(
      child: Center(
        child: Text('Item $index'),
      ),
    );
  },
)
```

- **GridView.count**: This constructor is a more convenient option when you want to define the number of columns in the grid. It does not require a `SliverGridDelegate` and is suitable for static data sets.

Example:

```
//dart
```

```
GridView.count(

  crossAxisCount: 3,  // Number of columns
  children: List.generate(20, (index) {
    return Card(
      child: Center(
        child: Text('Item $index'),
      ),
    );
  }),
)
```

- **GridView.extent**: This constructor allows you to define the maximum extent of each grid item, either by the number of pixels or by the available space. This is useful when you want the grid items to have a specific size but don't necessarily need to specify the number of columns.

Example:

```
//dart
GridView.extent(

  maxCrossAxisExtent: 200.0,  // Maximum width of each
item
  children: List.generate(20, (index) {
    return Card(
      child: Center(
        child: Text('Item $index'),
      ),
    );
  }),
)
```

In Flutter, `GridView` offers more flexibility than traditional web-based grid layouts, as it allows for dynamic creation and handling of items that can change during the app's lifecycle, such as adding or removing items on the fly. The lazy loading system, coupled with Flutter's efficient widget tree system, makes it possible to display grids with hundreds or thousands of items without sacrificing performance.

7.6 CSS Grids vs Flutter GridView

CSS grids are widely used in web development to create complex layouts, especially for responsive design. A CSS grid layout can define both rows and columns, and it allows for precise control over the placement of elements within a grid container. However, when transitioning from a web-based layout to a mobile environment, Flutter offers a more optimized and specialized approach with its `GridView`.

In CSS, grids are defined using the `display: grid` property, where the grid container specifies rows and columns. The items inside the grid are then placed according to these specifications. Let's compare how a simple grid layout is constructed in CSS versus Flutter.

CSS Grid Example

```
<!-- html -->
<div class="grid-container">
  <div class="grid-item">Item 1</div>
  <div class="grid-item">Item 2</div>
  <div class="grid-item">Item 3</div>
  <div class="grid-item">Item 4</div>
  <div class="grid-item">Item 5</div>
  <div class="grid-item">Item 6</div>
</div>

<style>
  .grid-container {
    display: grid;
    grid-template-columns: repeat(3, 1fr); /* 3 equal-
width columns */
    gap: 10px;
  }
  .grid-item {
    background-color: lightgray;
    padding: 20px;
    text-align: center;
  }
</style>
```

In the above CSS code, the `.grid-container` is set to `display: grid`, and the `grid-template-columns` property defines that the grid should have three equal-width columns. The `gap` property controls the spacing between the items.

Flutter GridView Equivalent

```
//dart
GridView.count(
  crossAxisCount: 3,  // Number of columns
  crossAxisSpacing: 10.0,  // Space between columns
  mainAxisSpacing: 10.0,  // Space between rows
  children: List.generate(6, (index) {
    return Card(
      child: Center(
        child: Text('Item ${index + 1}'),
      ),
    );
  }),
)
```

In the Flutter example, the `GridView.count` constructor is used to create a grid with 3 columns. The `crossAxisSpacing` and `mainAxisSpacing` properties define the spacing between columns and rows, similar to the CSS `gap` property.

Key Differences Between CSS Grid and Flutter GridView:

- **CSS Grid** relies heavily on CSS properties to define grid structures and item placement. The layout is determined by the browser's rendering engine, and although CSS grids are very flexible, they are not as optimized for mobile environments.
- **Flutter GridView** is designed specifically for mobile environments. It optimizes the layout for performance, with features like lazy loading and efficient widget rendering. Flutter's grid system is designed to handle complex layouts in a way that doesn't compromise app performance, even when dealing with hundreds or thousands of items.
- **Responsiveness**: While CSS grids are highly responsive by default due to their inherent nature in web design, Flutter requires you to manually adjust grid layouts based on the screen size or device type using techniques such as `LayoutBuilder` or `MediaQuery`.

7.7 Adding Interactivity to List Items

Adding interactivity to list items is an important aspect of building mobile applications. Interactivity enables users to engage with the content, trigger actions, and navigate through the app. In Flutter, interactivity can be added by wrapping the grid or list items in gesture recognition widgets, such as `GestureDetector`, `InkWell`, or `ListTile`.

Using GestureDetector for List Item Interactions

The `GestureDetector` widget in Flutter allows you to detect various gestures, including taps, drags, and swipes. By wrapping the list items or grid items in a `GestureDetector`, you can easily capture user interactions.

Example:

```
//dart
GridView.builder(
  itemCount: 10,
  gridDelegate: SliverGridDelegateWithFixedCrossAxisCount(
    crossAxisCount: 3,
  ),
  itemBuilder: (context, index) {
    return GestureDetector(
      onTap: () {
        print('Tapped on item $index');
      },
      child: Card(
        child: Center(
          child: Text('Item $index'),
        ),
      ),
    );
  },
)
```

In this example, each item in the grid is wrapped in a `GestureDetector`. When a user taps on any item, the `onTap` callback is triggered, and the index of the tapped item is printed to the console.

Using InkWell for Material Design Interaction

The `InkWell` widget is another popular choice for adding interactivity, especially when you want the material ripple effect on tap. It provides a visual feedback when the user taps on an item.

Example:

```
//dart
GridView.builder(
  itemCount: 10,
  gridDelegate: SliverGridDelegateWithFixedCrossAxisCount(
    crossAxisCount: 3,
  ),
  itemBuilder: (context, index) {
    return InkWell(
      onTap: () {
        print('Tapped on item $index');
      },
      child: Card(
        child: Center(
          child: Text('Item $index'),
        ),
      ),
    );
  },
)
```

In this case, when the user taps on an item, the `InkWell` widget shows the ripple effect, providing visual feedback, making it more consistent with Material Design guidelines.

Adding Swipe Gestures for Advanced Interactions

Sometimes, it is useful to allow users to swipe left or right to perform certain actions, such as deleting an item or navigating to another page. You can implement swipe gestures in Flutter using the `Dismissible` widget.

Example:

```
//dart
GridView.builder(
  itemCount: 10,
  gridDelegate: SliverGridDelegateWithFixedCrossAxisCount(
    crossAxisCount: 3,
  ),
  itemBuilder: (context, index) {
    return Dismissible(
      key: Key('item_$index'),
```

```
      onDismissed: (direction) {
        print('Item $index dismissed');
      },
      child: Card(
        child: Center(
          child: Text('Item $index'),
        ),
      ),
    );
  },
)
```

In this example, a `Dismissible` widget is used to wrap each grid item. When the user swipes an item, the item is dismissed (i.e., removed from the grid), and the `onDismissed` callback is triggered.

7.8 Sample Code: Dynamic Lists in HTML and Flutter

Now let's compare how dynamic lists are implemented in HTML and Flutter. HTML typically uses JavaScript to dynamically generate lists, while Flutter uses its declarative UI framework to build lists.

HTML and JavaScript Example

```
<!-- html -->
<!DOCTYPE html>
<html lang="en">
<head>
  <meta charset="UTF-8">
  <meta name="viewport" content="width=device-width,
initial-scale=1.0">
  <title>Dynamic List Example</title>
</head>
<body>
  <ul id="item-list"></ul>

  <script>
    const items = ["Apple", "Banana", "Orange", "Mango"];
    const listContainer = document.getElementById("item-
list");
```

```
    items.forEach(item => {
      const listItem = document.createElement("li");
      listItem.textContent = item;
      listContainer.appendChild(listItem);
    });
  </script>
</body>
</html>
```

In this HTML/JavaScript example, an unordered list (`<ul>`) is dynamically populated with items using JavaScript. The `forEach` method loops through an array and creates `<li>` elements for each item, which are appended to the list container.

Flutter Equivalent Example

```
//dart
class ItemList extends StatelessWidget {
  final List<String> items = ["Apple", "Banana", "Orange",
"Mango"];

  @override
  Widget build(BuildContext context) {
    return ListView.builder(
      itemCount: items.length,
      itemBuilder: (context, index) {
        return ListTile(
          title: Text(items[index]),
        );
      },
    );
  }
}
```

In this Flutter example, a `ListView.builder` widget is used to build the list dynamically. The `items` list is passed as a data source, and the `itemBuilder` callback generates each list item based on the index.

Summary

- **GridView** in Flutter offers a powerful way to create grid-based layouts, with several constructors to choose from, such as `GridView.builder`,

GridView.count, and GridView.extent.

- **CSS Grids** and **Flutter GridView** serve similar purposes, but Flutter's grid system is more optimized for mobile devices and can handle dynamic item loading more efficiently.
- **Interactivity** can be easily added to grid and list items in Flutter using widgets like GestureDetector, InkWell, and Dismissible, allowing for a variety of user interactions such as taps, swipes, and long presses.
- Comparing dynamic list generation in **HTML** and **Flutter**, both systems rely on their respective language's capabilities to generate content dynamically. However, Flutter's declarative style makes it easier to manage state and rebuild UI elements efficiently.

By leveraging these techniques and understanding the fundamental differences between HTML/CSS and Flutter layouts, developers can create highly interactive and efficient mobile applications.

Examples

1 HTML List with JavaScript Dynamic Population

```
<!-- html -->
<!DOCTYPE html>
<html lang="en">
<head>
  <meta charset="UTF-8">
  <meta name="viewport" content="width=device-width,
initial-scale=1.0">
  <title>Dynamic List Example</title>
</head>
<body>
  <ul id="item-list"></ul>

  <script>
    const items = ["Apple", "Banana", "Orange", "Mango"];
    const listContainer = document.getElementById("item-
list");

    items.forEach(item => {
      const listItem = document.createElement("li");
      listItem.textContent = item;
```

```
      listContainer.appendChild(listItem);
    });
  </script>
</body>
</html>
```

This example uses HTML to create a basic unordered list (`<ul>`) and populates it dynamically using JavaScript. The list items are created in the JavaScript part and appended to the HTML list container.

2 Flutter List with ListView.builder

```
//dart
class ItemList extends StatelessWidget {
  final List<String> items = ["Apple", "Banana", "Orange",
"Mango"];

  @override
  Widget build(BuildContext context) {
    return ListView.builder(
      itemCount: items.length,
      itemBuilder: (context, index) {
        return ListTile(
          title: Text(items[index]),
        );
      },
    );
  }
}
```

This Flutter code creates a dynamic list using `ListView.builder`. The list of items is passed, and each item is displayed using `ListTile`. The `itemCount` is set to the length of the `items` list, and `itemBuilder` creates the individual list item widgets.

3 HTML Grid Layout Using CSS Grid

```
<!-- html -->
<!DOCTYPE html>
<html lang="en">
<head>
  <meta charset="UTF-8">
  <meta name="viewport" content="width=device-width,
```

```
initial-scale=1.0">
  <title>Grid Layout Example</title>
  <style>
    .grid-container {
      display: grid;
      grid-template-columns: repeat(3, 1fr);
      gap: 10px;
    }
    .grid-item {
      background-color: #4CAF50;
      color: white;
      padding: 20px;
      text-align: center;
    }
  </style>
</head>
<body>
  <div class="grid-container">
    <div class="grid-item">Item 1</div>
    <div class="grid-item">Item 2</div>
    <div class="grid-item">Item 3</div>
    <div class="grid-item">Item 4</div>
    <div class="grid-item">Item 5</div>
    <div class="grid-item">Item 6</div>
  </div>
</body>
</html>
```

This HTML and CSS example creates a simple grid layout using the `grid` display property in CSS. The grid has three equal-width columns, and the items are placed inside each grid cell, with a gap between the items.

4 Flutter Grid with GridView.count

```
//dart
class GridExample extends StatelessWidget {
  final List<String> items = ["Item 1", "Item 2", "Item
3", "Item 4", "Item 5", "Item 6"];

  @override
  Widget build(BuildContext context) {
    return GridView.count(
```

```
      crossAxisCount: 3,
      children: items.map((item) {
        return Card(
          color: Colors.green,
          child: Center(
            child: Text(item, style: TextStyle(color:
Colors.white)),
          ),
        );
      }).toList(),
    );
  }
}
```

In this Flutter example, the `GridView.count` widget is used to create a grid layout with three columns (`crossAxisCount: 3`). Each item in the list is mapped to a `Card` widget containing the item's name displayed in a `Text` widget.

Tips

- **Responsiveness in Grid Layouts:** In HTML/CSS, grids are often made responsive using media queries. Flutter, on the other hand, can achieve this by using `MediaQuery` and adjusting `crossAxisCount` based on screen size or orientation, providing more flexibility.
- **Reusability of Widgets in Flutter:** Both in lists and grids, Flutter's declarative UI system allows you to build reusable widgets. By creating separate widgets for list/grid items, you can reuse them across multiple views.
- **Performance Considerations:** For large data sets, Flutter's `ListView.builder` and `GridView.builder` are optimized to render only the items visible on the screen, improving performance. Similarly, in HTML, you can improve performance by lazy-loading list items using JavaScript.

Actionable Strategies

- **Optimize Flutter List Performance:** Use `ListView.builder` for lists with a large number of items. This ensures that only the visible items are rendered, reducing memory usage and improving the performance of your app. This is similar to how you would implement lazy loading for lists in JavaScript for HTML.

- **Use CSS Grid for Flexible Layouts:** In HTML, `CSS Grid` is a powerful tool to create complex layouts. Implement responsive grids by using CSS `grid-template-columns` with percentages or `fr` units, and adjust them based on screen size with media queries. For instance, setting `grid-template-columns: repeat(auto-fill, minmax(200px, 1fr));` will make sure the grid adjusts based on the available space.

- **Implement Grid and List Features with Gesture Detection:** In Flutter, both lists and grids are ideal for adding interactive gestures like tapping, swiping, and long-pressing. Use widgets like `GestureDetector` or `InkWell` to capture user interactions, allowing for actions like item selection, deletion, or even navigation.

- **Create Custom List and Grid Items:** Whether in Flutter or HTML, custom item widgets are essential for better user experience. In HTML, you can define custom structures for list items by adding HTML elements, while in Flutter, you can easily create a custom widget for list/grid items and enhance their appearance and functionality.

- **Use Dynamic Data Binding:** In Flutter, make sure to leverage dynamic data binding by using `setState` or other state management solutions to ensure that your lists or grids are automatically updated when data changes. For HTML/JavaScript, using event listeners or frameworks like React or Vue can make the data-binding process more efficient and seamless.

By understanding how these structures work in both HTML/CSS and Flutter, developers can create more efficient, scalable, and responsive applications that take full advantage of the tools available in each environment. Whether dealing with lists or grids, the strategies provided allow for optimization, responsiveness, and improved user experience.

Chapter 8: Navigation and Routing

Navigation is a crucial part of user interaction in both web applications and mobile apps. The ability to transition between different pages or views while preserving the state and flow of the application enhances user experience and helps maintain organization. This chapter focuses on how navigation and routing work in web apps and Flutter, highlighting differences and similarities in approaches.

8.1 Understanding Navigation in Web Apps

In web development, navigation refers to the method by which users can move between different pages, sections, or components of an app or website. The navigation is typically handled by manipulating the browser's URL and re-rendering the corresponding view.

Key Concepts in Web Navigation:

- **URLs**: Web apps are often structured around URLs that map to different pages or resources. A URL can represent a route to a specific page, and the browser's address bar will update to reflect the current page.
- **Anchor Tags**: In traditional web apps, navigating between pages is often done using anchor tags (`<a href="...">`), which are tied to specific URLs. This causes the browser to reload the page.
- **Single Page Applications (SPA)**: SPAs use JavaScript frameworks (like React, Angular, Vue.js) to change the content of the page without reloading. The browser's address bar updates, but the page does not fully reload. SPAs use the `History API` or `Hash Routing` to manage navigation.

Example of Basic Web Navigation with HTML and JavaScript:

```
<!-- html -->
<!DOCTYPE html>
<html lang="en">
<head>
  <meta charset="UTF-8">
  <meta name="viewport" content="width=device-width,
initial-scale=1.0">
  <title>Basic Web Navigation</title>
</head>
```

```
<body>
  <nav>
    <a href="#home" onclick="navigate('home')">Home</a>
    <a href="#about" onclick="navigate('about')">About</a>
    <a href="#contact"
onclick="navigate('contact')">Contact</a>
  </nav>

  <div id="content"></div>

  <script>
    function navigate(page) {
      const contentDiv =
document.getElementById('content');
      if (page === 'home') {
        contentDiv.innerHTML = '<h1>Home Page</h1>';
      } else if (page === 'about') {
        contentDiv.innerHTML = '<h1>About Us</h1>';
      } else if (page === 'contact') {
        contentDiv.innerHTML = '<h1>Contact Us</h1>';
      }
    }
  </script>
</body>
</html>
```

In this example, the JavaScript `navigate()` function handles the dynamic loading of content into the `#content` div without a full page reload. The browser's URL is not updated, but the app remains responsive and dynamic.

Benefits of Web Navigation:

1. **State Preservation**: With SPAs, the app can retain the state without refreshing the entire page.
2. **Smooth User Experience**: Instant content changes enhance user experience by preventing delays caused by page reloads.
3. **History Management**: The browser's history is manipulated to allow users to navigate backward and forward in the app's view.

8.2 Flutter Navigator: Navigating Screens

In Flutter, navigation and routing are handled using the `Navigator` class, which manages a stack of routes. Each screen or page is pushed to or popped from the stack based on the user's actions.

The Navigator Class

The `Navigator` class in Flutter is used to manage the app's routes. It maintains a stack of pages and handles navigation between them by either pushing new screens or popping existing ones.

Flutter Navigation Basics:

- **Push**: This operation adds a new route to the stack, making the new route the current screen.
- **Pop**: This removes the top-most route from the stack, reverting the app to the previous screen.

Example of Basic Navigation in Flutter Using `Navigator.push`:

```
//dart
import 'package:flutter/material.dart';

void main() {
  runApp(MyApp());
}

class MyApp extends StatelessWidget {
  @override
  Widget build(BuildContext context) {
    return MaterialApp(
      home: HomeScreen(),
    );
  }
}

class HomeScreen extends StatelessWidget {
  @override
  Widget build(BuildContext context) {
    return Scaffold(
      appBar: AppBar(title: Text("Home Screen")),
      body: Center(
        child: ElevatedButton(
```

```
          onPressed: () {
            Navigator.push(
              context,
              MaterialPageRoute(builder: (context) =>
SecondScreen()),
            );
          },
          child: Text("Go to Second Screen"),
        ),
      ),
    );
  }
}

class SecondScreen extends StatelessWidget {
  @override
  Widget build(BuildContext context) {
    return Scaffold(
      appBar: AppBar(title: Text("Second Screen")),
      body: Center(
        child: ElevatedButton(
          onPressed: () {
            Navigator.pop(context);
          },
          child: Text("Back to Home"),
        ),
      ),
    );
  }
}
```

In this example:

- `Navigator.push` adds the `SecondScreen` to the stack when the button is clicked.
- `Navigator.pop` removes the current screen from the stack, returning to the previous screen.

Advantages of Flutter Navigation:

- **Declarative Approach**: Flutter's navigation uses a declarative paradigm where the app's structure and flow are defined by widget trees.

- **Ease of Use**: With simple navigation methods like `Navigator.push` and `Navigator.pop`, navigation is straightforward to implement and manage.
- **Custom Transitions**: Flutter allows developers to define custom screen transitions between pages, providing flexibility in animations.

8.3 Using Routes for Multi-Screen Apps

In more complex applications, managing navigation can get cumbersome when screens or pages are dynamically generated. Flutter offers a route-based navigation system that allows developers to define named routes, simplifying navigation between multiple screens.

Named Routes in Flutter:

Named routes provide a way to navigate to a specific screen by referencing a string, rather than by passing widget objects directly. This method is useful for large apps with many screens, as it keeps navigation organized and easily maintainable.

Defining and Using Named Routes:

```
//dart
import 'package:flutter/material.dart';

void main() {
  runApp(MyApp());
}

class MyApp extends StatelessWidget {
  @override
  Widget build(BuildContext context) {
    return MaterialApp(
      initialRoute: '/',
      routes: {
        '/': (context) => HomeScreen(),
        '/second': (context) => SecondScreen(),
        '/third': (context) => ThirdScreen(),
      },
    );
  }
}
```

```
class HomeScreen extends StatelessWidget {
  @override
  Widget build(BuildContext context) {
    return Scaffold(
      appBar: AppBar(title: Text("Home Screen")),
      body: Center(
        child: ElevatedButton(
          onPressed: () {
            Navigator.pushNamed(context, '/second');
          },
          child: Text("Go to Second Screen"),
        ),
      ),
    );
  }
}

class SecondScreen extends StatelessWidget {
  @override
  Widget build(BuildContext context) {
    return Scaffold(
      appBar: AppBar(title: Text("Second Screen")),
      body: Center(
        child: ElevatedButton(
          onPressed: () {
            Navigator.pushNamed(context, '/third');
          },
          child: Text("Go to Third Screen"),
        ),
      ),
    );
  }
}

class ThirdScreen extends StatelessWidget {
  @override
  Widget build(BuildContext context) {
    return Scaffold(
      appBar: AppBar(title: Text("Third Screen")),
      body: Center(
        child: ElevatedButton(
          onPressed: () {
```

```
              Navigator.popUntil(context,
ModalRoute.withName('/'));
            },
            child: Text("Back to Home"),
          ),
        ),
      );
  }
}
```

In this example:

- The `MaterialApp` widget defines routes as a map, where each route is associated with a screen widget.
- `Navigator.pushNamed(context, '/second')` navigates to the `SecondScreen`.
- The `Navigator.popUntil` method is used to pop back to the home screen, skipping over intermediate screens.

Benefits of Named Routes:

1. **Centralized Management**: Routes can be defined in one place, making it easy to modify navigation behavior.
2. **Code Maintainability**: Named routes make the navigation flow more readable and less error-prone, especially in large apps.
3. **Improved Navigation Management**: The ability to navigate between screens by names rather than widget objects provides better control over the app's flow.

8.4 Passing Data Between Screens

In complex applications, passing data between screens is a fundamental feature. Both web apps and Flutter handle data passing, but the techniques differ slightly.

Passing Data in Web Apps:

In web applications, data is typically passed between screens by embedding the data in the URL (query parameters) or using JavaScript to manipulate global variables or session/local storage.

Example of Passing Data in Web Apps Using Query Parameters:

```
<!-- html -->
<!DOCTYPE html>
<html lang="en">
<head>
  <meta charset="UTF-8">
  <meta name="viewport" content="width=device-width,
initial-scale=1.0">
  <title>Data Passing Example</title>
</head>
<body>
  <a href="second.html?name=John">Go to Second Page</a>
</body>
</html>
```

In `second.html`, the data can be accessed using JavaScript by parsing the URL:

```
//javascript
const urlParams = new
URLSearchParams(window.location.search);
const name = urlParams.get('name');
document.getElementById("content").innerHTML = `Hello, $
{name}!`;
```

Passing Data in Flutter:

In Flutter, data can be passed between screens via the `Navigator` or by using arguments in named routes. The data is passed as parameters to the route.

Passing Data Using `Navigator.push`:

```
//dart
Navigator.push(
  context,
  MaterialPageRoute(
    builder: (context) => SecondScreen(data: 'Hello from
Home'),
  ),
);
```

In the `SecondScreen`, the data is accessed through the constructor:

```dart
//dart
class SecondScreen extends StatelessWidget {
  final String data;

  SecondScreen({required this.data});

  @override
  Widget build(BuildContext context) {
    return Scaffold(
      appBar: AppBar(title: Text("Second Screen")),
      body: Center(child: Text(data)),
    );
  }
}
```

Passing Data Using Named Routes:

```dart
//dart
Navigator.pushNamed(context, '/second', arguments: 'Hello
from Home');
```

In the `SecondScreen`, the data is retrieved from the `ModalRoute`:

```dart
//dart
class SecondScreen extends StatelessWidget {
  @override
  Widget build(BuildContext context) {
    final String data =
ModalRoute.of(context)?.settings.arguments as String;

    return Scaffold(
      appBar: AppBar(title: Text("Second Screen")),
      body: Center(child: Text(data)),
    );
  }
}
```

Tips for Passing Data Between Screens:

- **Use constructors for simple data**: Passing data via constructors works well when only a small amount of data needs to be passed.
- **Use `ModalRoute` for more complex data passing**: For larger or more complex data, you can use `ModalRoute.of(context)` to pass arguments.

- **Avoid overloading constructors**: If a screen has too many parameters, consider using a data model class to encapsulate all the data and pass it as one object.

8.5 Handling Back Navigation

In modern mobile applications, back navigation is one of the most important aspects of user experience. In Flutter, handling back navigation involves understanding the behavior of the `Navigator` class, which controls the stack of routes. Back navigation ensures that users can move backward through the navigation stack when they press the device's back button, either on Android or iOS. Flutter's approach to back navigation is deeply tied to its route management system.

In Flutter, the back navigation process is automatic. When you navigate to a new screen (route) using `Navigator.push()`, the new screen is pushed onto the navigation stack. Pressing the back button (or calling `Navigator.pop()`) pops the top screen off the stack and returns the user to the previous screen.

The Role of `Navigator.pop()`

The most common way to handle back navigation in Flutter is by calling `Navigator.pop()`. This method removes the current screen from the stack and reveals the previous screen. When you press the physical back button on Android or the back gesture on iOS, Flutter automatically triggers `Navigator.pop()` to revert to the previous screen.

Here's an example of how `Navigator.pop()` works in practice:

```
//dart
// Pushing a new screen
Navigator.push(
  context,
  MaterialPageRoute(builder: (context) => SecondScreen()),
);

// Back navigation using Navigator.pop()
Navigator.pop(context);
```

When `Navigator.pop(context)` is called, the `SecondScreen` is removed from the stack, and the `HomeScreen` becomes the active screen again.

Handling Back Button on Android

On Android, the system provides a physical back button, which can be customized to perform different actions. Flutter allows developers to intercept and handle back button presses to customize behavior. You can override the back button using the `WillPopScope` widget, which wraps a widget and listens for back button presses.

Here's an example of how to customize the back button behavior:

```
//dart
class MyScreen extends StatelessWidget {
  @override
  Widget build(BuildContext context) {
    return WillPopScope(
      onWillPop: () async {
        // Custom back navigation logic
        return true; // Allow back navigation
      },
      child: Scaffold(
        appBar: AppBar(title: Text("My Screen")),
        body: Center(child: Text("Press back button")),
      ),
    );
  }
}
```

In this example, the `WillPopScope` widget listens for the back button press and triggers the `onWillPop` callback, allowing the app to perform custom behavior before allowing the navigation to pop.

Handling Back Button on iOS

iOS does not have a physical back button, but users can swipe from the left edge of the screen to go back. Flutter automatically handles this swipe gesture with the native back navigation behavior. However, developers can still intercept the back navigation using `WillPopScope` to trigger custom actions before the screen is popped.

Customizing Back Navigation

Sometimes, the default back navigation behavior may not be sufficient. For instance, when you need to confirm if the user wants to leave a screen, you can use a dialog to ask for confirmation.

Here's an example of confirming back navigation:

```
//dart
class MyScreen extends StatelessWidget {
  @override
  Widget build(BuildContext context) {
    return WillPopScope(
      onWillPop: () async {
        bool shouldExit = await showDialog(
          context: context,
          builder: (context) {
            return AlertDialog(
              title: Text("Are you sure?"),
              content: Text("Do you really want to leave
this screen?"),
              actions: [
                TextButton(
                  onPressed: () {
                    Navigator.of(context).pop(false); //
Don't pop
                  },
                  child: Text("No"),
                ),
                TextButton(
                  onPressed: () {
                    Navigator.of(context).pop(true); // Do
pop
                  },
                  child: Text("Yes"),
                ),
              ],
            );
          },
        );
        return shouldExit ?? false; // Allow or deny
navigation
      },
      child: Scaffold(
        appBar: AppBar(title: Text("My Screen")),
        body: Center(child: Text("Press back button")),
```

```
        ),
      );
    }
}
```

This example presents a confirmation dialog when the user tries to navigate away from the current screen.

8.6 Deep Linking in Flutter vs Web URL Routing

Deep linking allows users to navigate directly to a specific page within an application from a URL, bypassing the home screen or any intermediary screens. In Flutter, deep linking is supported through the use of package libraries and platform-specific solutions. On the web, deep linking is accomplished through URL routing, where different URLs correspond to different pages within the application.

Deep Linking in Flutter

Deep linking in Flutter is handled using the `url_launcher` package or `flutter_webview_plugin` for opening specific URLs. There's also a more advanced solution through the `uni_links` package, which allows Flutter apps to handle incoming deep links, either from external sources (e.g., other apps) or from URLs shared with the app.

Here's an example of handling deep links using the `uni_links` package:

```
//dart
import 'package:uni_links/uni_links.dart';

class DeepLinkScreen extends StatefulWidget {
  @override
  _DeepLinkScreenState createState() =>
_DeepLinkScreenState();
}

class _DeepLinkScreenState extends State<DeepLinkScreen> {
  String _deepLink = "No link yet";

  @override
  void initState() {
    super.initState();
```

```
    _initDeepLink();
  }

  Future<void> _initDeepLink() async {
    // Handling incoming deep link
    try {
      Uri? initialLink = await getInitialLink();
      setState(() {
        _deepLink = initialLink?.toString() ?? "No link
found";
      });
    } catch (e) {
      setState(() {
        _deepLink = "Failed to get link";
      });
    }

    // Listening to changes in deep link
    linkStream.listen((String? link) {
      setState(() {
        _deepLink = link ?? "No link received";
      });
    });
  }

  @override
  Widget build(BuildContext context) {
    return Scaffold(
      appBar: AppBar(title: Text("Deep Link Example")),
      body: Center(child: Text("Deep Link: $_deepLink")),
    );
  }
}
```

In this example, Flutter listens for incoming deep links and displays them within the `DeepLinkScreen`. The app responds to the incoming URL and processes the navigation accordingly.

Web URL Routing

On the web, deep linking is inherently supported through the use of URLs. When a user visits a URL, the browser communicates with the server, which responds with the appropriate content for that page. In modern web applications, client-side routing libraries like React Router (for React apps) or Vue Router (for Vue.js apps) allow for deep linking by mapping specific URL paths to components or pages.

Here's an example of deep linking in a React app using React Router:

```
//javascript
import React from 'react';
import { BrowserRouter as Router, Route, Link } from
'react-router-dom';

function HomePage() {
  return <h2>Home Page</h2>;
}

function AboutPage() {
  return <h2>About Page</h2>;
}

function App() {
  return (
    <Router>
      <nav>
        <Link to="/">Home</Link>
        <Link to="/about">About</Link>
      </nav>
      <Route path="/" exact component={HomePage} />
      <Route path="/about" component={AboutPage} />
    </Router>
  );
}

export default App;
```

In this example, React Router maps the `/` and `/about` paths to their respective components, creating deep links that users can navigate to directly via URLs.

8.7 Animating Transitions Between Pages

Transitions between pages enhance the user experience by providing a fluid and engaging visual journey as users move from one screen to another. Flutter offers various ways to animate page transitions using its powerful animation framework, which includes built-in transition types like `SlideTransition`, `FadeTransition`, and `ScaleTransition`.

Default Navigation Animations

By default, Flutter provides a sliding animation when navigating between screens using `Navigator.push()`. The new screen slides in from the right, while the previous screen slides out to the left. This default animation provides a smooth, intuitive transition between pages.

However, Flutter allows for custom page transition animations to be created by extending the `PageRouteBuilder` class. The `PageRouteBuilder` allows developers to create custom transitions by specifying animations for both the entering and exiting screens.

Here's an example of customizing page transitions using `PageRouteBuilder`:

```
//dart
Navigator.push(
  context,
  PageRouteBuilder(
    pageBuilder: (context, animation, secondaryAnimation)
{
      return SecondScreen();
    },
    transitionsBuilder: (context, animation,
secondaryAnimation, child) {
      const begin = Offset(1.0, 0.0); // Start off-screen
to the right
      const end = Offset.zero;
      const curve = Curves.easeInOut;

      var tween = Tween(begin: begin, end:
end).chain(CurveTween(curve: curve));
      var offsetAnimation = animation.drive(tween);

      return SlideTransition(position: offsetAnimation,
child: child);
    },
  ),
);
```

This example customizes the transition by using `SlideTransition`, which slides the new screen in from the right when navigating forward and slides it out when navigating backward.

Custom Animation Effects

Flutter allows developers to create sophisticated animations, such as zoom-in effects, fade-ins, or scale transitions, giving you full control over the appearance and behavior of the page transitions. By combining different types of transitions and animation curves, you can create rich and highly customized user experiences.

Example:

```
//dart
Navigator.push(
  context,
  PageRouteBuilder(
    pageBuilder: (context, animation, secondaryAnimation)
{
      return SecondScreen();
    },
    transitionsBuilder: (context, animation,
secondaryAnimation, child) {
      var scaleTween = Tween(begin: 0.0, end: 1.0);
      var scaleAnimation = animation.drive(scaleTween);

      return ScaleTransition(scale: scaleAnimation, child:
child);
    },
  ),
);
```

This example creates a scaling transition, where the new screen grows from the center, creating a zoom-in effect.

8.8 Sample Code: HTML Links vs Flutter Navigation

In web applications, navigation is usually handled using URLs, where links (<a> tags) connect different pages. In Flutter, navigation is handled using the `Navigator` widget, and screen transitions are not based on URLs but on route pushing and popping. Despite the differences, both web and Flutter navigation share similar concepts.

HTML Link Example:

```
<!-- html -->
<a href="/about">Go to About Page</a>
```

This simple HTML link takes the user to the `/about` page by modifying the browser's URL.

Flutter Navigation Example:

```
//dart
Navigator.pushNamed(context, '/about');
```

In Flutter, the `Navigator.pushNamed()` method is used to navigate to a named route. Unlike web applications, Flutter doesn't rely on changing the URL; instead, it manipulates the route stack internally.

Navigating to a Specific URL:

For Flutter, handling deep linking can achieve a similar result to clicking on an HTML link. Here's how you might navigate to a specific page based on a deep link:

```
//dart
Navigator.pushNamed(context, '/profile', arguments:
userId);
```

This example is similar to an HTML link, where the `'/profile'` path corresponds to the user profile screen in Flutter.

Example Codes

HTML: Simple Navigation with Links

In HTML, navigation is often handled using anchor (<a>) tags that link to other pages or sections within the page.

```
<!-- html -->
<!DOCTYPE html>

<html lang="en">
<head>
    <meta charset="UTF-8">
    <meta name="viewport" content="width=device-width,
```

```
initial-scale=1.0">
    <title>HTML Navigation Example</title>
</head>
<body>
    <nav>
        <ul>
            <li><a href="home.html">Home</a></li>
            <li><a href="about.html">About</a></li>
            <li><a href="contact.html">Contact</a></li>
        </ul>
    </nav>
</body>
</html>
```

This structure uses anchor tags to route to different pages. The `href` attribute defines the target URL, and when a user clicks the link, the browser navigates to the specified page.

Flutter: Navigation with `Navigator.push`

Flutter provides a more dynamic approach to navigation, relying on the `Navigator` widget, which manages a stack of routes.

```
//dart
import 'package:flutter/material.dart';


void main() {
  runApp(MyApp());
}

class MyApp extends StatelessWidget {
  @override
  Widget build(BuildContext context) {
    return MaterialApp(
      home: HomePage(),
    );
  }
}

class HomePage extends StatelessWidget {
  @override
```

```
  Widget build(BuildContext context) {
    return Scaffold(
      appBar: AppBar(title: Text('Home')),
      body: Center(
        child: ElevatedButton(
          onPressed: () {
            Navigator.push(
              context,
              MaterialPageRoute(builder: (context) =>
AboutPage()),
            );
          },
          child: Text('Go to About'),
        ),
      ),
    );
  }
}

class AboutPage extends StatelessWidget {
  @override
  Widget build(BuildContext context) {
    return Scaffold(
      appBar: AppBar(title: Text('About')),
      body: Center(child: Text('This is the About Page')),
    );
  }
}
```

This example shows how navigation is handled with `Navigator.push`, which pushes a new route (page) onto the navigation stack. The `MaterialPageRoute` helps to specify the target page.

HTML: Handling Anchor Links for Page Sections

Anchor links in HTML can also navigate within the same page. This is often used for single-page applications (SPAs).

```
<!-- html -->
<!DOCTYPE html>

<html lang="en">
```

```html
<head>
    <meta charset="UTF-8">
    <meta name="viewport" content="width=device-width,
initial-scale=1.0">
    <title>HTML Section Navigation</title>
</head>
<body>
    <nav>
        <ul>
            <li><a href="#home">Home</a></li>
            <li><a href="#services">Services</a></li>
            <li><a href="#contact">Contact</a></li>
        </ul>
    </nav>

    <section id="home">
        <h2>Home</h2>
        <p>Welcome to the home section.</p>
    </section>

    <section id="services">
        <h2>Services</h2>
        <p>Details about our services.</p>
    </section>

    <section id="contact">
        <h2>Contact</h2>
        <p>Contact details.</p>
    </section>
</body>
</html>
```

Here, instead of navigating to another page, the `href="#home"` anchors the link to the corresponding section within the same page.

Flutter: Navigation with `Navigator.pop`

In Flutter, you can also pop a page off the navigation stack to go back to the previous screen using `Navigator.pop`.

```
//dart
```

```
import 'package:flutter/material.dart';


void main() {
  runApp(MyApp());
}

class MyApp extends StatelessWidget {
  @override
  Widget build(BuildContext context) {
    return MaterialApp(
      home: FirstPage(),
    );
  }
}

class FirstPage extends StatelessWidget {
  @override
  Widget build(BuildContext context) {
    return Scaffold(
      appBar: AppBar(title: Text('First Page')),
      body: Center(
        child: ElevatedButton(
          onPressed: () {
            Navigator.push(
              context,
              MaterialPageRoute(builder: (context) =>
SecondPage()),
            );
          },
          child: Text('Go to Second Page'),
        ),
      ),
    );
  }
}

class SecondPage extends StatelessWidget {
  @override
  Widget build(BuildContext context) {
    return Scaffold(
      appBar: AppBar(title: Text('Second Page')),
```

```
        body: Center(
          child: ElevatedButton(
            onPressed: () {
              Navigator.pop(context); // Go back to
FirstPage
            },
            child: Text('Go Back'),
          ),
        ),
      );
  }
}
```

This demonstrates how a user can navigate back using `Navigator.pop()`. It removes the current route and returns to the previous page.

Tips

- Use `Navigator.pushReplacement` if you want to replace the current page with a new one rather than adding a new page to the stack. This is useful when you no longer need the previous page.
- In Flutter, wrap your route changes in `MaterialPageRoute` or `CupertinoPageRoute` to specify the transition style you want (e.g., material vs. Cupertino).
- Make use of `Navigator.pushNamed` for named routes in larger Flutter applications. It makes your navigation easier to manage by using route names instead of widget instances.

Actionable Strategies

- **Consistency in Navigation**: Ensure that your navigation structure is consistent across your web or mobile application. For instance, always keep the main menu or navigation bar in the same location, whether in the header of a website or as a consistent widget in your Flutter app.
- **Deep Linking**: Implement deep linking in Flutter to handle URLs that open specific pages within your app, similar to how you use anchor tags in HTML for specific sections. Use `onGenerateRoute` to capture deep link paths and route users accordingly.

- **Lazy Loading Routes**: For performance optimization, use lazy loading for routes. In Flutter, this can be done by delaying the loading of certain screens until needed, improving the app's initial load time, just like how pages are only loaded when a user clicks a link in HTML.
- **Animation Transitions**: Use animated transitions when navigating between screens or pages. Flutter supports smooth page transitions using widgets like `PageRouteBuilder`, which gives you control over the transition's animation. On the web, you can achieve this with CSS transitions or JavaScript-based animations.
- **Testing Navigation**: Just like in traditional web development where you ensure that links are working correctly across different browsers, in Flutter, test navigation thoroughly using the `flutter_test` package. Write test cases to verify that navigation works as expected under various scenarios.

By focusing on these strategies, you will be able to create a more efficient and user-friendly navigation system in both your web and mobile applications.

Chapter 9: Handling User Input

Handling user input forms a critical part of both web and mobile app development. Whether it's gathering data, validating information, or providing an interface for interaction, understanding how to implement forms in HTML and Flutter is essential. This chapter will comprehensively examine the techniques for handling forms, input fields, validation, and form state management in both HTML/CSS/JavaScript and Flutter.

9.1 HTML Forms vs Flutter Forms

HTML Forms:

HTML forms are a fundamental part of web development. They allow developers to gather user input and submit it to a server for processing. The form element in HTML provides a way to group various input elements such as text fields, radio buttons, checkboxes, and buttons that allow the user to enter data.

Here's a simple HTML form example:

```
<!-- html -->
<!DOCTYPE html>
<html lang="en">
<head>
    <meta charset="UTF-8">
    <meta name="viewport" content="width=device-width,
initial-scale=1.0">
    <title>Simple HTML Form</title>
</head>
<body>
    <form action="/submit" method="POST">
        <label for="name">Name:</label>
        <input type="text" id="name" name="name"
required><br><br>

        <label for="email">Email:</label>
        <input type="email" id="email" name="email"
required><br><br>

        <label for="password">Password:</label>
```

```
        <input type="password" id="password"
name="password" required><br><br>

        <button type="submit">Submit</button>
    </form>
</body>
</html>
```

In this example, a user is prompted to enter their name, email, and password. The form uses the `POST` method to submit the data to a specified URL (`/submit`), where it can be processed by the server.

HTML forms are easy to set up, but they require a backend server or JavaScript to handle the user input and submission process.

Flutter Forms:

Flutter doesn't have an HTML form equivalent. Instead, user input is managed through widgets such as `TextFormField`, `TextField`, and buttons like `RaisedButton` or `FlatButton` to collect and submit data. Flutter's approach to forms is more dynamic and requires more programming compared to traditional HTML forms.

Here is an example of how forms are implemented in Flutter:

```
//dart
import 'package:flutter/material.dart';

void main() => runApp(MyApp());

class MyApp extends StatelessWidget {
  @override
  Widget build(BuildContext context) {
    return MaterialApp(
      home: Scaffold(
        appBar: AppBar(title: Text('Flutter Form
Example')),
        body: Padding(
          padding: const EdgeInsets.all(16.0),
          child: MyForm(),
        ),
      ),
    );
  }
```

```
}

class MyForm extends StatefulWidget {
  @override
  _MyFormState createState() => _MyFormState();
}

class _MyFormState extends State<MyForm> {
  final _formKey = GlobalKey<FormState>();

  final TextEditingController _nameController =
TextEditingController();
  final TextEditingController _emailController =
TextEditingController();
  final TextEditingController _passwordController =
TextEditingController();

  void _submitForm() {
    if (_formKey.currentState!.validate()) {
      ScaffoldMessenger.of(context).showSnackBar(
        SnackBar(content: Text('Processing Data')),
      );
    }
  }

  @override
  Widget build(BuildContext context) {
    return Form(
      key: _formKey,
      child: Column(
        crossAxisAlignment: CrossAxisAlignment.start,
        children: <Widget>[
          TextFormField(
            controller: _nameController,
            decoration: InputDecoration(labelText:
'Name'),
            validator: (value) {
              if (value == null || value.isEmpty) {
                return 'Please enter your name';
              }
              return null;
            },
```

```
          ),
          TextFormField(
            controller: _emailController,
            decoration: InputDecoration(labelText:
'Email'),
            validator: (value) {
              if (value == null || value.isEmpty) {
                return 'Please enter your email';
              }
              if (!RegExp(r'\S+@\S+\.
\S+').hasMatch(value)) {
                return 'Please enter a valid email';
              }
              return null;
            },
          ),
          TextFormField(
            controller: _passwordController,
            decoration: InputDecoration(labelText:
'Password'),
            obscureText: true,
            validator: (value) {
              if (value == null || value.isEmpty) {
                return 'Please enter a password';
              }
              return null;
            },
          ),
          Padding(
            padding: const EdgeInsets.symmetric(vertical:
16.0),
            child: ElevatedButton(
              onPressed: _submitForm,
              child: Text('Submit'),
            ),
          ),
        ],
      ),
    );
  }
}
```

In this Flutter example, the form is implemented using the `TextFormField` widget inside a `Form` widget. Flutter provides validation within the `FormState` object, allowing for more control and validation before form submission.

9.2 Using the Input vs TextField Widget

HTML Input Elements:

In HTML, the `<input>` element is used to create form fields, where users can enter data. This element can take various types, including `text`, `password`, `email`, `number`, and others, depending on the kind of data you want to collect.

```
<!-- html -->
<input type="text" id="username" name="username"
placeholder="Enter your username">
<input type="password" id="password" name="password"
placeholder="Enter your password">
<input type="email" id="email" name="email"
placeholder="Enter your email">
```

The `type` attribute determines the behavior of the input element. For instance, `type="password"` hides the input text, and `type="email"` allows email-specific validation.

Flutter TextField Widget:

In Flutter, the `TextField` widget serves as the primary widget for collecting user input. The `TextField` can be customized with controllers, input decorations, and validation functions. It is also used with the `TextFormField` widget, which allows for better validation and error handling within a form context.

Here's an example of how a basic `TextField` widget is used in Flutter:

```
//dart
TextField(
  controller: _controller,
  decoration: InputDecoration(
    labelText: 'Username',
    hintText: 'Enter your username',
    border: OutlineInputBorder(),
  ),
)
```

The `TextField` widget in Flutter provides a lot of customization options, including the ability to define the keyboard type, adjust styling, and handle text input focus. For forms, it's often wrapped inside a `Form` widget for validation.

9.3 Managing Form States

HTML Forms State Management:

In HTML, form state is managed by tracking the values of input fields via JavaScript. You can use JavaScript to retrieve form values and validate or process the data before submitting it to the server.

```
<!-- html -->
<form id="myForm">
  <label for="username">Username:</label>
  <input type="text" id="username"
name="username"><br><br>

  <label for="email">Email:</label>
  <input type="email" id="email" name="email"><br><br>

  <input type="submit" value="Submit">
</form>

<script>
  const form = document.getElementById("myForm");
  form.onsubmit = function(event) {
    event.preventDefault();
    const username =
document.getElementById("username").value;
    const email = document.getElementById("email").value;
    console.log("Username: " + username);
    console.log("Email: " + email);
  }
</script>
```

This JavaScript code captures the input values when the form is submitted. By using the `onsubmit` event, it prevents the default form submission behavior, allowing custom validation or submission actions to be taken.

Flutter Form State Management:

In Flutter, the `Form` widget is used to manage the state of form fields and validation.

Each form field is tied to a `TextEditingController` for tracking input, and the `FormState` is responsible for handling validation and submitting the form.

```
//dart
final _formKey = GlobalKey<FormState>();

void _submitForm() {
  if (_formKey.currentState!.validate()) {
    // Process data
  }
}
```

The `FormState` object, which is accessed via the `GlobalKey<FormState>()`, manages the form's overall state, including validation and submission. Each individual form field can also have its state tracked using the `TextFormField` widget, which validates input based on the conditions defined in the `validator` property.

9.4 Adding Validation to Flutter Forms

HTML Form Validation:

HTML5 introduces built-in form validation features, where input fields can be validated automatically based on their type. The `required` attribute can be used to mark fields that must be filled in before submission. HTML also provides the ability to create custom validation with JavaScript.

Here is an example of HTML form validation:

```
<!-- html -->
<form action="/submit" method="POST">
  <label for="username">Username:</label>
  <input type="text" id="username" name="username"
required><br><br>

  <label for="email">Email:</label>
  <input type="email" id="email" name="email"
required><br><br>

  <input type="submit" value="Submit">
</form>
```

In this case, the `required` attribute on both the `username` and `email` fields ensures that these fields cannot be left empty. If the user tries to submit the form without filling in these fields, the browser will prevent the submission and prompt the user to enter valid data.

Flutter Form Validation:

Flutter offers robust form validation capabilities through the `TextFormField` widget and the `FormState`. The `TextFormField` allows you to define validation logic in the `validator` property, which is a function that checks the input and returns an error message if the input is invalid.

```
//dart
TextFormField(
  controller: _emailController,
  decoration: InputDecoration(labelText: 'Email'),
  validator: (value) {
    if (value == null || value.isEmpty) {
      return 'Please enter your email';
    }
    if (!RegExp(r'\S+@\S+\.\S+').hasMatch(value)) {
      return 'Please enter a valid email';
    }
    return null;
  },
)
```

This example performs two validations for the email input:

1. It checks whether the field is empty.
2. It uses a regular expression to ensure the input matches the format of a valid email address.

Flutter's `TextFormField` makes it easy to handle form validation dynamically, which provides a seamless user experience, especially in mobile apps. By checking the validity of the form fields, you can provide real-time feedback to users, guiding them through the process of entering valid data.

9.5 Handling Button Clicks

Handling button clicks is a fundamental aspect of building interactive applications, both in web development and mobile app development. Buttons are one of the most common UI elements, used to trigger actions such as submitting forms, navigating between screens, or sending data. The way buttons are implemented and how click events are handled varies between HTML and Flutter. Let's examine how button clicks are handled in both technologies, diving into their respective structures, functionalities, and differences.

Button Handling in HTML

In HTML, a button is typically defined using the `<button>` tag. It can be styled using CSS and made interactive with JavaScript. The basic structure of a button in HTML looks like this:

```
<!-- html -->
<button id="submitButton" type="button">Submit</button>
```

In this example, a button with the text "Submit" is created. The `type="button"` attribute indicates that it is a button element, as opposed to a form submit button. To add interactivity, JavaScript is used to detect and respond to user clicks. Here's how you might handle a click event in HTML using JavaScript:

```
<!-- html -->
<script>

document.getElementById("submitButton").addEventListener("
click", function() {
    alert("Button clicked!");
  });
</script>
```

In this example, when the user clicks the button, a JavaScript event listener is triggered. The `addEventListener` method listens for the `click` event and executes a callback function that shows an alert message.

For more complex button behavior, JavaScript can also interact with other elements of the page, modify the DOM, or trigger AJAX requests to fetch data without refreshing the page. This makes buttons in HTML highly dynamic and customizable.

Button Handling in Flutter

In Flutter, button handling is slightly more abstracted, as Flutter uses the `GestureDetector` or `ElevatedButton` widgets for detecting tap interactions. The Flutter equivalent of an HTML button is typically an `ElevatedButton` widget or a `FlatButton` widget (deprecated in Flutter 3.0 in favor of `TextButton` and

ElevatedButton). Let's look at an example of button handling in Flutter:

```
//dart
ElevatedButton(
  onPressed: () {
    print("Button clicked!");
  },
  child: Text('Submit'),
)
```

In this example, the `ElevatedButton` widget is used to create a button. The `onPressed` callback is executed when the user clicks the button. Inside the callback, you can define the action to take place upon button press, such as printing a message to the console, navigating to another screen, or performing any other task.

The difference between HTML and Flutter button handling is that Flutter relies on a more declarative approach where UI components are created and managed through widgets, and the state changes are handled automatically when certain actions occur, like pressing a button.

Additionally, in Flutter, button clicks are typically used in the context of a larger widget tree, and the state management often includes updating the UI dynamically in response to a user action.

9.6 Input Decorations and Customizations

When dealing with forms and inputs in web and mobile applications, user experience is greatly enhanced when inputs are visually appealing and easy to interact with. Input decorations and customizations allow developers to adjust the appearance of text fields, add icons, customize borders, and modify the behavior of inputs to suit the needs of the application. Let's break down how input decorations are handled in both HTML/CSS and Flutter.

Input Decorations in HTML/CSS

In HTML, form elements such as text inputs can be styled using CSS. Basic input fields are created using the `<input>` tag, and their styles can be customized by targeting specific attributes. Here's an example of how you can style an input field:

```
<!-- html -->
<input type="text" id="username" placeholder="Enter your
```

```
username" class="input-field">
```

This simple input field has a placeholder text "Enter your username." The `class="input-field"` allows you to apply custom styles using CSS. Below is an example of how you might customize the input field with CSS:

```
/* css */
.input-field {
  padding: 10px;
  border: 2px solid #ccc;
  border-radius: 5px;
  font-size: 16px;
  width: 100%;
}

.input-field:focus {
  border-color: #4CAF50;
  outline: none;
}
```

In this CSS example, the input field has padding, a solid border, and a border-radius for rounded corners. When the input is focused, the border color changes to green, enhancing the user interaction.

You can also add icons or images inside the input fields using CSS. For example, to add a search icon inside an input field:

```
<!-- html -->
<div class="input-container">
  <input type="text" placeholder="Search">
  <i class="search-icon">&#128269;</i>
</div>
/* css */
.input-container {
  position: relative;
  display: inline-block;
}

.search-icon {
  position: absolute;
  top: 10px;
  left: 10px;
  font-size: 18px;
  color: #888;
```

```
}
```

This customizes the input field by adding an icon that remains inside the input field, making the design more intuitive.

Input Decorations in Flutter

Flutter offers a much more comprehensive approach to input decoration through its `InputDecoration` class, which allows developers to fully customize the appearance of text fields. You can easily style text fields by passing an `InputDecoration` to the `TextField` or `TextFormField` widget. Here's an example of how you can customize the decoration of a text field in Flutter:

```
//dart
TextField(
  decoration: InputDecoration(
    labelText: 'Username',
    hintText: 'Enter your username',
    border: OutlineInputBorder(),
    prefixIcon: Icon(Icons.person),
  ),
)
```

In this example, the `InputDecoration` class is used to add a label, hint text, and a prefix icon to the input field. The border of the field is also customized with an `OutlineInputBorder`, which adds a solid border around the field.

Here are some of the key properties of the `InputDecoration` class that can be used to customize inputs:

- `labelText`: Adds a label above the text field.
- `hintText`: Adds placeholder text inside the text field when it's empty.
- `prefixIcon`: Adds an icon at the beginning of the input field.
- `suffixIcon`: Adds an icon at the end of the input field.
- `border`: Customizes the border around the input field.
- `focusedBorder` and `enabledBorder`: Allows you to define the border when the field is focused or enabled.

Customizing input fields in Flutter is extremely flexible, allowing for complex UI designs with minimal effort.

9.7 Debugging Input Issues in Flutter

Debugging input issues is crucial to ensure that user data is collected correctly, and any potential issues are addressed before releasing the application. Flutter provides a number of tools and techniques to help developers identify and fix issues with input fields.

Common Input Issues in Flutter

1. **Invalid Input Validation**: Often, developers need to validate user input before it's submitted. Flutter provides the `TextFormField` widget in combination with a `Form` widget, which allows for advanced input validation. However, sometimes inputs may fail to validate properly due to improper logic or regular expressions.

2. **Focus Issues**: Sometimes, when working with multiple input fields, the user may have trouble focusing on the correct field, or the keyboard might not pop up when the input field is tapped. This is usually caused by improper widget layouts or a missing `FocusNode` for the text fields.

3. **State Management**: If the state of the application is not managed properly, input fields may fail to update dynamically, or changes made by the user may not be reflected correctly in the UI.

Debugging Tools in Flutter

1. **Flutter DevTools**: Flutter provides a set of tools known as Flutter DevTools that can be used to debug and inspect the UI. These tools allow developers to inspect the widget tree, view widget layouts, check performance, and analyze state changes. The "Inspect Widget" feature in DevTools is especially useful for identifying issues with form fields.

2. **Print Statements**: While debugging, using print statements to check the values of variables and the state of the input fields is a simple but effective approach. For example, printing the value of a `TextField` to the console when the user submits the form can help verify that the correct data is being collected.

3. **Form Validation Feedback**: Flutter provides built-in support for form validation, and you can use the `validator` property of the `TextFormField` widget to check user input before it's submitted. The `FormState` class also provides methods like `validate` and `save` to help manage form validation in

a structured way.

9.8 Sample Code: Forms in HTML and Flutter

Let's take a look at a sample code comparison for creating forms in HTML and Flutter. These examples will highlight how form elements are structured and how interactivity is implemented in both technologies.

HTML Form Example

Here's an example of a basic form in HTML:

```
<!-- html -->
<form id="userForm">
  <label for="username">Username</label>
  <input type="text" id="username" name="username"
required>

  <label for="email">Email</label>
  <input type="email" id="email" name="email" required>

  <button type="submit" id="submitButton">Submit</button>
</form>

<script>

document.getElementById("userForm").addEventListener("subm
it", function(event) {
    event.preventDefault();
    alert("Form submitted!");
  });
</script>
```

In this example, the form consists of two input fields for username and email. The JavaScript code prevents the default form submission and shows an alert when the form is submitted.

Flutter Form Example

Here's how the same form could be implemented in Flutter:

```
//dart
```

```
import 'package:flutter/material.dart';

void main() {
  runApp(MyApp());
}

class MyApp extends StatelessWidget {
  @override
  Widget build(BuildContext context) {
    return MaterialApp(
      home: Scaffold(
        appBar: AppBar(title: Text("Form Example")),
        body: Padding(
          padding: EdgeInsets.all(16.0),
          child: UserForm(),
        ),
      ),
    );
  }
}

class UserForm extends StatefulWidget {
  @override
  _UserFormState createState() => _UserFormState();
}

class _UserFormState extends State<UserForm> {
  final _formKey = GlobalKey<FormState>();

  String? username;
  String? email;

  @override
  Widget build(BuildContext context) {
    return Form(
      key: _formKey,
      child: Column(
        children: <Widget>[
          TextFormField(
            decoration: InputDecoration(labelText:
'Username'),
            validator: (value) {
```

```
            if (value == null || value.isEmpty) {
              return 'Please enter a username';
            }
            return null;
          },
          onSaved: (value) {
            username = value;
          },
        ),
        TextFormField(
          decoration: InputDecoration(labelText:
'Email'),
          validator: (value) {
            if (value == null || value.isEmpty) {
              return 'Please enter an email';
            }
            return null;
          },
          onSaved: (value) {
            email = value;
          },
        ),
        ElevatedButton(
          onPressed: () {
            if (_formKey.currentState?.validate() ??
false) {
              _formKey.currentState?.save();
              showDialog(
                context: context,
                builder: (context) => AlertDialog(
                  content: Text('Form submitted with
username: $username and email: $email'),
                ),
              );
            }
          },
          child: Text('Submit'),
        ),
      ],
    ),
  );
}
```

```
}
```

This Flutter form uses a `TextFormField` widget for both the username and email input fields. The form validation is handled using the `validator` property, and when the form is submitted, it shows a dialog displaying the entered data.

In both web and mobile app development, handling user input is crucial for building interactive and dynamic applications. The differences between HTML forms and Flutter forms illustrate the varying approaches to creating forms, handling button clicks, customizing input fields, and validating data. While HTML relies heavily on JavaScript for interactivity and styling through CSS, Flutter offers a more declarative approach using widgets for UI components and built-in validation mechanisms. Understanding these differences and mastering the tools available in each platform ensures that you can build seamless, user-friendly applications across both web and mobile platforms.

Examples:

HTML/CSS Form with Text Input and Submit Button vs. Flutter Form

HTML/CSS:

```
<!-- html -->
<form id="userForm">
  <label for="username">Username:</label>
  <input type="text" id="username" name="username">
  <button type="submit">Submit</button>
</form>
```

Flutter:

```
//dart
TextEditingController usernameController =
TextEditingController();

@override
Widget build(BuildContext context) {
  return Scaffold(
    appBar: AppBar(title: Text('User Form')),
    body: Padding(
      padding: const EdgeInsets.all(16.0),
      child: Column(
```

```
        children: [
          TextField(
            controller: usernameController,
            decoration: InputDecoration(labelText:
'Username'),
          ),
          ElevatedButton(
            onPressed: () {
              // handle submit logic here
            },
            child: Text('Submit'),
          ),
        ],
      ),
    ),
  );
}
```

Comparison:

1. In HTML/CSS, a simple form structure with an `<input>` element and a `<button>` is used. The form has implicit form submission handling, which can be customized using JavaScript.
2. In Flutter, the `TextField` widget is used for text input, and a `TextEditingController` is employed to manage the input's state. The `ElevatedButton` handles the user action and triggers the form submission logic.

HTML/CSS Form Validation vs. Flutter Form Validation

HTML/CSS:

```
<!-- html -->
<form id="loginForm">
  <label for="email">Email:</label>
  <input type="email" id="email" name="email" required>
  <button type="submit">Login</button>
</form>
```

Flutter:

```
//dart
```

```
final GlobalKey<FormState> _formKey =
GlobalKey<FormState>();

@override
Widget build(BuildContext context) {
  return Scaffold(
    appBar: AppBar(title: Text('Login Form')),
    body: Padding(
      padding: const EdgeInsets.all(16.0),
      child: Form(
        key: _formKey,
        child: Column(
          children: [
            TextFormField(
              validator: (value) {
                if (value!.isEmpty) {
                  return 'Please enter a valid email';
                }
                return null;
              },
              decoration: InputDecoration(labelText:
'Email'),
            ),
            ElevatedButton(
              onPressed: () {
                if (_formKey.currentState?.validate() ??
false) {
                  // Process data
                }
              },
              child: Text('Login'),
            ),
          ],
        ),
      ),
    ),
  );
}
```

Comparison:

2 In HTML/CSS, the `required` attribute is used for basic validation on the form input, ensuring the field cannot be left blank before submission.

3 In Flutter, the `Form` and `TextFormField` widgets are used for form validation. A `GlobalKey` helps in managing the form state, and custom validation logic is applied within the `validator` callback function.

JavaScript Handling Input with Event Listeners vs. Flutter Handling Input with Gesture Detectors

HTML/JavaScript:

```
<!-- html -->
<input type="text" id="nameInput">
<button id="submitBtn">Submit</button>

<script>

document.getElementById('submitBtn').addEventListener('cli
ck', function() {
    const name =
document.getElementById('nameInput').value;
    alert('Hello, ' + name);
  });
</script>
```

Flutter:

```
//dart
TextEditingController nameController =
TextEditingController();

@override
Widget build(BuildContext context) {
  return Scaffold(
    appBar: AppBar(title: Text('Input Handling')),
    body: Padding(
      padding: const EdgeInsets.all(16.0),
      child: Column(
        children: [
          TextField(
            controller: nameController,
            decoration: InputDecoration(labelText: 'Enter
your name'),
```

```
          ),
          GestureDetector(
            onTap: () {
              String name = nameController.text;
              showDialog(
                context: context,
                builder: (context) => AlertDialog(
                  content: Text('Hello, $name'),
                ),
              );
            },
            child: Container(
              padding: EdgeInsets.all(10),
              color: Colors.blue,
              child: Text('Submit', style:
TextStyle(color: Colors.white)),
            ),
          ),
        ],
      ),
    ),
  );
}
```

Comparison:

3 In JavaScript, the `addEventListener` method is used to bind the `click` event to the button, and input data is retrieved directly from the DOM using `getElementById`.

4 In Flutter, a `TextEditingController` is used for managing the input's state. Instead of traditional button clicks, a `GestureDetector` widget can be used to detect tap gestures and trigger the corresponding logic.

HTML Select Dropdown vs. Flutter Dropdown Menu

HTML/CSS:

```
<!-- html -->
<select id="languageSelect">
  <option value="en">English</option>
  <option value="es">Spanish</option>
  <option value="fr">French</option>
```

```
</select>
```

Flutter:

```
//dart
String dropdownValue = 'English';

@override
Widget build(BuildContext context) {
  return Scaffold(
    appBar: AppBar(title: Text('Language Selector')),
    body: Padding(
      padding: const EdgeInsets.all(16.0),
      child: DropdownButton<String>(
        value: dropdownValue,
        onChanged: (String? newValue) {
          setState(() {
            dropdownValue = newValue!;
          });
        },
        items: <String>['English', 'Spanish', 'French']
            .map<DropdownMenuItem<String>>((String value)
{
          return DropdownMenuItem<String>(
            value: value,
            child: Text(value),
          );
        }).toList(),
      ),
    ),
  );
}
```

Comparison:

4 The HTML `<select>` element is used for creating a dropdown list, and the `<option>` elements define the selectable options.

5 In Flutter, the `DropdownButton` widget is used, where the current selection is tracked through a state variable (`dropdownValue`), and the options are mapped into `DropdownMenuItem` widgets.

Tips:

1. **Use Proper Controllers for Input Fields**: In Flutter, always use a `TextEditingController` for handling input values. This provides direct access to the text entered and ensures easy manipulation of input field values.
2. **Utilize `Form` Widgets for Complex Validations**: When you need to manage more complex form validation logic in Flutter, use the `Form` widget along with `TextFormField`. This allows you to validate multiple fields and provides better control over form submission.
3. **Leverage `GestureDetector` for Custom Interactions**: Flutter's `GestureDetector` is a powerful widget to capture user interactions such as taps, drags, or swipes. You can replace traditional buttons and implement custom UI actions in response to user input.

Actionable Strategies:

1. **Improve Input Validation with Feedback**: Whether you're working with HTML forms or Flutter widgets, always provide feedback to users when they submit invalid inputs. In HTML, use `required`, `pattern`, or `maxlength` attributes. In Flutter, make use of `TextFormField` validation with `FormState`.
2. **Optimize User Experience by Using Custom Input Decorations**: In Flutter, use `InputDecoration` to customize the appearance of input fields, including icons, labels, and hints. Similarly, in HTML, use `placeholder` and `label` for a clean and user-friendly interface.
3. **Minimize Input Errors with Auto-Correction and Auto-Complete**: To help users input data correctly, enable auto-correction and auto-completion features. In Flutter, set `keyboardType` and `textInputAction` for better control over the input behavior. In HTML, consider using `autocorrect` and `autocomplete` attributes.
4. **Implement Input Masking for Consistency**: Input masking helps users enter data in a specific format, such as phone numbers or credit card details. In Flutter, use third-party packages like `flutter_masked_text` to implement input masking. In HTML, JavaScript-based solutions like `inputmask` can achieve

the same.

5 **Test Across Platforms**: Always ensure that your form handles input correctly across different platforms and devices. Test for responsiveness in HTML by using media queries, and for Flutter, test on both Android and iOS simulators to ensure a consistent user experience.

Chapter 10: Working with Images and Media

10.1 Displaying Images in HTML vs Flutter

HTML/CSS:

In HTML, images are embedded using the `<img>` tag. The `src` attribute specifies the path to the image file, and optional attributes like `alt` and `title` provide alternative text and additional information. The `width` and `height` attributes allow resizing, and the `style` attribute can be used for inline CSS styling.

Example:

```
<!-- html -->
<img src="images/sample.jpg" alt="Sample Image"
width="300" height="200">
```

- The `src` attribute can contain a relative path (like `"images/sample.jpg"`) or an absolute URL (`"http://example.com/sample.jpg"`).
- The `alt` attribute provides alternative text if the image cannot be loaded.
- The `width` and `height` attributes control the image size directly.

If CSS is used to style the image, you can control aspects such as borders, margins, shadows, and other properties.

```
<!-- html -->
<style>
  img {
    border: 2px solid black;
    border-radius: 10px;
    box-shadow: 5px 5px 15px rgba(0, 0, 0, 0.3);
  }
</style>

<img src="images/sample.jpg" alt="Sample Image">
```

Flutter:

In Flutter, images can be displayed using the `Image` widget. Flutter provides several constructors for different types of image sources. The `Image.asset()` constructor is used to load images from assets, while `Image.network()` is used to load images from the internet.

Example:

```
//dart
Image.asset('assets/sample.jpg', width: 300, height: 200)
```

```
//dart
Image.network('https://example.com/sample.jpg', width:
300, height: 200)
```

- The `width` and `height` parameters control the image size in Flutter.
- Flutter supports both network and local images seamlessly using the appropriate constructors.

In Flutter, the `Image` widget provides more flexibility. It can be customized using properties such as `fit` for resizing the image, `alignment` for positioning the image, and `color` for applying color filters.

Example with a fit:

```
//dart
Image.network('https://example.com/sample.jpg', fit:
BoxFit.cover)
```

In this example, `BoxFit.cover` ensures the image covers the available space while maintaining its aspect ratio.

10.2 Image Widget Basics

HTML/CSS:

In HTML, images are simple to implement using the `<img>` tag. However, when working with media-rich content such as images with specific effects, HTML relies on additional elements or CSS styling.

For instance, you can use CSS for transformations, such as scaling or rotating images.

```
<!-- html -->
<style>
  .rotate {
    transform: rotate(45deg);
```

```
  }
</style>

<img src="images/sample.jpg" alt="Sample Image"
class="rotate">
```

- The `transform` property is used to apply rotations, translations, and other transformations to images.

To create responsive images in HTML, you can use the `max-width: 100%` CSS rule, which ensures the image scales down to fit within the container while maintaining its aspect ratio.

```
/* css */
img {
  max-width: 100%;
  height: auto;
}
```

This ensures that images are responsive, scaling appropriately on different screen sizes.

Flutter:

In Flutter, images are represented using the `Image` widget. The `Image` widget comes with several constructors, such as `Image.asset`, `Image.network`, and `Image.memory`. Each of these is designed to load images from different sources. The `Image` widget in Flutter also allows for transformations using the `Transform` widget.

Basic image widget example:

```
//dart
Image.asset('assets/sample.jpg')
```

You can modify the image's properties using the `fit` property to scale it within its container, just as in CSS.

```
//dart
Image.asset(
  'assets/sample.jpg',
  fit: BoxFit.contain,
)
```

Flutter's `BoxFit` provides different options for resizing the image to fit the available space, including `fill`, `contain`, `cover`, and others.

You can also apply more advanced transformations, like rotating or scaling an image, by wrapping the `Image` widget in a `Transform` widget.

```
//dart
Transform.rotate(
  angle: 0.5, // 0.5 radians
  child: Image.asset('assets/sample.jpg'),
)
```

This example rotates the image by 0.5 radians.

10.3 Adding Network and Asset Images

HTML/CSS:

In HTML, images can be either local (stored within the project directory) or fetched from a remote server (network images). For local images, you simply use the relative path in the `src` attribute. For remote images, you provide the full URL.

```
<!-- html -->
<!-- Local image -->
<img src="images/sample.jpg" alt="Sample Image">

<!-- Remote image -->
<img src="https://example.com/sample.jpg" alt="Sample
Image">
```

For styling purposes, the CSS `background-image` property can be used to set an image as a background for a container or element.

```
/* css */
.container {
  background-image: url('images/sample.jpg');
  width: 500px;
  height: 300px;
```

```
}
```

Flutter:

In Flutter, local images are placed in the `assets` directory and are referenced using the `Image.asset` constructor. First, ensure that the image file is included in the `pubspec.yaml` file under the assets section.

```
//yaml
flutter:
  assets:
    - assets/images/sample.jpg
```

Then, load the image in your Flutter app:

```
//dart
Image.asset('assets/images/sample.jpg')
```

For network images, Flutter provides the `Image.network` constructor, which loads the image from the specified URL.

```
//dart
Image.network('https://example.com/sample.jpg')
```

Flutter also allows you to manage image loading with caching using the `CachedNetworkImage` widget, which automatically handles caching and retrieval of images from the network.

```
//dart
CachedNetworkImage(
  imageUrl: 'https://example.com/sample.jpg',
  placeholder: (context, url) =>
CircularProgressIndicator(),
  errorWidget: (context, url, error) => Icon(Icons.error),
)
```

In this example, a loading indicator (`CircularProgressIndicator`) is shown while the image is being fetched, and an error icon is displayed if the image cannot be loaded.

10.4 Using Image Filters and Transformations

HTML/CSS:

HTML and CSS provide various ways to apply filters and transformations to images. The CSS `filter` property is commonly used for applying visual effects like blur, grayscale, brightness, contrast, and more.

Example of applying a blur filter:

```
/* css */
img {
  filter: blur(5px);
}
```

This applies a 5-pixel blur to the image. Other filters can also be used:

```
/* css */
img {
  filter: grayscale(100%) contrast(200%);
}
```

In this example, the image is converted to grayscale, and its contrast is increased by 200%.

To apply transformations such as rotation or scaling, the `transform` property is used:

```
/* css */
img {
  transform: scale(1.5) rotate(30deg);
}
```

This scales the image by 1.5 times its original size and rotates it by 30 degrees.

Flutter:

In Flutter, the `ImageFiltered` widget is used to apply filters to images. Filters are applied using the `ImageFilter` class. Flutter provides many filters like blur, brightness, and other effects. Here's an example of applying a blur filter:

```
//dart
ImageFiltered(
  imageFilter: ImageFilter.blur(sigmaX: 5.0, sigmaY: 5.0),
  child: Image.asset('assets/sample.jpg'),
)
```

In this example, a blur effect with a radius of 5 pixels is applied to the image. The `sigmaX` and `sigmaY` parameters control the blur amount horizontally and vertically.

Flutter also allows for custom transformations. For instance, you can rotate or scale an image by wrapping it in a `Transform` widget.

Example of rotating an image:

```
//dart
Transform.rotate(
  angle: 0.5, // 0.5 radians
  child: Image.asset('assets/sample.jpg'),
)
```

The `angle` property controls the rotation angle. You can also apply other transformations such as scaling, translation, and skewing.

Code Examples Summary:

- **Displaying Images:**

HTML:

```
<!-- html -->
<img src="images/sample.jpg" alt="Sample Image"
width="300" height="200">
```

Flutter:

```
//dart
```

```
Image.asset('assets/sample.jpg', width: 300, height: 200)
```

- **Applying Filters:**

HTML:
```
/* css */
img {
  filter: grayscale(100%) contrast(200%);
}
```

Flutter:
```
//dart
ImageFiltered(
  imageFilter: ImageFilter.blur(sigmaX: 5.0, sigmaY: 5.0),
  child: Image.asset('assets/sample.jpg'),
)
```

1 **Network Images:**

HTML:
```
<!-- html -->
<img src="https://example.com/sample.jpg" alt="Sample
Image">
```

Flutter:
```
//dart
Image.network('https://example.com/sample.jpg')
```

Key Tips:

- **Ensure Responsiveness**: Use CSS properties like `max-width: 100%` for responsive images in HTML, and `BoxFit` properties for scalable images in Flutter.
- **Use Filters Effectively**: CSS filters in HTML provide quick ways to modify image appearances, while Flutter's `ImageFiltered` widget offers a powerful way to apply more advanced effects.
- **Optimization**: Always optimize your images (compressing them for the web or mobile) to improve load times and performance.

10.5 Embedding Videos in Flutter

Videos are an essential element in modern web and mobile applications, serving as a powerful tool for engagement, education, and entertainment. Embedding videos is a straightforward task in both HTML and Flutter, but the approaches differ based on the platform's requirements and capabilities. In this section, we will compare how videos are embedded in HTML, CSS, JavaScript, and Flutter, looking at both the simplest use cases and more complex implementations.

Embedding Videos in HTML

In HTML, the `<video>` element is used to embed video files. This tag is versatile and can handle a wide variety of video formats, including MP4, WebM, and Ogg. It also offers built-in controls for play, pause, volume, and fullscreen, without requiring any external plugins. You can easily add video files from local sources or link to videos hosted on a server or video platform like YouTube.

Basic Video Embedding

A simple example to embed a video in HTML:

```
<!-- html -->
<video width="640" height="360" controls>
  <source src="video/sample.mp4" type="video/mp4">
  <source src="video/sample.webm" type="video/webm">
  <source src="video/sample.ogv" type="video/ogv">
  Your browser does not support the video tag.
</video>
```

- **`<video>` tag**: This defines the video element.
- **`controls` attribute**: This adds the default video controls like play, pause, and volume.
- **`<source>` tag**: Multiple sources can be added to support different video formats. The browser will try to play the first supported format.
- **`width` and `height`**: These attributes set the video size in pixels.

The video will be displayed with standard controls, and the user can interact with the video, such as playing or pausing it, adjusting volume, or changing playback speed. The browser will automatically choose the appropriate format based on the user's environment.

Embedding Videos in Flutter

In Flutter, embedding videos is not as simple as HTML due to the absence of a native `<video>` tag. However, Flutter offers a variety of packages that enable the use of videos. The most popular package for embedding videos is `video_player`. This package provides a `VideoPlayerController` that can load video content from various sources, including assets, network URLs, and file systems.

Setting Up the `video_player` Package

First, add the `video_player` package to the `pubspec.yaml` file:

```
//yaml
dependencies:
  flutter:
    sdk: flutter
  video_player: ^2.3.0
```

Next, run `flutter pub get` to install the dependencies. Now, you can use the `VideoPlayerController` to load and play videos.

Basic Video Embedding in Flutter

Here's a simple example of how to embed a video from assets using the `video_player` package:

```
//dart
import 'package:flutter/material.dart';
import 'package:video_player/video_player.dart';

class VideoScreen extends StatefulWidget {
  @override
  _VideoScreenState createState() => _VideoScreenState();
}

class _VideoScreenState extends State<VideoScreen> {
  late VideoPlayerController _controller;

  @override
  void initState() {
    super.initState();
    _controller = VideoPlayerController.asset('assets/
video/sample.mp4')
      ..initialize().then((_) {
```

```
        setState(() {});
      });
  }

  @override
  void dispose() {
    super.dispose();
    _controller.dispose();
  }

  @override
  Widget build(BuildContext context) {
    return Scaffold(
      appBar: AppBar(title: Text('Flutter Video Player')),
      body: Center(
        child: _controller.value.isInitialized
            ? AspectRatio(
                aspectRatio:
_controller.value.aspectRatio,
                child: VideoPlayer(_controller),
              )
            : CircularProgressIndicator(),
      ),
      floatingActionButton: FloatingActionButton(
        onPressed: () {
          setState(() {
            if (_controller.value.isPlaying) {
              _controller.pause();
            } else {
              _controller.play();
            }
          });
        },
        child: Icon(
          _controller.value.isPlaying ? Icons.pause :
Icons.play_arrow,
        ),
      ),
    );
  }
}
```

- **`VideoPlayerController.asset`**: Loads the video from the app's assets directory.
- **`initialize()`**: Initializes the video controller.
- **`AspectRatio`**: Ensures the video maintains its original aspect ratio.
- **`VideoPlayer`**: Displays the video.
- **`FloatingActionButton`**: Controls playback, allowing the user to toggle between play and pause.

This code snippet demonstrates how to load and display a video, play and pause it, and show a loading indicator while the video is initializing. The `video_player` package also supports video streaming from URLs using `VideoPlayerController.network`.

Video Streaming Example in Flutter

For streaming videos from a remote source, you can use the `VideoPlayerController.network` constructor:

```
//dart
_controller = VideoPlayerController.network('https://
www.example.com/sample.mp4')
  ..initialize().then((_) {
    setState(() {});
  });
```

Key Differences Between HTML and Flutter Video Embedding

- **HTML**: Embedding a video in HTML requires a single tag, `<video>`, along with the `controls` attribute for built-in functionality.
- **Flutter**: Flutter does not have a native `<video>` element. You need a third-party package, such as `video_player`, to handle video embedding and controls.

While HTML simplifies the process of embedding videos with built-in support, Flutter offers more flexibility by allowing the integration of custom controls and enabling video streaming.

10.6 Handling Media Responsiveness

Responsiveness is crucial for modern web and mobile applications. As users access content across a variety of devices with different screen sizes, it is essential that media like images, videos, and other media elements adjust to the screen dimensions. In this section, we'll examine how to handle media responsiveness in both HTML/CSS and Flutter.

Media Responsiveness in HTML/CSS

HTML and CSS provide several tools for ensuring media elements, such as images and videos, are responsive. A commonly used technique for responsive images is using CSS rules that automatically adjust the image size based on the screen width.

Responsive Images in HTML

To make images responsive, you can use the `max-width` property in CSS:

```
/* css */
img {
  max-width: 100%;
  height: auto;
}
```

- **`max-width: 100%`**: Ensures that the image will never exceed the width of its container, and it will scale down when the container shrinks.
- **`height: auto`**: Maintains the image's aspect ratio.

Responsive Videos in HTML

Videos can also be made responsive by using CSS. One popular approach is to wrap the video inside a container and use the `padding-top` technique to maintain the aspect ratio.

```
<!-- html -->
<div class="video-container">
  <video width="640" height="360" controls>
    <source src="video/sample.mp4" type="video/mp4">
  </video>
</div>

<style>
  .video-container {
    position: relative;
```

```
    width: 100%;
    padding-top: 56.25%; /* 16:9 aspect ratio */
    height: 0;
    overflow: hidden;
  }

  .video-container video {
    position: absolute;
    top: 0;
    left: 0;
    width: 100%;
    height: 100%;
  }
</style>
```

- **`padding-top: 56.25%`**: This creates a responsive container with a 16:9 aspect ratio (calculated as 9/16 * 100).
- **`position: absolute`**: This ensures that the video fills the container.

This method keeps the video responsive while maintaining its aspect ratio across different screen sizes.

Media Responsiveness in Flutter

In Flutter, responsive media can be handled by using widgets that adjust based on the screen size. Flutter provides tools like `MediaQuery` and `LayoutBuilder` to manage screen size and layout adaptively. For example, you can create responsive images and videos by adjusting the widget size based on the screen width.

Responsive Images in Flutter

To make images responsive in Flutter, you can use the `MediaQuery` to get the screen size and adjust the image accordingly.

```
//dart
import 'package:flutter/material.dart';

class ResponsiveImage extends StatelessWidget {
  @override
  Widget build(BuildContext context) {
    double screenWidth =
MediaQuery.of(context).size.width;
```

```
    return Image.asset(
      'assets/sample.jpg',
      width: screenWidth * 0.8, // 80% of screen width
    );
  }
}
```

- **`MediaQuery.of(context).size.width`**: Retrieves the width of the screen.
- **`width: screenWidth * 0.8`**: Adjusts the image to take up 80% of the screen width.

Responsive Videos in Flutter

For videos, responsiveness can be managed similarly by using the `AspectRatio` widget, which adjusts the video's aspect ratio based on the screen size.

```
//dart
import 'package:flutter/material.dart';
import 'package:video_player/video_player.dart';

class ResponsiveVideo extends StatefulWidget {
  @override
  _ResponsiveVideoState createState() =>
_ResponsiveVideoState();
}

class _ResponsiveVideoState extends State<ResponsiveVideo>
{
  late VideoPlayerController _controller;

  @override
  void initState() {
    super.initState();
    _controller = VideoPlayerController.asset('assets/
video/sample.mp4')
      ..initialize().then((_) {
        setState(() {});
      });
  }
```

```
  @override
  Widget build(BuildContext context) {
    double screenWidth =
MediaQuery.of(context).size.width;

    return Scaffold(
      appBar: AppBar(title: Text('Responsive Video')),
      body: Center(
        child: _controller.value.isInitialized
            ? AspectRatio(
                aspectRatio:
_controller.value.aspectRatio,
                child: VideoPlayer(_controller),
              )
            : CircularProgressIndicator(),
      ),
    );
  }
}
```

This code ensures that the video adapts to the screen size while preserving its aspect ratio.

Key Points for Media Responsiveness

- **HTML**: Use CSS properties like `max-width: 100%` for images and the `padding-top` technique for videos to make them responsive.
- **Flutter**: Use `MediaQuery` and `AspectRatio` to dynamically adjust the size and aspect ratio of images and videos based on the screen size.

10.7 Lazy Loading in Flutter

Lazy loading is a technique used to delay the loading of media elements (such as images and videos) until they are needed, typically when they are about to appear on the screen. This improves the performance of web and mobile apps by reducing the initial load time and saving memory. Lazy loading is crucial for content-heavy applications, especially when dealing with large numbers of images and videos.

Lazy Loading Images in Flutter

To implement lazy loading for images in Flutter, you can use the `CachedNetworkImage` widget, which is part of the `cached_network_image` package. This widget automatically caches images and only loads them when they are about to be displayed on the screen.

Implementing Lazy Loading for Images

```
//dart
import 'package:flutter/material.dart';
import 'package:cached_network_image/
cached_network_image.dart';

class LazyLoadingImages extends StatelessWidget {
  final List<String> imageUrls = [
    'https://example.com/image1.jpg',
    'https://example.com/image2.jpg',
    // Add more URLs here
  ];

  @override
  Widget build(BuildContext context) {
    return Scaffold(
      appBar: AppBar(title: Text('Lazy Loading Images')),
      body: ListView.builder(
        itemCount: imageUrls.length,
        itemBuilder: (context, index) {
          return CachedNetworkImage(
            imageUrl: imageUrls[index],
            placeholder: (context, url) =>
CircularProgressIndicator(),
            errorWidget: (context, url, error) =>
Icon(Icons.error),
          );
        },
      ),
    );
  }
}
```

- **`CachedNetworkImage`**: Automatically handles image caching and lazy loading.
- **`placeholder`**: A widget that displays while the image is being loaded.
- **`errorWidget`**: Displays an error widget if the image fails to load.

This implementation ensures that images are loaded only when needed, improving performance, especially for long lists.

Lazy Loading Videos in Flutter

Lazy loading videos can be implemented using a similar approach. However, since videos are larger and more resource-intensive, you may want to load them only when they come into view.

```
//dart
import 'package:flutter/material.dart';
import 'package:video_player/video_player.dart';

class LazyLoadingVideos extends StatelessWidget {
  final List<String> videoUrls = [
    'https://example.com/video1.mp4',
    'https://example.com/video2.mp4',
    // Add more URLs here
  ];

  @override
  Widget build(BuildContext context) {
    return Scaffold(
      appBar: AppBar(title: Text('Lazy Loading Videos')),
      body: ListView.builder(
        itemCount: videoUrls.length,
        itemBuilder: (context, index) {
          return LazyLoadVideoPlayer(url:
videoUrls[index]);
        },
      ),
    );
  }
}

class LazyLoadVideoPlayer extends StatefulWidget {
  final String url;

  LazyLoadVideoPlayer({required this.url});

  @override
  _LazyLoadVideoPlayerState createState() =>
_LazyLoadVideoPlayerState();
```

```
}

class _LazyLoadVideoPlayerState extends
State<LazyLoadVideoPlayer> {
  late VideoPlayerController _controller;

  @override
  void initState() {
    super.initState();
    _controller =
VideoPlayerController.network(widget.url);
  }

  @override
  Widget build(BuildContext context) {
    return GestureDetector(
      onTap: () {
        if (_controller.value.isPlaying) {
          _controller.pause();
        } else {
          _controller.play();
        }
      },
      child: AspectRatio(
        aspectRatio: 16 / 9,
        child: VideoPlayer(_controller),
      ),
    );
  }
}
```

In this example, the video is loaded and displayed only when it is about to appear in the viewport.

Key Considerations for Lazy Loading

- **Images**: Lazy loading improves performance by loading images only when they come into view, using the `CachedNetworkImage` widget.
- **Videos**: Lazy loading videos involves only initializing video players when the video is about to be displayed on the screen, reducing memory consumption.

10.8 Sample Code: Images in HTML vs Flutter

Now, let's compare how images are implemented in HTML and Flutter using side-by-side code examples. These examples will demonstrate how to embed images in both platforms, highlighting the similarities and differences in their approaches.

HTML Example for Embedding an Image

```
<!-- html -->
<!DOCTYPE html>
<html lang="en">
<head>
  <meta charset="UTF-8">
  <meta name="viewport" content="width=device-width,
initial-scale=1.0">
  <title>Image in HTML</title>
</head>
<body>
  <img src="image/sample.jpg" alt="Sample Image"
width="300" height="200">
</body>
</html>
```

- The `img` tag is used to display an image.
- The `src` attribute specifies the path to the image.
- The `alt` attribute provides alternative text for the image.
- The `width` and `height` attributes define the size of the image.

Flutter Example for Embedding an Image

```
//dart
import 'package:flutter/material.dart';

class ImageExample extends StatelessWidget {
  @override
  Widget build(BuildContext context) {
    return Scaffold(
      appBar: AppBar(title: Text('Image in Flutter')),
      body: Center(
        child: Image.asset('assets/sample.jpg'),
      ),
```

```
    );
  }
}
```

- **Image.asset** is used to load the image from the app's asset directory.
- Flutter does not require `width` and `height` attributes directly in the code, though you can manage image size using `width` and `height` properties of the `Image` widget.

Key Differences:

- **HTML**: Directly embeds the image using the `<img>` tag and requires attributes for size and alternative text.
- **Flutter**: Uses the `Image.asset` or `Image.network` widget, depending on whether the image is local or hosted on a remote server. It offers a more programmatic approach with flexible sizing options.

Examples for Chapter 10: Working with Images and Media: HTML vs Flutter

Embedding an Image in HTML (Using `<img>` Tag) HTML makes it easy to embed an image using the `<img>` tag, specifying the path to the image file via the `src` attribute. The tag can also include attributes like `alt`, `width`, and `height` for better accessibility and layout control.

```
<!-- html -->
<!DOCTYPE html>

<html lang="en">
  <head>
    <meta charset="UTF-8">
    <meta name="viewport" content="width=device-width,
initial-scale=1.0">
    <title>Embedding Image in HTML</title>
  </head>
  <body>
    <img src="images/logo.png" alt="Logo" width="300"
height="200">
  </body>
</html>
```

In this example:

1. The `src` specifies the image file's path.
2. `alt` provides an accessible description for screen readers.
3. `width` and `height` specify the image's dimensions.

Using CSS for Image Styling (HTML and CSS Integration) CSS allows you to style images in ways that HTML alone cannot. You can modify the image size, apply borders, shadows, and other styles directly from your stylesheet.

```
<!-- html -->
<html>

  <head>
    <style>
      .image-style {
        width: 50%;
        border: 3px solid #ddd;
        border-radius: 8px;
        box-shadow: 5px 5px 15px rgba(0,0,0,0.3);
      }
    </style>
  </head>
  <body>
    <img src="images/sample.jpg" alt="Sample Image"
class="image-style">
  </body>
</html>
```

This example uses CSS to style the image, making it responsive and adding visual effects like borders and shadows.

Handling Images with JavaScript (Dynamic Image Loading) JavaScript is often used to load images dynamically based on user actions or events. Below is an example of using JavaScript to change an image on a button click.

```
<!-- html -->
<html>

  <head>
```

```
    <script>
      function changeImage() {
        document.getElementById("myImage").src = "images/
new-image.jpg";
      }
    </script>
  </head>
  <body>
    <img id="myImage" src="images/initial-image.jpg"
alt="Initial Image" width="300">
    <button onclick="changeImage()">Change Image</button>
  </body>
</html>
```

In this example, JavaScript is used to modify the `src` attribute of an image, effectively changing the image when the button is clicked.

Displaying Images in Flutter (Using `Image.asset` and `Image.network`) In Flutter, images can be loaded either from local assets or from the web. The `Image.asset` widget is used for local assets, while `Image.network` is used to load images from a URL.

```
//dart
import 'package:flutter/material.dart';


class ImageExample extends StatelessWidget {
  @override
  Widget build(BuildContext context) {
    return Scaffold(
      appBar: AppBar(title: Text('Image in Flutter')),
      body: Column(
        children: [
          // Local image
          Image.asset('assets/images/local-image.png'),

          // Remote image
          Image.network('https://example.com/remote-
image.jpg'),
        ],
      ),
    );
```

```
    }
}
```

This Flutter example shows how to use `Image.asset` to display local images and `Image.network` for loading images from the internet.

Tips for Working with Images and Media: HTML vs Flutter

- **Optimize Image Size for Web and Mobile**
  Images can significantly impact performance. Make sure you optimize images for faster loading times on both web and mobile platforms. Use tools like Photoshop, TinyPNG, or ImageOptim to compress your images before uploading.

- **Responsive Images**
  In HTML, use the `srcset` attribute in the `<img>` tag to provide multiple image sizes for different devices. In Flutter, use the `MediaQuery` class to dynamically adjust image sizes according to the screen dimensions.

- **Lazy Loading for Better Performance**
  Both HTML and Flutter can benefit from lazy loading. In HTML, you can use the `loading="lazy"` attribute to defer loading images until they are in the viewport. Flutter's `CachedNetworkImage` widget provides built-in support for lazy loading images from the web.

Actionable Strategies for Working with Images and Media

- **Leverage Image Caching in Both HTML and Flutter** For mobile and web applications, caching images can greatly improve load times and performance. In Flutter, the `cached_network_image` package provides automatic caching of images, while in HTML, you can use Service Workers to cache images for offline use.

- **Use Image Compression and Next-Gen Formats** Reduce image file sizes by using next-gen formats like WebP for web applications and AVIF for mobile applications. Compressing images reduces the amount of data transferred, enhancing the performance of your website or app.

- **Responsive Design with CSS and Media Queries** Use CSS media queries to serve different image sizes based on the screen size. Combine this with the `srcset` attribute in HTML to ensure that images are loaded appropriately based on the user's device, reducing unnecessary bandwidth consumption.

- **Add Fallback Images and Error Handling** Whether working with HTML or Flutter, it's crucial to handle errors gracefully. In HTML, use the `onerror` event on images to show a fallback if an image fails to load. In Flutter, use the `errorWidget` property in the `CachedNetworkImage` widget to display an error icon or placeholder when the image cannot be loaded.
- **Apply Image Transformations for Better UX** Both Flutter and HTML allow you to apply transformations to images. In HTML, you can use CSS properties like `transform`, `rotate`, `scale`, and `skew` to animate and adjust the image's position or scale. In Flutter, you can use the `Transform` widget to rotate, scale, or translate images and other UI elements in response to user actions or animations.

Additional Considerations for Flutter and HTML Image Handling

HTML Image Loading with Progressive Enhancement In HTML, you can use the `picture` element to implement responsive images, which allows you to specify different image formats for different screen sizes and resolutions. For example, you can provide a higher-quality image for users on high-resolution devices (Retina screens).

```
<!-- html -->
<picture>

  <source srcset="images/high-res.jpg" media="(min-width:
600px)">
  <source srcset="images/low-res.jpg" media="(max-width:
599px)">
  <img src="images/default.jpg" alt="Image">
</picture>
```

This allows you to serve images optimized for various device configurations.

Handling Image Aspect Ratio in HTML and Flutter Maintaining the aspect ratio of images is essential for maintaining consistent UI layouts. In HTML, you can use CSS to preserve the aspect ratio by setting the `object-fit` property to `cover` or `contain`. In Flutter, the `BoxFit` property in the `Image` widget allows you to achieve similar results.

```
<!-- html -->
<style>

  img {
    object-fit: cover;
    width: 100%;
    height: 200px;
  }
</style>
```

```
//dart
Image.asset(
  'assets/image.jpg',
  fit: BoxFit.cover, // Preserves aspect ratio
);
```

Video Integration in HTML vs Flutter When working with videos, HTML provides the `<video>` tag, allowing you to embed and control video playback. Flutter also supports video playback via the `video_player` package, which provides native-like control for video streaming on both Android and iOS.

HTML Video Example:

```
<!-- html -->
<video width="400" controls>

  <source src="video/movie.mp4" type="video/mp4">
  Your browser does not support the video tag.
</video>
```

Flutter Video Example:

```
//dart
import 'package:video_player/video_player.dart';

class VideoExample extends StatefulWidget {
  @override
```

```
  _VideoExampleState createState() =>
_VideoExampleState();
}

class _VideoExampleState extends State<VideoExample> {
  late VideoPlayerController _controller;

  @override
  void initState() {
    super.initState();
    _controller = VideoPlayerController.network('https://
www.example.com/video.mp4')
      ..initialize().then((_) {
        setState(() {});
      });
  }

  @override
  Widget build(BuildContext context) {
    return Scaffold(
      appBar: AppBar(title: Text('Video Example')),
      body: Center(
        child: _controller.value.isInitialized
            ? AspectRatio(
                aspectRatio:
_controller.value.aspectRatio,
                child: VideoPlayer(_controller),
              )
            : CircularProgressIndicator(),
      ),
    );
  }

  @override
  void dispose() {
    super.dispose();
    _controller.dispose();
  }
}
```

In conclusion, both HTML and Flutter offer robust capabilities for handling images and media. While HTML utilizes tags and CSS for basic image embedding and styling,

Flutter provides an intuitive, widget-based system that allows for more dynamic control over images and media. By understanding these technologies and applying the tips and strategies listed, developers can create engaging, performant, and responsive applications across platforms.

Chapter 11: State Management Simplified

11.1 Understanding State in React Native

State management is a cornerstone of building dynamic and interactive applications. In React Native, "state" refers to a mutable object within a component that determines how it behaves and what it renders. A component's state can change over time, typically in response to user actions or network data updates. React Native provides a structured way to manage state through its component-based architecture.

Core Concepts of State in React Native:

- **State vs. Props:**
    - **State**: A local component's mutable data that determines its rendering. Changes in state cause the component to re-render.
    - **Props**: Immutable and passed from parent to child components to configure the child's behavior.
- **Updating State with `setState()`:**
  In class-based components, `setState()` is used to update the state. For functional components, React Hooks like `useState` are used.

Example: Simple State in React Native (Functional Component)

```
//javascript
import React, { useState } from 'react';
import { View, Text, Button } from 'react-native';

const CounterApp = () => {
  const [count, setCount] = useState(0);

  return (
    <View>
      <Text>Count: {count}</Text>
      <Button title="Increase" onPress={() =>
setCount(count + 1)} />
    </View>
  );
};
```

```
export default CounterApp;
```

In this example:

- `useState` is used to define the `count` state variable.
- `setCount` updates the state and triggers a re-render.

Key Advantages of React Native's State Management:

- **Reactivity:** Any change in the state automatically re-renders the component.
- **Component Isolation:** State is scoped to individual components, enabling modular development.
- **Predictability:** A clear flow of state changes ensures predictable updates.

11.2 Managing State in Flutter Apps

In Flutter, state management is equally critical. Flutter widgets can be categorized as "stateful" or "stateless" based on whether they manage state internally.

Stateless vs. Stateful Widgets:

- **Stateless Widgets:** Widgets that do not require mutable state and rely solely on immutable data.
- **Stateful Widgets:** Widgets that require state changes to manage their dynamic behavior.

Example: Simple Stateful Widget in Flutter

```
//dart
import 'package:flutter/material.dart';

class CounterApp extends StatefulWidget {
  @override
  _CounterAppState createState() => _CounterAppState();
}

class _CounterAppState extends State<CounterApp> {
  int count = 0;

  void incrementCounter() {
    setState(() {
      count++;
```

```
    });
  }

  @override
  Widget build(BuildContext context) {
    return Scaffold(
      appBar: AppBar(title: Text("Counter App")),
      body: Center(
        child: Column(
          mainAxisAlignment: MainAxisAlignment.center,
          children: [
            Text("Count: $count"),
            ElevatedButton(
              onPressed: incrementCounter,
              child: Text("Increase"),
            ),
          ],
        ),
      ),
    );
  }
}
```

In this example:

- `setState` triggers the widget to rebuild whenever the `count` state is updated.
- Flutter encourages an explicit structure to define how UI reacts to state changes.

React Native vs. Flutter State Comparison:

Feature	**React Native**	**Flutter**
State Definition	Hooks like `useState`, `useReducer`	Stateful Widgets
State Update	`setState()` in classes, `setCount` hook	`setState()`
UI Rebuilding	Virtual DOM reconciliation	Widget tree re-render
Modularity	Component-based	Widget-based

11.3 The Provider Package Overview

The `Provider` package is one of the most popular state management solutions in Flutter. It simplifies state sharing across the widget tree while adhering to Flutter's reactive nature.

Key Features of Provider:

1. **Scoped Access:** Share state with specific parts of the widget tree.
2. **Reactivity:** Automatically rebuilds widgets when the provided state changes.
3. **Extensibility:** Integrates seamlessly with other state management tools.

Example: Using Provider in Flutter

1. **Define the State Model:**

```
//dart
import 'package:flutter/foundation.dart';

class CounterModel with ChangeNotifier {
  int _count = 0;

  int get count => _count;

  void increment() {
    _count++;
    notifyListeners();
  }
}
```

2. **Wrap the App with Provider:**

```
//dart
import 'package:flutter/material.dart';
import 'package:provider/provider.dart';
import 'counter_model.dart';

void main() {
  runApp(
```

```
    ChangeNotifierProvider(
      create: (_) => CounterModel(),
      child: MyApp(),
    ),
  );
}
```

3 **Access and Update State:**

```
//dart
class CounterScreen extends StatelessWidget {
  @override
  Widget build(BuildContext context) {
    final counter = Provider.of<CounterModel>(context);

    return Scaffold(
      appBar: AppBar(title: Text("Provider Example")),
      body: Center(
        child: Column(
          mainAxisAlignment: MainAxisAlignment.center,
          children: [
            Text("Count: ${counter.count}"),
            ElevatedButton(
              onPressed: counter.increment,
              child: Text("Increase"),
            ),
          ],
        ),
      ),
    );
  }
}
```

Tips for Using Provider Effectively:

- Use `ChangeNotifierProvider` for models that notify listeners.
- Leverage `Consumer` or `context.watch` for optimal reactivity.
- Avoid unnecessary state sharing by scoping providers.

11.4 When to Use Stateful vs Stateless Widgets

Choosing between stateful and stateless widgets in Flutter depends on the app's behavior and requirements. Mismanagement of this choice can lead to performance issues or unnecessary complexity.

Guidelines for Stateless Widgets:

- Use for widgets that depend only on immutable data.
- Ideal for static UI elements like buttons, text labels, or icons.

Example of Stateless Widget:

```
//dart
class Greeting extends StatelessWidget {
  final String name;

  Greeting({required this.name});

  @override
  Widget build(BuildContext context) {
    return Text("Hello, $name!");
  }
}
```

Guidelines for Stateful Widgets:

- Use when the widget requires dynamic changes or user interactions.
- Necessary for features like animations, forms, or real-time updates.

Example of Stateful Widget:

```
//dart
class ToggleButton extends StatefulWidget {
  @override
  _ToggleButtonState createState() =>
_ToggleButtonState();
}

class _ToggleButtonState extends State<ToggleButton> {
  bool isToggled = false;

  void toggleButton() {
    setState(() {
```

```
      isToggled = !isToggled;
    });
  }

  @override
  Widget build(BuildContext context) {
    return ElevatedButton(
      onPressed: toggleButton,
      child: Text(isToggled ? "ON" : "OFF"),
    );
  }
}
```

Comparison of Stateless and Stateful Widgets:

Criteria	Stateless Widgets	Stateful Widgets
Data Dependency	Immutable data	Mutable data
Performance	Lightweight, faster rendering	More overhead due to reactivity
Use Cases	Static UI elements	Interactive or dynamic behavior

Best Practices for Choosing Widget Type:

- Prefer stateless widgets for predictable and consistent UI.
- Use stateful widgets sparingly, relying on external state management when feasible.
- Avoid deeply nested stateful widgets to reduce complexity.

Actionable Takeaways:

- React Native's `useState` and Flutter's `setState` offer similar simplicity for local state.
- Choose between `Provider` or React Context API for global state needs.
- Avoid overcomplicating apps by managing too much state locally.

11.5 Lifting State Up in the Widget Tree

State lifting refers to moving shared state to the nearest common ancestor of multiple components or widgets. This technique is crucial when different parts of the UI depend on the same piece of state, enabling efficient updates and centralized control.

The Need for Lifting State:

- **Avoiding Redundancy:** Keeping shared state in one place reduces duplication and inconsistencies.
- **Facilitating Communication:** Enables sibling components to share and update state through a common parent.
- **Streamlined Updates:** Ensures a single source of truth for state changes, improving maintainability.

Example: Lifting State in React Native

```
//javascript
import React, { useState } from 'react';
import { View, Text, TextInput } from 'react-native';

const ParentComponent = () => {
  const [sharedText, setSharedText] = useState('');

  return (
    <View>
      <ChildInput onTextChange={setSharedText} />
      <ChildDisplay text={sharedText} />
    </View>
  );
};

const ChildInput = ({ onTextChange }) => {
  return (
    <TextInput
      placeholder="Type here..."
      onChangeText={onTextChange}
      style={{ borderWidth: 1, padding: 10 }}
    />
  );
};

const ChildDisplay = ({ text }) => {
```

```
  return (
    <Text>Entered Text: {text}</Text>
  );
};

export default ParentComponent;
```

Key Points in the Example:

- The `ParentComponent` manages the `sharedText` state.
- `ChildInput` updates the state using the `onTextChange` prop.
- `ChildDisplay` receives the updated state through the `text` prop.

Lifting State in Flutter:

Flutter follows a similar pattern, but with widgets. Stateful widgets manage the state, and it is passed to child widgets via constructors or callback functions.

Example: Lifting State in Flutter

```
//dart
import 'package:flutter/material.dart';

class ParentWidget extends StatefulWidget {
  @override
  _ParentWidgetState createState() =>
_ParentWidgetState();
}

class _ParentWidgetState extends State<ParentWidget> {
  String sharedText = "";

  void updateText(String newText) {
    setState(() {
      sharedText = newText;
    });
  }

  @override
  Widget build(BuildContext context) {
    return Column(
```

```
      children: [
        ChildInput(onTextChange: updateText),
        ChildDisplay(text: sharedText),
      ],
    );
  }
}

class ChildInput extends StatelessWidget {
  final Function(String) onTextChange;

  ChildInput({required this.onTextChange});

  @override
  Widget build(BuildContext context) {
    return TextField(
      decoration: InputDecoration(border:
OutlineInputBorder(), hintText: "Type here..."),
      onChanged: onTextChange,
    );
  }
}

class ChildDisplay extends StatelessWidget {
  final String text;

  ChildDisplay({required this.text});

  @override
  Widget build(BuildContext context) {
    return Text("Entered Text: $text");
  }
}
```

Comparison of React Native and Flutter State Lifting:

Feature	React Native	Flutter
State Management	`useState` or `setState`	`setState`
Parent-Child Sharing	Props for passing data	Widget constructors or callbacks

UI Updates	Automatic re-rendering	Explicit widget rebuilding

11.6 Debugging State Management Issues

Debugging state management issues can be challenging, especially in complex applications. Common problems include unexpected behavior, stale state, and performance bottlenecks.

Strategies for Debugging in React Native:

React Developer Tools:
Inspect the component tree and analyze props and state for each component.

Console Logs:
Add `console.log` statements to trace state changes or function calls.

Example: Logging State Changes

```
//javascript
const [count, setCount] = useState(0);


useEffect(() => {
  console.log("Count updated: ", count);
}, [count]);
```

Breakpoints in Debugger:
Use IDE tools to set breakpoints and inspect variables at runtime.

Strategies for Debugging in Flutter:

Flutter Inspector:
Analyze the widget tree and debug UI-related issues.

Logging with `print`:
Log state changes or errors directly in the console.

Example: Logging in Flutter

```
//dart

void incrementCounter() {
  print("Counter updated: $count");
  setState(() {
    count++;
  });
}
```

DevTools:
Visualize performance metrics and state changes.

Common Issues and Their Resolutions:

Problem	React Native Solution	Flutter Solution
State not updating	Verify `setState` or `useState` usage	Check `setState` placement
Excessive re-renders	Optimize component hierarchy	Use `shouldRebuild` or `Keys`
Stale state	Ensure asynchronous operations are handled	Utilize `FutureBuilder` or `Streams`

11.7 Sample Code: State in React Native vs Flutter

React Native Example: Counter App with Context API

```
//javascript
import React, { createContext, useState, useContext } from
'react';

const CounterContext = createContext();

const CounterProvider = ({ children }) => {
  const [count, setCount] = useState(0);

  return (
```

```
    <CounterContext.Provider value={{ count, setCount }}>
      {children}
    </CounterContext.Provider>
  );
};

const CounterDisplay = () => {
  const { count } = useContext(CounterContext);
  return <Text>Count: {count}</Text>;
};

const CounterButton = () => {
  const { setCount } = useContext(CounterContext);
  return <Button title="Increment" onPress={() =>
setCount((prev) => prev + 1)} />;
};

const App = () => (
  <CounterProvider>
    <View>
      <CounterDisplay />
      <CounterButton />
    </View>
  </CounterProvider>
);

export default App;
```

Flutter Example: Counter App with Provider

```
//dart
import 'package:flutter/material.dart';
import 'package:provider/provider.dart';

class CounterModel with ChangeNotifier {
  int _count = 0;

  int get count => _count;

  void increment() {
    _count++;
```

```
    notifyListeners();
  }
}

void main() {
  runApp(
    ChangeNotifierProvider(
      create: (_) => CounterModel(),
      child: MyApp(),
    ),
  );
}

class MyApp extends StatelessWidget {
  @override
  Widget build(BuildContext context) {
    return MaterialApp(
      home: CounterScreen(),
    );
  }
}

class CounterScreen extends StatelessWidget {
  @override
  Widget build(BuildContext context) {
    final counter = Provider.of<CounterModel>(context);

    return Scaffold(
      appBar: AppBar(title: Text("Provider Counter")),
      body: Column(
        mainAxisAlignment: MainAxisAlignment.center,
        children: [
          Text("Count: ${counter.count}"),
          ElevatedButton(
            onPressed: counter.increment,
            child: Text("Increment"),
          ),
        ],
      ),
    );
  }
}
```

11.8 Advanced State Management Libraries

State management becomes increasingly complex as applications grow. Advanced libraries provide more robust solutions.

Popular State Management Libraries in React Native:

- **Redux:** A predictable state container with strict rules for state updates.
- **MobX:** Reactive state management with observable data structures.
- **Recoil:** Minimal boilerplate for managing shared state.

Popular State Management Libraries in Flutter:

- **Provider:** Simplifies state management with a reactive approach.
- **Bloc (Business Logic Component):** Separates business logic from UI.
- **Riverpod:** An improved version of Provider with more flexibility.

Tips for Choosing a Library:

- Start with simple solutions like `useState` or `Provider`.
- Scale up to Redux or Bloc for enterprise-level apps.
- Prioritize maintainability and team expertise.

These sections demonstrate how React Native and Flutter streamline state management, offering developers flexibility to build scalable applications.

Examples

Managing State with Vanilla JavaScript and React Native

JavaScript:

```
<!-- html -->

<input id="textInput" oninput="updateText()" />
<p id="displayText"></p>
<script>
  function updateText() {
    const input =
document.getElementById('textInput').value;
    document.getElementById('displayText').innerText =
`You typed: ${input}`;
  }
```

```
</script>
```

React Native:

```
//javascript

import React, { useState } from 'react';
import { View, TextInput, Text } from 'react-native';

const App = () => {
  const [text, setText] = useState('');

  return (
    <View>
      <TextInput placeholder="Type here"
onChangeText={setText} />
      <Text>You typed: {text}</Text>
    </View>
  );
};

export default App;
```

CSS State Styling vs Flutter Dynamic Styling

CSS:

```
<!-- html -->

<style>
  .button {
    background-color: blue;
    color: white;
  }
  .button:hover {
    background-color: darkblue;
  }
</style>
<button class="button">Hover me</button>
```

Flutter:

```
//dart
```

```
ElevatedButton(
  style: ElevatedButton.styleFrom(
    primary: Colors.blue,
    onPrimary: Colors.white,
  ),
  onPressed: () {},
  child: Text("Hover me"),
);
```

HTML Event Handling vs Flutter Gesture Detectors

HTML:

```
<!-- html -->
<button onclick="alert('Button Clicked!')">Click me</
button>
```

Flutter:

```
//dart
GestureDetector(
  onTap: () {
    print("Button Clicked!");
  },
  child: Container(
    padding: EdgeInsets.all(10),
    color: Colors.blue,
    child: Text("Click me"),
  ),
);
```

Dynamic Class Application in CSS vs Conditional Widget Rendering in Flutter

CSS:<!-- html -->

```
<style>
  .active {
    background-color: green;
  }
  .inactive {
    background-color: red;
```

```
  }
</style>
<div class="active">Active State</div>
```

Flutter:

```
//dart
bool isActive = true;

Container(
  color: isActive ? Colors.green : Colors.red,
  child: Text(isActive ? "Active State" : "Inactive
State"),
);
```

Tips

- When transitioning between front-end technologies like HTML, CSS, and JavaScript to Flutter, focus on learning Flutter's **stateful widgets**, which combine UI and state management into a single entity.
- Use **React Native hooks** (`useState`, `useEffect`) and **Flutter's setState or Provider** for state control, keeping application logic consistent and intuitive.
- Simplify state-related issues by modularizing the logic, making it reusable and easily debuggable across different frameworks.

Actionable Strategies

- **Modularize State Logic**: Break state into manageable parts by defining distinct areas of responsibility (e.g., separating UI state and application logic). Use custom hooks in React Native or inherited widgets in Flutter to manage complexity.
- **Adopt Cross-Framework Patterns**: Leverage universal patterns like lifting state up, callback functions, and state immutability. For example, in both JavaScript and Flutter, rely on parent-child communication to maintain a clear data flow.
- **Implement Robust Debugging Practices**: Use built-in tools like React Developer Tools and Flutter Inspector to visualize the state flow. Enhance debugging efficiency by introducing consistent naming conventions for variables and state keys.
- **Optimize for Performance**: Limit re-renders by memoizing components in React Native (`React.memo`) and using efficient widget rebuild practices in

Flutter (e.g., `const` constructors or `shouldRebuild`).

- **Standardize State Management Across Teams**: Introduce state management libraries like Redux for React Native and Bloc for Flutter to streamline the development process. Maintain clear documentation and examples for team onboarding.

Chapter 12: Adding Animations and Transitions

Animations and transitions play a significant role in modern applications, providing a fluid and engaging user experience. Whether building web applications using HTML, CSS, and JavaScript or developing mobile applications with Flutter, understanding how animations are implemented and structured is essential.

12.1 Animations in Web Apps vs Flutter

Web technologies like HTML, CSS, and JavaScript have well-established methods for creating animations. CSS provides declarative animations, while JavaScript allows more control with imperative logic. In Flutter, animations are tightly integrated into the framework, offering powerful tools for both basic and advanced transitions.

Declarative Animations in CSS

CSS simplifies animations through properties like `@keyframes`, `animation`, and `transition`.

Example:

```
<!-- html -->
<style>
  .fade-in {
    opacity: 0;
    animation: fadeIn 2s forwards;
  }

  @keyframes fadeIn {
    from {
      opacity: 0;
    }
    to {
      opacity: 1;
    }
  }
</style>
<div class="fade-in">Hello, World!</div>
```

JavaScript-Controlled Animations

JavaScript allows more dynamic and interactive animations, often in response to user input or events.

Example:

```
<!-- html -->
<div id="box" style="width:100px; height:100px;
background-color:red;"></div>
<script>
  const box = document.getElementById('box');
  box.addEventListener('click', () => {
    box.style.transition = 'transform 1s';
    box.style.transform = 'translateX(200px)';
  });
</script>
```

Flutter's Declarative Animation Approach

In Flutter, animations are widget-centric, integrating seamlessly into the widget tree. Flutter widgets such as `AnimatedContainer`, `Hero`, and custom `AnimationController` offer flexibility for creating animations.

Example:

```
//dart
AnimatedContainer(
  duration: Duration(seconds: 2),
  color: Colors.blue,
  width: isExpanded ? 200 : 100,
  height: isExpanded ? 200 : 100,
  child: GestureDetector(
    onTap: () {
      setState(() {
        isExpanded = !isExpanded;
      });
```

```
    },
  ),
);
```

12.2 The AnimatedContainer Widget

The `AnimatedContainer` widget in Flutter simplifies animations by allowing developers to transition between different property values like size, color, and alignment.

Key Features of AnimatedContainer:

- **Ease of Use**: Automatically animates changes to properties.
- **Declarative Syntax**: Integrates into the widget tree with minimal code.
- **Customization**: Supports curve modifications like `Curves.easeInOut`.

Example: Animating Size and Color Changes

```
//dart
class AnimatedBox extends StatefulWidget {
  @override
  _AnimatedBoxState createState() => _AnimatedBoxState();
}

class _AnimatedBoxState extends State<AnimatedBox> {
  bool isExpanded = false;

  @override
  Widget build(BuildContext context) {
    return Scaffold(
      body: Center(
        child: AnimatedContainer(
          duration: Duration(seconds: 1),
          width: isExpanded ? 200 : 100,
          height: isExpanded ? 200 : 100,
          color: isExpanded ? Colors.blue : Colors.red,
          curve: Curves.easeInOut,
          child: GestureDetector(
            onTap: () {
              setState(() {
                isExpanded = !isExpanded;
```

```
                    });
                },
            ),
        ),
      ),
    );
  }
}
```

12.3 Hero Animations for Page Transitions

Hero animations allow seamless transitions between screens, providing a visually consistent experience. This is often used in applications where an element's visual representation is maintained across routes.

HTML and CSS Example for Page Transition

```
<!-- html -->
<style>
  .page {
    position: absolute;
    width: 100%;
    height: 100%;
    transition: transform 1s ease;
  }

  .page.hidden {
    transform: translateX(100%);
  }
</style>

<div id="page1" class="page">Page 1</div>
<div id="page2" class="page hidden">Page 2</div>
<script>
  const page1 = document.getElementById('page1');
  const page2 = document.getElementById('page2');

  page1.addEventListener('click', () => {
    page1.classList.add('hidden');
    page2.classList.remove('hidden');
  });
</script>
```

Flutter Hero Widget Example

Flutter simplifies page transitions using the `Hero` widget. The `tag` property ensures that the element is tracked between screens.

```
//dart
Hero(
  tag: 'imageHero',
  child: GestureDetector(
    onTap: () {
      Navigator.push(context, MaterialPageRoute(builder:
(_) {
        return SecondPage();
      }));
    },
    child: Image.network(
      'https://example.com/image.jpg',
      width: 100,
    ),
  ),
);
```

12.4 Custom Animations Using AnimationController

For complex animations, `AnimationController` provides granular control over the animation lifecycle. It allows developers to define their own animations and manage states programmatically.

JavaScript Equivalent for Custom Animation

```
<!-- html -->
<div id="box" style="width:100px; height:100px;
background-color:red;"></div>
<script>
  const box = document.getElementById('box');
  let position = 0;

  function animate() {
    if (position < 200) {
      position++;
```

```
      box.style.transform = `translateX(${position}px)`;
      requestAnimationFrame(animate);
    }
  }

  box.addEventListener('click', animate);
</script>
```

Flutter AnimationController Example

```
//dart
class CustomAnimation extends StatefulWidget {
  @override
  _CustomAnimationState createState() =>
_CustomAnimationState();
}

class _CustomAnimationState extends State<CustomAnimation>
    with SingleTickerProviderStateMixin {
  late AnimationController _controller;
  late Animation<double> _animation;

  @override
  void initState() {
    super.initState();
    _controller = AnimationController(
      duration: Duration(seconds: 2),
      vsync: this,
    );
    _animation = Tween<double>(begin: 0, end:
200).animate(_controller)
      ..addListener(() {
        setState(() {});
      });

    _controller.forward();
  }

  @override
  void dispose() {
    _controller.dispose();
```

```
    super.dispose();
  }

  @override
  Widget build(BuildContext context) {
    return Scaffold(
      body: Center(
        child: Container(
          width: _animation.value,
          height: _animation.value,
          color: Colors.blue,
        ),
      ),
    );
  }
}
```

Highlighted Tips

- Use **ease-in-out curves** for smooth and visually appealing animations.
- Minimize the duration for interactive animations to keep the app responsive.
- Leverage `AnimatedBuilder` in Flutter to reuse and optimize animation logic for multiple widgets.

Actionable Takeaways

- **Integrate Animations Thoughtfully**: Ensure animations enhance user experience without overwhelming the design. For example, subtle hover effects in web apps or smooth transitions in mobile apps.
- **Combine Animation Techniques**: Blend declarative animations (`AnimatedContainer`) with imperative controls (`AnimationController`) for dynamic user interfaces.
- **Optimize for Performance**: Use lightweight animations with efficient rendering techniques, such as limiting DOM updates in JavaScript or widget rebuilds in Flutter.
- **Focus on Accessibility**: Make animations optional or offer alternatives for users with motion sensitivity by providing settings to disable animations.
- **Experiment with Advanced Frameworks**: Explore libraries like `GSAP` for JavaScript and `rive` for Flutter to create high-performance and visually striking animations.

12.5 Staggered Animations

Staggered animations involve animating multiple elements sequentially with a delay between their start times. This technique enhances visual hierarchy and provides a polished look.

CSS Example for Staggered Animations

CSS achieves staggered animations using `animation-delay`. Each element has a delayed start, creating the staggered effect.

```
<!-- html -->
<style>
  .box {
    width: 50px;
    height: 50px;
    background-color: blue;
    margin: 10px;
    animation: slideIn 1s forwards;
  }

  .box:nth-child(1) {
    animation-delay: 0s;
  }

  .box:nth-child(2) {
    animation-delay: 0.5s;
  }

  .box:nth-child(3) {
    animation-delay: 1s;
  }

  @keyframes slideIn {
    from {
      transform: translateX(-100px);
    }
    to {
      transform: translateX(0);
    }
  }
</style>
```

```
<div class="box"></div>
<div class="box"></div>
<div class="box"></div>
```

Flutter Example for Staggered Animations

Flutter offers a programmatic way to handle staggered animations using the `AnimationController` and `Future.delayed` for introducing delays.

```
//dart
class StaggeredAnimation extends StatefulWidget {
  @override
  _StaggeredAnimationState createState() =>
_StaggeredAnimationState();
}

class _StaggeredAnimationState extends
State<StaggeredAnimation>
    with SingleTickerProviderStateMixin {
  late AnimationController _controller;
  late Animation<double> _animation1;
  late Animation<double> _animation2;

  @override
  void initState() {
    super.initState();

    _controller = AnimationController(
      duration: Duration(seconds: 2),
      vsync: this,
    );

    _animation1 = Tween<double>(begin: 0, end:
100).animate(
      CurvedAnimation(
        parent: _controller,
        curve: Interval(0.0, 0.5, curve:
Curves.easeInOut),
      ),
    );
```

```
    _animation2 = Tween<double>(begin: 0, end:
100).animate(
      CurvedAnimation(
        parent: _controller,
        curve: Interval(0.5, 1.0, curve:
Curves.easeInOut),
      ),
    );

    _controller.forward();
  }

  @override
  Widget build(BuildContext context) {
    return Scaffold(
      body: Column(
        mainAxisAlignment: MainAxisAlignment.center,
        children: [
          AnimatedBuilder(
            animation: _animation1,
            builder: (context, child) {
              return Container(
                width: _animation1.value,
                height: 50,
                color: Colors.blue,
              );
            },
          ),
          SizedBox(height: 20),
          AnimatedBuilder(
            animation: _animation2,
            builder: (context, child) {
              return Container(
                width: _animation2.value,
                height: 50,
                color: Colors.green,
              );
            },
          ),
        ],
      ),
    );
```

```
  }
}
```

12.6 Interactive Animations with GestureDetector

Interactive animations respond to user input, creating a dynamic and engaging experience. They are implemented using gesture recognition combined with animations.

Interactive Animations in HTML and JavaScript

In web applications, animations can respond to gestures or events such as clicks, drags, or hovers.

```
<!-- html -->
<div id="box" style="width:100px; height:100px;
background-color:blue;"></div>
<script>
  const box = document.getElementById('box');

  box.addEventListener('mousedown', () => {
    box.style.transition = 'transform 0.5s';
    box.style.transform = 'scale(1.2)';
  });

  box.addEventListener('mouseup', () => {
    box.style.transform = 'scale(1)';
  });
</script>
```

Interactive Animations in Flutter

Flutter's `GestureDetector` widget enables interaction, paired with animations for creating responsive UIs.

```
//dart
class InteractiveAnimation extends StatefulWidget {
  @override
  _InteractiveAnimationState createState() =>
_InteractiveAnimationState();
}
```

```dart
class _InteractiveAnimationState extends
State<InteractiveAnimation> {
  double _scale = 1.0;

  @override
  Widget build(BuildContext context) {
    return Scaffold(
      body: Center(
        child: GestureDetector(
          onTapDown: (_) => setState(() => _scale = 1.2),
          onTapUp: (_) => setState(() => _scale = 1.0),
          child: AnimatedContainer(
            duration: Duration(milliseconds: 300),
            transform: Matrix4.identity()..scale(_scale),
            width: 100,
            height: 100,
            color: Colors.blue,
          ),
        ),
      ),
    );
  }
}
```

12.7 Debugging Animation Errors

Animations can be challenging to debug, especially when dealing with complex interactions or performance issues. Both web and Flutter provide tools to identify and resolve these challenges.

Common Animation Issues

1. **Janky or Stuttering Animations**: Caused by excessive rendering or blocking operations.
2. **Incorrect Timing**: Animations may not synchronize due to incorrect durations or delays.
3. **Unintended Behavior**: Errors in animation logic can lead to unexpected results.

Debugging Animations in Web Apps

- Use browser developer tools to inspect animations and identify performance bottlenecks.
- Check the computed styles and animation timelines for proper execution.

```
<!-- html -->
<style>
  .box {
    width: 100px;
    height: 100px;
    background-color: red;
    animation: move 1s infinite;
  }

  @keyframes move {
    from {
      transform: translateX(0);
    }
    to {
      transform: translateX(200px);
    }
  }
</style>
<div class="box"></div>
```

In the browser's developer tools, inspect the `.box` element and monitor the `@keyframes` execution.

Debugging Animations in Flutter

Flutter provides tools like `PerformanceOverlay` and `DevTools` to analyze and improve animations.

```
//dart
MaterialApp(
  debugShowCheckedModeBanner: false,
  showPerformanceOverlay: true,
  home: MyApp(),
);
```

Tips for Debugging:

- Use `print` statements to track animation state.
- Leverage the `AnimationStatus` callback to monitor the animation lifecycle.

12.8 Sample Code: CSS Animations vs Flutter Animations

Comparing how animations are structured in CSS and Flutter highlights their differences in approach.

CSS Animation Example

CSS animations are declarative and defined using styles.

```
<!-- html -->
<style>
  .fade-in {
    opacity: 0;
    animation: fadeIn 2s forwards;
  }

  @keyframes fadeIn {
    from {
      opacity: 0;
    }
    to {
      opacity: 1;
    }
  }
</style>
<div class="fade-in">Hello World</div>
```

Flutter Animation Example

Flutter animations are widget-based and require more boilerplate for dynamic behavior.

```
//dart
class FadeInWidget extends StatefulWidget {
  @override
  _FadeInWidgetState createState() =>
_FadeInWidgetState();
}

class _FadeInWidgetState extends State<FadeInWidget>
    with SingleTickerProviderStateMixin {
```

```
  late AnimationController _controller;
  late Animation<double> _animation;

  @override
  void initState() {
    super.initState();
    _controller = AnimationController(
      duration: Duration(seconds: 2),
      vsync: this,
    );
    _animation = Tween<double>(begin: 0, end:
1).animate(_controller);

    _controller.forward();
  }

  @override
  Widget build(BuildContext context) {
    return Scaffold(
      body: FadeTransition(
        opacity: _animation,
        child: Center(child: Text('Hello World')),
      ),
    );
  }
}
```

Key Takeaways

1. Staggered animations enhance user experience by creating structured transitions between elements.
2. Interactive animations increase engagement and can be achieved using gestures in Flutter or events in web apps.
3. Debugging animations requires careful analysis of timing, performance, and logic.
4. Comparing CSS and Flutter animations reveals the declarative vs. programmatic nature of these technologies.

Examples

Smooth Button Hover Animation

HTML, CSS, and JavaScript:

```
<!-- html -->
<button class="hover-btn">Hover Me</button>

<style>
  .hover-btn {
    padding: 10px 20px;
    font-size: 16px;
    background-color: #007BFF;
    color: white;
    border: none;
    cursor: pointer;
    transition: background-color 0.3s ease, transform 0.3s
ease;
  }
  .hover-btn:hover {
    background-color: #0056b3;
    transform: scale(1.1);
  }
</style>
```

Flutter:

```
//dart

GestureDetector(
  onTap: () {
    print("Button Pressed");
  },
  child: AnimatedContainer(
    duration: Duration(milliseconds: 300),
    decoration: BoxDecoration(
      color: _hovering ? Colors.blue[800] : Colors.blue,
      borderRadius: BorderRadius.circular(8),
    ),
    padding: EdgeInsets.symmetric(horizontal: 20,
vertical: 10),
    transform: Matrix4.identity()..scale(_hovering ? 1.1 :
1.0),
    child: Text(
```

```
      "Hover Me",
      style: TextStyle(color: Colors.white, fontSize: 16),
    ),
  ),
)
```

Image Carousel Transition

HTML, CSS, and JavaScript:

```
<!-- html -->
<div class="carousel">

  <div class="carousel-item">Image 1</div>
  <div class="carousel-item">Image 2</div>
  <div class="carousel-item">Image 3</div>
</div>
<style>
  .carousel {
    display: flex;
    overflow: hidden;
    width: 300px;
  }
  .carousel-item {
    min-width: 100%;
    transition: transform 0.5s ease-in-out;
  }
</style>
<script>
  let index = 0;
  const items = document.querySelectorAll('.carousel-
item');
  setInterval(() => {
    index = (index + 1) % items.length;
    items.forEach((item, i) => {
      item.style.transform = `translateX(-${index *
100}%)`;
    });
  }, 3000);
</script>
```

Flutter:

```
//dart
CarouselSlider(
  items: [
    Image.asset('assets/image1.png'),
    Image.asset('assets/image2.png'),
    Image.asset('assets/image3.png'),
  ],
  options: CarouselOptions(
    height: 200.0,
    autoPlay: true,
    enlargeCenterPage: true,
    autoPlayCurve: Curves.fastOutSlowIn,
    enableInfiniteScroll: true,
    autoPlayInterval: Duration(seconds: 3),
  ),
)
```

Sidebar Slide Animation

HTML, CSS, and JavaScript:

```
<!-- html -->
<div id="sidebar" class="sidebar"></div>

<button id="toggle">Toggle Sidebar</button>
<style>
  .sidebar {
    position: fixed;
    left: -250px;
    width: 250px;
    height: 100%;
    background: #333;
    color: white;
    transition: left 0.5s ease;
  }
  .sidebar.open {
    left: 0;
```

```
  }
</style>
<script>
  const sidebar = document.getElementById('sidebar');
  const toggle = document.getElementById('toggle');
  toggle.addEventListener('click', () => {
    sidebar.classList.toggle('open');
  });
</script>
```

Flutter:

```
//dart

Scaffold(
  drawer: Drawer(
    child: ListView(
      children: <Widget>[
        DrawerHeader(
          child: Text("Menu"),
          decoration: BoxDecoration(color: Colors.blue),
        ),
        ListTile(
          title: Text("Item 1"),
          onTap: () {},
        ),
      ],
    ),
  ),
  appBar: AppBar(
    title: Text("Sidebar Animation"),
  ),
  body: Center(child: Text("Swipe from left to open the
sidebar.")),
)
```

Progress Bar Animation

HTML, CSS, and JavaScript:

```
<!-- html -->
<div class="progress-bar">

  <div class="fill"></div>
</div>
<style>
  .progress-bar {
    width: 100%;
    height: 20px;
    background: #ddd;
    overflow: hidden;
    border-radius: 10px;
  }
  .fill {
    width: 0%;
    height: 100%;
    background: #007BFF;
    transition: width 2s linear;
  }
</style>
<script>
  setTimeout(() => {
    document.querySelector('.fill').style.width = '100%';
  }, 1000);
</script>
```

Flutter:

```
//dart
LinearProgressIndicator(
  value: _progressValue, // 0.0 to 1.0
  backgroundColor: Colors.grey[300],
  valueColor: AlwaysStoppedAnimation<Color>(Colors.blue),
)
```

Tips

- **Understand Transition Principles:** Transition timing functions such as `ease-in`, `ease-out`, and `ease-in-out` in CSS correlate with Flutter's `Curves` class (`Curves.easeIn`, `Curves.easeOut`, etc.), so understanding how these ease patterns affect user experience can help replicate smooth animations across platforms.

- **Use Keyframes Strategically:** CSS keyframe animations align closely with Flutter's `AnimationController` and `Tween` for defining intermediate states. Breaking complex animations into simpler states is useful for debugging and performance optimization.
- **Test Responsiveness Early:** For both web and Flutter animations, ensure responsiveness by testing on multiple screen sizes and devices to guarantee seamless transitions and animations.

Actionable Strategies

- **Start with Simplified Animations:** Before implementing complex animations, focus on simpler transitions like hover effects, color changes, and scaling. This ensures foundational elements of your animation library work correctly.
- **Sync Animation Timing Across Components:** Ensure that the duration and timing of animations in one part of the app are consistent with others to create a cohesive experience. For example, Flutter's `duration` property should align with CSS's `transition-duration`.
- **Optimize for Performance:** In web development, use hardware-accelerated properties like `transform` and `opacity` for smooth animations. In Flutter, prefer `AnimatedBuilder` or `Hero` transitions for better performance.
- **Leverage Community Packages:** Use tools like Animate.css in web development and `flutter_animate` in Flutter to accelerate development time for common animation patterns.
- **Track Animation Errors Early:** Use browser developer tools for CSS and JavaScript debugging. For Flutter, rely on the `debugPrint` function and widget inspection to troubleshoot animation bugs effectively.

Chapter 13: Responsive Design in Flutter

Creating applications that adapt to different screen sizes and devices is essential for a seamless user experience. This chapter addresses responsive design fundamentals in Flutter and its comparison with traditional web technologies like HTML, CSS, and JavaScript. With Flutter's powerful widgets and layout tools, building applications for mobile, web, and desktop becomes a more structured and dynamic process.

13.1 Responsive Web Design Basics

Responsive web design ensures that the application's layout and content dynamically adapt to various screen sizes and resolutions. Traditional web technologies achieve this using CSS media queries, flexible layouts, and fluid grids.

Example (HTML and CSS): Responsive Layout

```
<!-- html -->
<!DOCTYPE html>
<html lang="en">
<head>
  <meta name="viewport" content="width=device-width,
initial-scale=1.0">
  <style>
    .container {
      display: flex;
      flex-wrap: wrap;
    }
    .box {
      flex: 1 1 100%;
    }
    @media (min-width: 768px) {
      .box {
        flex: 1 1 50%;
      }
    }
    @media (min-width: 1024px) {
      .box {
        flex: 1 1 33.33%;
      }
    }
```

```
  </style>
</head>
<body>
  <div class="container">
    <div class="box" style="background: lightblue;">Box
1</div>
    <div class="box" style="background: lightgreen;">Box
2</div>
    <div class="box" style="background: lightcoral;">Box
3</div>
  </div>
</body>
</html>
```

In this example, the `@media` rules define how the layout changes across different screen sizes.

Flutter Comparison: Flutter uses widgets like `MediaQuery`, `LayoutBuilder`, and flexible layout widgets to achieve similar responsiveness. Instead of relying on CSS, developers leverage Flutter's rich widget library to adjust layout properties.

```
//dart
class ResponsiveLayout extends StatelessWidget {
  @override
  Widget build(BuildContext context) {
    final screenWidth = MediaQuery.of(context).size.width;

    return Scaffold(
      body: screenWidth < 768
          ? Column(
              children: [
                Container(color: Colors.blue, height: 100,
width: double.infinity),
                Container(color: Colors.green, height:
100, width: double.infinity),
                Container(color: Colors.red, height: 100,
width: double.infinity),
              ],
            )
          : Row(
              children: [
                Expanded(child: Container(color:
Colors.blue, height: double.infinity)),
```

```
                Expanded(child: Container(color:
Colors.green, height: double.infinity)),
                Expanded(child: Container(color:
Colors.red, height: double.infinity)),
              ],
            ),
    );
  }
}
```

In Flutter, the `MediaQuery` widget accesses the screen width and adjusts the layout dynamically.

13.2 MediaQuery in Flutter

`MediaQuery` is a core Flutter widget for responsive design, providing information about the screen size, device orientation, pixel density, and more. It acts as the foundation for determining how the layout should adapt.

Common Properties of MediaQuery:

- `MediaQuery.of(context).size`: Returns the dimensions of the screen.
- `MediaQuery.of(context).orientation`: Determines whether the device is in portrait or landscape mode.
- `MediaQuery.of(context).devicePixelRatio`: Provides the pixel density of the device.

Example: Responsive Text Size

```
//dart
class ResponsiveText extends StatelessWidget {
  @override
  Widget build(BuildContext context) {
    final screenWidth = MediaQuery.of(context).size.width;

    return Text(
      "Responsive Text",
      style: TextStyle(
        fontSize: screenWidth < 600 ? 16 : 24,
      ),
```

```
    );
  }
}
```

HTML and CSS Equivalent:

```
<!-- html -->
<p class="responsive-text">Responsive Text</p>
<style>
  .responsive-text {
    font-size: 16px;
  }
  @media (min-width: 600px) {
    .responsive-text {
      font-size: 24px;
    }
  }
</style>
```

While CSS requires media queries for size adjustments, Flutter achieves this dynamically through `MediaQuery`.

13.3 Using Flexible and Expanded Widgets

Flutter's `Flexible` and `Expanded` widgets allow layouts to adjust dynamically within a `Row` or `Column`. These widgets enable children to occupy available space proportionally.

Flexible vs. Expanded:

- `Flexible`: Adapts its size within the constraints of its parent but doesn't necessarily occupy all the remaining space.
- `Expanded`: Forces the child to fill all available space.

Example: Responsive Grid with Expanded

```
//dart
class ResponsiveGrid extends StatelessWidget {
  @override
  Widget build(BuildContext context) {
    return Scaffold(
```

```
        body: Row(
          children: [
            Expanded(
              flex: 1,
              child: Container(color: Colors.blue),
            ),
            Expanded(
              flex: 2,
              child: Container(color: Colors.green),
            ),
            Expanded(
              flex: 1,
              child: Container(color: Colors.red),
            ),
          ],
        ),
      );
    }
  }
```

HTML and CSS Equivalent:

```
<!-- html -->
<div class="grid">
  <div class="col" style="flex: 1; background: blue;"></
div>
  <div class="col" style="flex: 2; background: green;"></
div>
  <div class="col" style="flex: 1; background: red;"></
div>
</div>
<style>
  .grid {
    display: flex;
  }
</style>
```

Both approaches achieve proportional layouts, but Flutter's declarative nature integrates the layout and responsiveness directly into the widget tree.

13.4 Building Apps for Mobile, Web, and Desktop

Flutter's ability to target multiple platforms makes it a versatile framework. However, building responsive apps across mobile, web, and desktop requires additional considerations like input methods, aspect ratios, and navigation paradigms.

Key Strategies for Cross-Platform Responsiveness:

- Use `LayoutBuilder` to adjust layouts based on parent constraints.
- Implement adaptive navigation patterns (`Drawer` for mobile, `Rail` for desktop).
- Handle pointer and touch events differently for desktop and mobile platforms.

Example: Adaptive Navigation

```
//dart
class AdaptiveScaffold extends StatelessWidget {
  @override
  Widget build(BuildContext context) {
    final screenWidth = MediaQuery.of(context).size.width;

    return Scaffold(
      body: Center(child: Text("Responsive App")),
      drawer: screenWidth < 600 ? Drawer(child:
Text("Mobile Menu")) : null,
      appBar: AppBar(title: Text("Adaptive Navigation")),
      endDrawer: screenWidth >= 600 ? Drawer(child:
Text("Desktop Menu")) : null,
    );
  }
}
```

HTML and CSS Equivalent:

```
<!-- html -->
<nav class="navbar">
  <div class="menu mobile-menu">Mobile Menu</div>
  <div class="menu desktop-menu">Desktop Menu</div>
</nav>
<style>
  .mobile-menu {
```

```
    display: block;
  }
  .desktop-menu {
    display: none;
  }
  @media (min-width: 600px) {
    .mobile-menu {
      display: none;
    }
    .desktop-menu {
      display: block;
    }
  }
</style>
```

This demonstrates how navigation adjusts to screen size, offering an optimized experience for both mobile and desktop users.

Tips and Examples Highlighted:

- Flutter widgets like `MediaQuery` and `LayoutBuilder` serve as dynamic alternatives to CSS media queries.
- `Expanded` and `Flexible` widgets make proportional layouts intuitive without external dependencies.
- The unified widget tree in Flutter simplifies managing responsiveness across platforms.
- **Key Tip:** Always test your Flutter app on different devices (simulators, emulators, real devices) to validate responsive behaviors.
- **Example Code Insights:** Use `MediaQuery` for retrieving device dimensions and `Flexible` widgets for proportional layouts.

13.5 SafeArea and Platform-Specific Design

When designing cross-platform applications, developers must account for varying screen layouts and special regions like notches, status bars, and bottom navigation bars. The `SafeArea` widget in Flutter ensures that content is displayed within the usable screen area, avoiding obstruction by these elements.

Using SafeArea in Flutter

`SafeArea` is a widget that pads its child widget to ensure it is not obscured by system UI components. It is particularly useful for devices with unique screen features like notches or rounded corners.

Example: SafeArea Usage in Flutter

```
//dart
import 'package:flutter/material.dart';

class SafeAreaExample extends StatelessWidget {
  @override
  Widget build(BuildContext context) {
    return Scaffold(
      body: SafeArea(
        child: Center(
          child: Text(
            "This text is safe from notches!",
            style: TextStyle(fontSize: 20),
          ),
        ),
      ),
    );
  }
}
```

Without the `SafeArea` widget, the content could overlap with the device's system UI, leading to a poor user experience.

HTML and CSS Equivalent for Handling Safe Areas Although HTML and CSS lack a direct equivalent to `SafeArea`, padding can be added dynamically using environment variables in modern CSS:

```
/* css */
<style>
body {
  padding: env(safe-area-inset-top) env(safe-area-inset-
right)
           env(safe-area-inset-bottom) env(safe-area-
```

```
inset-left);
}
</style>
```

This CSS code ensures that the content respects the safe areas defined by the device.

Platform-Specific Design in Flutter

Adapting to platform-specific design conventions enhances user experience by aligning with familiar design patterns. Flutter provides tools to differentiate between platforms using the `Platform` class and widgets like `Cupertino` (for iOS-style design) and `Material` (for Android-style design).

Example: Platform-Specific Button

```
//dart
import 'dart:io';
import 'package:flutter/cupertino.dart';
import 'package:flutter/material.dart';

class PlatformSpecificButton extends StatelessWidget {
  @override
  Widget build(BuildContext context) {
    return Center(
      child: Platform.isIOS
          ? CupertinoButton(
              color: CupertinoColors.activeBlue,
              child: Text("iOS Button"),
              onPressed: () {},
            )
          : ElevatedButton(
              onPressed: () {},
              child: Text("Android Button"),
            ),
    );
  }
}
```

This approach ensures the app feels native on both iOS and Android platforms.

13.6 Adapting Layouts Dynamically

Dynamic layout adaptation involves modifying the application interface based on available screen dimensions or specific conditions.

Using LayoutBuilder for Adaptive Layouts

`LayoutBuilder` is a powerful widget for dynamically adjusting layouts. It provides the parent widget's constraints, enabling developers to decide how child widgets should be displayed.

Example: Responsive Grid with LayoutBuilder

```
//dart
class DynamicGrid extends StatelessWidget {
  @override
  Widget build(BuildContext context) {
    return Scaffold(
      body: LayoutBuilder(
        builder: (context, constraints) {
          if (constraints.maxWidth < 600) {
            return Column(
              children: [
                Container(color: Colors.blue, height:
100),
                Container(color: Colors.green, height:
100),
              ],
            );
          } else {
            return Row(
              children: [
                Expanded(child: Container(color:
Colors.blue)),
                Expanded(child: Container(color:
Colors.green)),
              ],
            );
          }
        },
      ),
    );
  }
}
```

This example demonstrates how `LayoutBuilder` adjusts the layout for different screen widths.

HTML and JavaScript Dynamic Layout

```
<!-- html -->
<div id="dynamic-layout"></div>
<script>
  const layout = document.getElementById('dynamic-
layout');
  if (window.innerWidth < 600) {
    layout.innerHTML = `
      <div style="background: blue; height: 100px;"></div>
      <div style="background: green; height: 100px;"></
div>
    `;
  } else {
    layout.innerHTML = `
      <div style="display: flex;">
        <div style="flex: 1; background: blue;"></div>
        <div style="flex: 1; background: green;"></div>
      </div>
    `;
  }
</script>
```

JavaScript dynamically updates the DOM, while Flutter directly adjusts widgets based on constraints.

13.7 Testing Responsiveness in Flutter

Testing is crucial to ensure that the application performs well across different screen sizes and orientations. Flutter provides tools for simulating different device configurations.

Using Flutter's Device Preview Package

The `device_preview` package enables testing how the application looks on various devices without requiring physical hardware.

Installation: Add the package to `pubspec.yaml`:

```
//yaml
dependencies:
  device_preview: ^0.9.0
```

Example: Simulating Devices

```
//dart
import 'package:device_preview/device_preview.dart';
import 'package:flutter/material.dart';

void main() {
  runApp(DevicePreview(
    enabled: true,
    builder: (context) => MyApp(),
  ));
}

class MyApp extends StatelessWidget {
  @override
  Widget build(BuildContext context) {
    return MaterialApp(
      useInheritedMediaQuery: true,
      builder: DevicePreview.appBuilder,
      home: Scaffold(
        appBar: AppBar(title: Text("Responsive Test")),
        body: Center(child: Text("Testing
Responsiveness")),
      ),
    );
  }
}
```

This package simplifies testing by emulating devices of various sizes and orientations.

13.8 Sample Code: Responsive Design in Web vs Flutter

To better understand responsive design in Flutter, comparing it with web technologies such as HTML, CSS, and JavaScript reveals similarities and differences.

HTML, CSS, and JavaScript Example: Responsive Navigation Bar

```
<!-- html -->
<nav class="navbar">
  <a href="#">Home</a>
  <a href="#">About</a>
  <a href="#">Contact</a>
</nav>
<style>
  .navbar {
    display: flex;
    justify-content: space-between;
    padding: 10px;
  }
  @media (max-width: 600px) {
    .navbar {
      flex-direction: column;
    }
  }
</style>
```

Flutter Equivalent: Responsive Navigation Bar

```
//dart
class ResponsiveNavBar extends StatelessWidget {
  @override
  Widget build(BuildContext context) {
    return Scaffold(
      appBar: AppBar(title: Text("Responsive
Navigation")),
      body: LayoutBuilder(
        builder: (context, constraints) {
          if (constraints.maxWidth < 600) {
            return Column(
              children: [
                Text("Home"),
                Text("About"),
                Text("Contact"),
              ],
            );
          } else {
```

```
            return Row(
              mainAxisAlignment:
MainAxisAlignment.spaceAround,
              children: [
                Text("Home"),
                Text("About"),
                Text("Contact"),
              ],
            );
          }
        },
      ),
    );
  }
}
```

Key Takeaways:

- `SafeArea` ensures content is visible and not obscured by device-specific UI elements.
- Dynamic layout adaptation in Flutter leverages widgets like `LayoutBuilder` and `MediaQuery`.
- Platform-specific designs in Flutter ensure apps feel native on both iOS and Android.
- Rigorous testing practices, including tools like `device_preview`, validate responsive behaviors.
- Comparisons with traditional web technologies demonstrate Flutter's declarative and efficient approach to responsive design.

These practices and examples highlight the versatility and power of Flutter for creating responsive, cross-platform applications.

Examples

Grid Layout Implementation

HTML/CSS:

```
<!-- html -->


<div class="grid-container">

  <div class="grid-item">1</div>
  <div class="grid-item">2</div>
```

```
  <div class="grid-item">3</div>
</div>
<style>
  .grid-container {
    display: grid;
    grid-template-columns: repeat(3, 1fr);
    gap: 10px;
  }
  .grid-item {
    background-color: lightblue;
    text-align: center;
    padding: 20px;
  }
</style>
```

Flutter:

```
//dart
import 'package:flutter/material.dart';

class GridLayout extends StatelessWidget {
  @override
  Widget build(BuildContext context) {
    return Scaffold(
      body: GridView.builder(
        gridDelegate:
SliverGridDelegateWithFixedCrossAxisCount(
          crossAxisCount: 3,
          crossAxisSpacing: 10,
          mainAxisSpacing: 10,
        ),
        itemBuilder: (context, index) {
          return Container(
            color: Colors.lightBlue,
            alignment: Alignment.center,
            child: Text("${index + 1}"),
          );
        },
        itemCount: 9,
      ),
    );
  }
```

```
}
```

Responsive Media Queries vs `MediaQuery`

CSS Media Queries:

```
/* css */

body {
  font-size: 16px;
}
@media (max-width: 768px) {
  body {
    font-size: 14px;
  }
}
```

Flutter `MediaQuery`:

```
//dart
class ResponsiveText extends StatelessWidget {
  @override
  Widget build(BuildContext context) {
    double screenWidth =
MediaQuery.of(context).size.width;

    return Text(
      "Responsive Text",
      style: TextStyle(
        fontSize: screenWidth < 768 ? 14 : 16,
      ),
    );
  }
}
```

Navigation Bars in Web vs Flutter

HTML/CSS:

```
<!-- html -->
<nav class="navbar">

  <a href="#">Home</a>
  <a href="#">About</a>
  <a href="#">Contact</a>
</nav>
<style>
  .navbar {
    display: flex;
    justify-content: space-between;
    background: #333;
    color: white;
    padding: 10px;
  }
  @media (max-width: 600px) {
    .navbar {
      flex-direction: column;
    }
  }
</style>
```

Flutter:

```
//dart
import 'package:flutter/material.dart';

class ResponsiveNavBar extends StatelessWidget {
  @override
  Widget build(BuildContext context) {
    return Scaffold(
      appBar: AppBar(title: Text("Responsive
Navigation")),
      body: LayoutBuilder(
        builder: (context, constraints) {
          if (constraints.maxWidth < 600) {
            return Column(
              children: [Text("Home"), Text("About"),
Text("Contact")],
```

```
            );
          } else {
            return Row(
              mainAxisAlignment:
MainAxisAlignment.spaceAround,
              children: [Text("Home"), Text("About"),
Text("Contact")],
            );
          }
        },
      ),
    );
  }
}
```

Flexbox vs Flutter Flex Widgets

CSS Flexbox:

```
<!-- html -->


<div class="container">

  <div class="item">1</div>
  <div class="item">2</div>
  <div class="item">3</div>
</div>
<style>
  .container {
    display: flex;
    justify-content: space-around;
  }
  .item {
    background-color: lightgray;
    padding: 20px;
  }
</style>
```

Flutter Flex Widgets:

```
//dart
import 'package:flutter/material.dart';
```

```
class FlexLayout extends StatelessWidget {
  @override
  Widget build(BuildContext context) {
    return Scaffold(
      body: Row(
        mainAxisAlignment: MainAxisAlignment.spaceAround,
        children: [
          Container(color: Colors.grey, padding:
EdgeInsets.all(20), child: Text("1")),
          Container(color: Colors.grey, padding:
EdgeInsets.all(20), child: Text("2")),
          Container(color: Colors.grey, padding:
EdgeInsets.all(20), child: Text("3")),
        ],
      ),
    );
  }
}
```

Tips

- Always test your layout on multiple screen sizes and orientations to ensure the UI adapts well to different devices. Tools like Flutter's `device_preview` package or browser dev tools can help simulate various screen configurations.
- Leverage Flutter's built-in `MediaQuery` and `LayoutBuilder` to dynamically adjust the layout instead of hardcoding dimensions. This ensures the design remains flexible across a wide range of devices.
- Use percentage-based widths and heights in CSS and constraints-based widgets in Flutter, such as `Flexible` and `Expanded`, to create scalable and fluid layouts.

Actionable Strategies

- Implement a grid system for your application to organize content effectively. In Flutter, you can use `GridView` or `SliverGridDelegate`, while on the web, CSS Grid is the go-to solution.
- Break down responsive design into manageable components. Use smaller widgets in Flutter and reusable classes in CSS to ensure consistency and maintainability.
- Optimize performance by loading only the necessary components for the screen size. For instance, avoid rendering heavy widgets or high-resolution images on

smaller devices.

- Adopt platform-specific designs where appropriate to provide a native look and feel. Use Flutter's `Platform.isIOS` or `Platform.isAndroid` for conditional rendering.
- Maintain a responsive typography system by scaling font sizes dynamically based on screen dimensions. In Flutter, `MediaQuery` can be combined with `TextStyle` for responsive text adjustments.

Chapter 14: Adding Interactivity with Gestures

In modern application development, user interactivity is one of the most critical components. Gesture-based interactions allow users to perform intuitive actions like tapping, swiping, dragging, and more. Flutter offers robust tools and widgets to enable gesture-based functionality, and its flexibility in combining animations and interactions enhances user experiences. This chapter explains how to incorporate gestures into Flutter applications, comparing them with web implementations using HTML, CSS, and JavaScript.

14.1 Handling Taps and Clicks

Tapping or clicking is the most basic form of interaction, and in Flutter, it is usually achieved using the `InkWell` or `GestureDetector` widgets.

Comparison of Web vs Flutter Handling of Clicks

HTML/JavaScript:

```
<!-- html -->
<button id="clickButton">Click Me</button>
<script>

document.getElementById("clickButton").addEventListener("c
lick", function () {
    alert("Button clicked!");
  });
</script>
```

Flutter:

```
//dart
import 'package:flutter/material.dart';

class TapExample extends StatelessWidget {
  @override
  Widget build(BuildContext context) {
    return Scaffold(
      body: Center(
        child: GestureDetector(
          onTap: () {
```

```
            print("Button tapped!");
          },
          child: Container(
            padding: EdgeInsets.all(20),
            color: Colors.blue,
            child: Text("Tap Me", style: TextStyle(color:
Colors.white)),
          ),
        ),
      ),
    );
  }
}
```

In Flutter, `GestureDetector` allows for flexibility. Beyond `onTap`, it supports other interactions like `onDoubleTap`, `onLongPress`, and more. Unlike web applications that require binding events explicitly via JavaScript, Flutter integrates gestures directly into its widget tree.

Key Considerations:

- In web development, a click handler can be added to almost any element. Flutter achieves similar flexibility but within a unified widget-based structure.
- Flutter's `InkWell` adds material design ripples, making it ideal for tap interactions on material-style buttons.

14.2 Swiping and Dragging Widgets

Swiping and dragging gestures provide dynamic user interfaces, such as dismissing items, revealing actions, or moving elements.

Web Swiping Example with JavaScript:

```
<!-- html -->
<div id="swipeArea" style="width: 300px; height: 100px;
background: lightgray;">
  Swipe Me
</div>
<script>
  let startX = 0;

document.getElementById("swipeArea").addEventListener("tou
```

```
chstart", (e) => {
    startX = e.touches[0].clientX;
  });


document.getElementById("swipeArea").addEventListener("tou
chend", (e) => {
    let endX = e.changedTouches[0].clientX;
    if (startX > endX) {
      alert("Swiped Left");
    } else {
      alert("Swiped Right");
    }
  });
</script>
```

Flutter Swipe Example:

```
//dart
import 'package:flutter/material.dart';

class SwipeExample extends StatelessWidget {
  @override
  Widget build(BuildContext context) {
    return Scaffold(
      body: Center(
        child: GestureDetector(
          onHorizontalDragEnd: (details) {
            if (details.velocity.pixelsPerSecond.dx > 0) {
              print("Swiped Right");
            } else {
              print("Swiped Left");
            }
          },
          child: Container(
            width: 300,
            height: 100,
            color: Colors.grey,
            alignment: Alignment.center,
            child: Text("Swipe Me"),
          ),
```

```
        ),
      ),
    );
  }
}
```

Comparison:

- On the web, touch gestures rely on `touchstart`, `touchmove`, and `touchend` events. Flutter uses high-level abstractions such as `onHorizontalDragEnd`, eliminating the need for manual touch-coordinate tracking.
- Flutter's drag events allow velocity tracking, enabling smooth animations based on swipe speed.

14.3 Using GestureDetector for Custom Actions

The `GestureDetector` widget in Flutter is incredibly versatile, capturing all kinds of gestures and allowing custom logic for each.

Custom Actions Example in Flutter:

```
//dart
import 'package:flutter/material.dart';

class CustomGesture extends StatelessWidget {
  @override
  Widget build(BuildContext context) {
    return Scaffold(
      body: Center(
        child: GestureDetector(
          onDoubleTap: () {
            print("Double tapped!");
          },
          onLongPress: () {
            print("Long pressed!");
          },
          child: Container(
            width: 150,
            height: 150,
            color: Colors.red,
            alignment: Alignment.center,
```

```
              child: Text("Try Gestures"),
            ),
          ),
        ),
      );
    }
  }
```

Web Equivalent Using JavaScript:

```
<!-- html -->
<div id="gestureArea" style="width: 150px; height: 150px;
background: red; text-align: center; line-height: 150px;
color: white;">
  Try Gestures
</div>
<script>
  let gestureArea =
document.getElementById("gestureArea");

  gestureArea.addEventListener("dblclick", () => {
    alert("Double clicked!");
  });

  gestureArea.addEventListener("contextmenu", (e) => {
    e.preventDefault();
    alert("Right-click or long press detected!");
  });
</script>
```

Differences:

- Flutter simplifies complex interactions such as long presses and double taps by providing high-level callbacks.
- JavaScript requires binding multiple event listeners for similar functionality.

Advantages of `GestureDetector`:

- Detects multiple gestures simultaneously.
- Works seamlessly with other Flutter widgets.
- Can trigger animations, navigation, or any custom logic.

14.4 Animating on Gestures

Gestures often trigger visual feedback or transitions. Flutter's integration with animation frameworks makes this process seamless.

Example: Animating a Box on Tap

Flutter:

```
//dart
import 'package:flutter/material.dart';

class AnimatedGesture extends StatefulWidget {
  @override
  _AnimatedGestureState createState() =>
_AnimatedGestureState();
}

class _AnimatedGestureState extends State<AnimatedGesture>
{
  double _size = 100;

  void _animateBox() {
    setState(() {
      _size = _size == 100 ? 150 : 100;
    });
  }

  @override
  Widget build(BuildContext context) {
    return Scaffold(
      body: Center(
        child: GestureDetector(
          onTap: _animateBox,
          child: AnimatedContainer(
            duration: Duration(milliseconds: 300),
            width: _size,
            height: _size,
            color: Colors.blue,
          ),
        ),
      ),
```

```
    );
  }
}
```

Web with CSS and JavaScript:

```
<!-- html -->
<div id="box" style="width: 100px; height: 100px;
background: blue; transition: all 0.3s;"></div>
<script>
  let box = document.getElementById("box");
  box.addEventListener("click", () => {
    box.style.width = box.style.width === "100px" ?
"150px" : "100px";
    box.style.height = box.style.height === "100px" ?
"150px" : "100px";
  });
</script>
```

Comparison:

- Flutter uses `AnimatedContainer`, encapsulating animation logic within the widget itself.
- On the web, animations often rely on external styles and manual JavaScript manipulation.

Tips

- Use `GestureDetector` for flexibility when adding interactivity to custom widgets or containers.
- Pair gestures with animations, such as `AnimatedContainer` or `Hero`, to provide a polished user experience.
- Keep gesture-based actions intuitive and aligned with platform conventions (e.g., swipe-to-delete on mobile).

Actionable Strategies

- Experiment with multi-touch gestures using Flutter's `onPanUpdate` for panning or dragging across the screen.
- Combine gesture detection with state management solutions like `Provider` or `Bloc` to handle complex gesture-triggered workflows.
- Test gesture behaviors across multiple devices to account for variations in screen

size, touch sensitivity, and user habits.

- Create accessible gesture alternatives (e.g., buttons with the same functionality as swipe gestures) to support diverse user needs.
- Incorporate visual cues, such as color changes or ripples, to indicate gesture recognition, improving user feedback and experience.

14.5 Debugging Gesture Issues

Handling gestures in Flutter can sometimes be challenging, especially when multiple gestures are registered simultaneously or when performance issues arise. Debugging gesture-related problems requires careful analysis of both the gesture detectors and the widgets involved. Below are strategies and techniques that can help identify and resolve common gesture-related issues.

Common Gesture Issues in Flutter

Gesture Conflicts: Multiple gesture recognizers in the same area might lead to conflicts. For instance, if you have both `onTap` and `onPanUpdate` on a widget, the `onTap` gesture might get overridden by the dragging action.

- **Solution**: Prioritize gestures by using `GestureDetector` in combination with `IgnorePointer` or `AbsorbPointer` to handle gesture blocking or delegation.

Example:

```
//dart
GestureDetector(

  onTap: () {
    print("Tap detected!");
  },
  onPanUpdate: (details) {
    print("Pan update detected!");
  },
  child: Container(
    color: Colors.blue,
    height: 200,
    width: 200,
  ),
);
```

In this case, when you swipe (pan), it might trigger both the `onTap` and `onPanUpdate`. To resolve this, use `AbsorbPointer` to prevent one gesture from being detected when the other is in progress.

```
//dart
AbsorbPointer(
  absorbing: _isSwiping, // Use this flag to conditionally
block gestures
  child: GestureDetector(
    onTap: () {
      print("Tap detected!");
    },
    onPanUpdate: (details) {
      print("Pan update detected!");
    },
    child: Container(
      color: Colors.blue,
      height: 200,
      width: 200,
    ),
  ),
);
```

Unresponsive Gesture Detectors: Sometimes gestures may not trigger, especially on custom widgets. This might be caused by the widget not receiving touch events or interference from other layers.

- **Solution**: Ensure the widget receiving the gesture is interactive. Sometimes wrapping a widget in a `GestureDetector` with an `InkWell` or similar widget might help.

Example:

```
//dart
GestureDetector(

  onTap: () {
    print("Tap detected");
  },
```

```
  child: Container(
    color: Colors.green,
    padding: EdgeInsets.all(20),
    child: Center(
      child: Text("Tap Me", style: TextStyle(color:
Colors.white)),
    ),
  ),
);
```

If tapping doesn't work, ensure the container is not obstructed by other widgets, especially if using a `Stack` layout.

Unintended Gesture Triggers: When gestures like `onPanUpdate` or `onLongPress` are triggered unintentionally, it may be due to misinterpretation of user input, especially on smaller screens or when touch sensitivity is high.

- **Solution**: Implement thresholds or delays in gesture recognition, allowing the user to interact in a more controlled manner.

Example:

```
//dart
GestureDetector(

  onLongPressStart: (details) {
    print("Long press started");
  },
  onLongPressEnd: (details) {
    print("Long press ended");
  },
  child: Container(
    width: 150,
    height: 150,
    color: Colors.blue,
  ),
);
```

Add additional handling logic, such as checking the duration of the gesture or its movement, before triggering the action.

14.6 Comparing Event Listeners in HTML and Flutter

In HTML, event listeners are typically bound to DOM elements using JavaScript, which allows developers to define actions in response to user input events like clicks, touches, or keyboard presses. Flutter, however, does not rely on a DOM and instead operates with a tree of widgets, offering a more declarative way of handling gestures and interactions.

Event Listeners in HTML

In HTML, interaction is often handled with JavaScript by binding event listeners to elements. Each interaction such as `click`, `mousedown`, `touchstart`, etc., can be attached to an element.

Example of a button click handler in HTML and JavaScript:

```
<!-- html -->
<button id="button">Click Me</button>
<script>

document.getElementById("button").addEventListener("click"
, function() {
    alert("Button clicked!");
  });
</script>
```

Here, the `click` event listener is added to the button element. When clicked, it triggers the function displaying an alert.

Event Listeners in Flutter

Flutter's approach to handling user interactions involves wrapping widgets with gesture detectors, which are triggered on certain events. These detectors can handle a wide variety of gestures without having to manually listen to events like in JavaScript.

Example in Flutter for handling taps:

```
//dart
GestureDetector(
  onTap: () {
    print("Button tapped!");
  },
```

```
  child: Container(
    color: Colors.blue,
    height: 100,
    width: 200,
    alignment: Alignment.center,
    child: Text("Tap Me", style: TextStyle(color:
Colors.white)),
  ),
)
```

Key Differences:

- **Declarative vs Imperative**: Flutter uses a declarative style for UI components, where user interactions are embedded within the widget tree. HTML and JavaScript use an imperative approach where you explicitly define event listeners and interactions.
- **State Management**: In Flutter, interactions with widgets are tightly coupled with state management and UI updates. In JavaScript, state changes typically require manual DOM manipulation or updating through frameworks like React.
- **Gesture Handling**: Flutter's `GestureDetector` abstracts away low-level touch events, providing high-level gesture recognizers like `onTap`, `onDoubleTap`, `onLongPress`, etc. JavaScript requires handling multiple touch events manually (`touchstart`, `touchmove`, `touchend`).

14.7 Sample Code: Interactive Elements in React Native vs Flutter

Both React Native and Flutter aim to provide a smooth and responsive user experience for mobile applications, but the methods of adding interactivity are quite different.

React Native Example:

In React Native, you can add interactivity using the `TouchableOpacity` component or `GestureResponder` API for custom gestures.

```
//js
import React from 'react';
import { TouchableOpacity, Text, Alert, View } from
'react-native';

const App = () => {
  const handlePress = () => {
    Alert.alert("Button Pressed!");
```

```
  };

  return (
    <View style={{ flex: 1, justifyContent: 'center',
alignItems: 'center' }}>
      <TouchableOpacity onPress={handlePress}>
        <View style={{ padding: 20, backgroundColor:
'blue' }}>
          <Text style={{ color: 'white' }}>Press Me</Text>
        </View>
      </TouchableOpacity>
    </View>
  );
};

export default App;
```

Flutter Example:

In Flutter, `GestureDetector` or `InkWell` are commonly used to add interactive behavior to widgets.

```
//dart
import 'package:flutter/material.dart';

class InteractiveElement extends StatelessWidget {
  @override
  Widget build(BuildContext context) {
    return Scaffold(
      body: Center(
        child: GestureDetector(
          onTap: () {
            print("Button tapped!");
          },
          child: Container(
            padding: EdgeInsets.all(20),
            color: Colors.blue,
            child: Text("Tap Me", style: TextStyle(color:
Colors.white)),
          ),
        ),
      ),
```

```
    );
  }
}

void main() => runApp(MaterialApp(home:
InteractiveElement()));
```

Key Differences:

- **React Native** uses `TouchableOpacity` or `TouchableHighlight` for simple interactivity, providing a wrapper that listens to touch events. For more complex gestures, React Native offers `PanResponder` and `GestureResponder`.
- **Flutter** relies on widgets like `GestureDetector`, `InkWell`, and `Button` that listen for interactions and provide more declarative control.

14.8 Best Practices for User Interactions

When building interactive apps, it is essential to follow best practices to ensure a seamless user experience. Below are some best practices when dealing with gestures in Flutter.

1. Prioritize Simplicity

Keep user interactions as intuitive and simple as possible. Complex interactions can confuse users and lead to frustration.

- **Tip**: Avoid overlapping gestures. For example, don't attach a drag gesture and tap gesture to the same area unless necessary. Consider a dedicated area for each action.

2. Provide Immediate Feedback

Users need immediate feedback when they interact with the UI. This could be visual feedback like color changes, ripple effects, or animations.

- **Tip**: Use `InkWell` or `InkResponse` to provide ripple effects on taps.
- **Tip**: Provide visual feedback for long-press actions, such as scaling or highlighting an item.

3. Optimize for Different Screen Sizes

Ensure that gestures are comfortable and functional across different devices. Larger screens may require larger touch targets, and smaller screens may require more careful placement of interactive elements.

- **Tip**: Test gestures on different screen sizes to ensure that tap targets are accessible.
- **Tip**: Use `MediaQuery` to adjust UI layouts for different screen sizes.

4. Handle Edge Cases for Performance

Gestures can often trigger actions that impact performance. Ensure that long-running tasks triggered by gestures, like animations or network requests, do not block the UI thread.

- **Tip**: Offload heavy tasks to background threads or isolate functions to keep the UI responsive.
- **Tip**: Use `FutureBuilder` or `StreamBuilder` to manage asynchronous tasks initiated by gestures without blocking the UI thread.

5. Create Accessible Interactions

Not all users can interact with your app using touch gestures alone. Consider accessibility features such as voice control or keyboard navigation.

- **Tip**: Provide accessible alternatives for gestures, like keyboard shortcuts or accessible buttons.
- **Tip**: Make sure your interactive elements are focusable for screen readers.

By following these best practices, you ensure that your app is not only interactive but also intuitive, performant, and accessible to a wider range of users.

Examples

HTML/CSS/JavaScript: Button Click Interaction

HTML and JavaScript allow you to easily add interactivity by attaching event listeners to elements. In this case, we create a button element that responds to clicks by displaying an alert.

```
<!-- html -->
```

```
<!DOCTYPE html>

<html lang="en">
  <head>
    <meta charset="UTF-8" />
    <meta name="viewport" content="width=device-width,
initial-scale=1.0" />
    <title>Button Interaction</title>
  </head>
  <body>
    <button id="myButton">Click Me</button>
    <script>

document.getElementById('myButton').addEventListener('clic
k', function () {
        alert('Button Clicked!');
      });
    </script>
  </body>
</html>
```

In this example, the `addEventListener` method is used to bind a `click` event to the button. Upon clicking the button, the alert message will be displayed.

React Native: Button Interaction

In React Native, the `TouchableOpacity` component is used to make elements interactive. The following example shows how to create a button that responds to a tap.

```
//jsx
import React from 'react';

import { TouchableOpacity, Text, Alert, View } from
'react-native';

const App = () => {
  const handlePress = () => {
    Alert.alert("Button Pressed!");
  };

  return (
    <View style={{ flex: 1, justifyContent: 'center',
```

```
alignItems: 'center' }}>
      <TouchableOpacity onPress={handlePress}>
        <View style={{ padding: 20, backgroundColor:
'blue' }}>
          <Text style={{ color: 'white' }}>Press Me</Text>
        </View>
      </TouchableOpacity>
    </View>
  );
};

export default App;
```

Here, `TouchableOpacity` is used to wrap the button, making it respond to user taps. The `onPress` event triggers the `handlePress` function that displays an alert.

Flutter: Button Interaction with GestureDetector

In Flutter, `GestureDetector` is commonly used for detecting gestures. This example shows how to use it to add tap functionality to a button.

```
//dart
import 'package:flutter/material.dart';

void main() {
  runApp(MyApp());
}

class MyApp extends StatelessWidget {
  @override
  Widget build(BuildContext context) {
    return MaterialApp(
      home: Scaffold(
        appBar: AppBar(title: Text("Button Interaction")),
        body: Center(
          child: GestureDetector(
            onTap: () {
              print("Button Pressed!");
            },
            child: Container(
              padding: EdgeInsets.all(20),
              color: Colors.blue,
```

```
              child: Text("Press Me", style:
TextStyle(color: Colors.white)),
            ),
          ),
        ),
      ),
    );
  }
}
```

The `GestureDetector` is used in Flutter to detect tap events on a container. When tapped, the text inside the container is printed to the console.

HTML/CSS/JavaScript: Hover Effect

In HTML, CSS, and JavaScript, hover effects can be used to enhance interactivity. The following code shows a hover effect using CSS and an event listener in JavaScript.

```
<!-- html -->
<!DOCTYPE html>

<html lang="en">
  <head>
    <meta charset="UTF-8" />
    <meta name="viewport" content="width=device-width,
initial-scale=1.0" />
    <title>Hover Effect</title>
    <style>
      .hover-button {
        padding: 20px;
        background-color: blue;
        color: white;
        cursor: pointer;
      }
      .hover-button:hover {
        background-color: darkblue;
      }
    </style>
  </head>
  <body>
    <button id="hoverButton" class="hover-button">Hover
Over Me</button>
```

```
    <script>

document.getElementById('hoverButton').addEventListener('m
ouseover', function () {
        console.log('Hovered Over!');
      });
    </script>
  </body>
</html>
```

The `:hover` CSS pseudo-class changes the button's background color when the mouse is hovered over it. Additionally, the JavaScript event listener listens for the `mouseover` event and logs the action.

Tips

- **Avoid Gesture Conflicts**: Ensure that multiple gestures attached to the same widget do not conflict with each other. For example, using both `onTap` and `onPanUpdate` on the same widget can result in undesired behavior. To prevent this, use `AbsorbPointer` or `IgnorePointer` to block unwanted gestures.
- **Optimize for Touch Sensitivity**: Mobile devices have different screen sizes and touch sensitivity. Ensure that touch targets are appropriately sized for accessibility, especially on smaller devices. The minimum size for interactive elements should generally be 48x48dp.
- **Provide Clear Feedback for Interactions**: Always provide immediate visual feedback when a user interacts with an element. This can include changes in color, size, or a ripple effect. For instance, `InkWell` in Flutter provides a ripple effect when a user taps an interactive element.

Actionable Strategies

- **Use Declarative Gesture Handling**: In Flutter, prefer using declarative gesture handling methods such as `GestureDetector` over low-level touch listeners. This improves code readability and maintainability, making it easier to manage interactions declaratively.
- **Leverage Built-in Gesture Libraries**: Both React Native and Flutter provide

built-in libraries and components like `TouchableOpacity` (React Native) and `GestureDetector` (Flutter) for handling gestures. Leverage these components rather than writing custom touch handlers from scratch to save time and ensure consistent behavior.

- **Test Interactions Across Devices**: Test your interactive elements on various devices, both on mobile and desktop. Flutter allows for cross-platform development, but it's important to ensure that your gestures perform well on all screen sizes. Adjustments may be required based on screen size and resolution.
- **Consider Performance and Efficiency**: When dealing with multiple gestures or complex animations, ensure that the interactions are optimized for performance. Use async operations for heavy tasks and avoid blocking the UI thread with expensive operations. Flutter's `FutureBuilder` and `StreamBuilder` are useful for handling async data without freezing the UI.
- **Create Responsive UI Designs**: Responsive layouts are critical for ensuring a good user experience across all devices. Use Flutter's `MediaQuery` or React Native's `Dimensions` API to build layouts that adjust based on the device's screen size and orientation. Ensure that interactive elements like buttons and text fields are appropriately scaled for mobile screens.

Chapter 15: Networking and APIs

Modern applications heavily rely on networking and API integration to provide dynamic and personalized experiences. In this chapter, we cover essential aspects of working with APIs in both Flutter and web technologies (HTML, CSS, JavaScript), emphasizing how to fetch data, manage asynchronous calls, and display results effectively.

15.1 Fetching Data from APIs

Fetching data is fundamental when integrating backend services. In web development, you typically use JavaScript's `fetch` API or libraries like Axios. In Flutter, the `http` package is a popular choice. Below are structured comparisons and implementations:

HTML, CSS, JavaScript Example: Fetching Data

JavaScript's `fetch` method simplifies making HTTP requests and processing responses. Here's how you fetch data from a sample API:

```
<!-- html -->
<!DOCTYPE html>
<html lang="en">
  <head>
    <meta charset="UTF-8" />
    <meta name="viewport" content="width=device-width,
initial-scale=1.0" />
    <title>API Fetch</title>
  </head>
  <body>
    <div id="data"></div>
    <script>
      fetch('https://jsonplaceholder.typicode.com/posts')
        .then((response) => response.json())
        .then((data) => {
          const container =
document.getElementById('data');
          data.slice(0, 5).forEach((post) => {
            const div = document.createElement('div');
            div.innerHTML = `<h3>${post.title}</h3><p>$
{post.body}</p>`;
```

```
            container.appendChild(div);
          });
        })
        .catch((error) => console.error('Error fetching
data:', error));
    </script>
  </body>
</html>
```

This example fetches posts from a placeholder API, processes the JSON response, and dynamically creates HTML elements to display data.

Flutter Example: Fetching Data

In Flutter, the `http` package is commonly used to perform HTTP requests. Below is an example that fetches similar data:

```
//dart
import 'package:flutter/material.dart';
import 'package:http/http.dart' as http;
import 'dart:convert';

void main() {
  runApp(MyApp());
}

class MyApp extends StatelessWidget {
  @override
  Widget build(BuildContext context) {
    return MaterialApp(
      home: Scaffold(
        appBar: AppBar(title: Text("Fetch API Data")),
        body: PostsPage(),
      ),
    );
  }
}

class PostsPage extends StatefulWidget {
  @override
  _PostsPageState createState() => _PostsPageState();
}
```

```
class _PostsPageState extends State<PostsPage> {
  late Future<List<Post>> posts;

  @override
  void initState() {
    super.initState();
    posts = fetchPosts();
  }

  Future<List<Post>> fetchPosts() async {
    final response =
        await http.get(Uri.parse('https://
jsonplaceholder.typicode.com/posts'));
    if (response.statusCode == 200) {
      final List<dynamic> jsonData =
json.decode(response.body);
      return jsonData.map((data) =>
Post.fromJson(data)).toList();
    } else {
      throw Exception('Failed to load posts');
    }
  }

  @override
  Widget build(BuildContext context) {
    return FutureBuilder<List<Post>>(
      future: posts,
      builder: (context, snapshot) {
        if (snapshot.connectionState ==
ConnectionState.waiting) {
          return Center(child:
CircularProgressIndicator());
        } else if (snapshot.hasError) {
          return Center(child: Text('Error: $
{snapshot.error}'));
        } else {
          return ListView.builder(
            itemCount: snapshot.data!.length,
            itemBuilder: (context, index) {
              final post = snapshot.data![index];
              return ListTile(
```

```
                title: Text(post.title),
                subtitle: Text(post.body),
              );
            },
          );
        }
      },
    );
  }
}

class Post {
  final String title;
  final String body;

  Post({required this.title, required this.body});

  factory Post.fromJson(Map<String, dynamic> json) {
    return Post(title: json['title'], body: json['body']);
  }
}
```

Here, `http.get` is used to fetch data, which is parsed into a list of `Post` objects. The `FutureBuilder` widget handles the asynchronous call and dynamically builds the UI.

15.2 The `http` Package in Flutter

The `http` package provides a straightforward API for making HTTP requests. Below are key features and methods:

- **GET Request**: Used to retrieve data.
- **POST Request**: Sends data to the server.
- **Headers**: Allows custom configuration for requests.
- **Error Handling**: Ensures robustness in network communication.

Example: Performing a POST Request

```
//dart
Future<void> createPost(String title, String body) async {
```

```
  final response = await http.post(
    Uri.parse('https://jsonplaceholder.typicode.com/
posts'),
    headers: {'Content-Type': 'application/json'},
    body: jsonEncode({'title': title, 'body': body,
'userId': 1}),
  );

  if (response.statusCode == 201) {
    print('Post created: ${response.body}');
  } else {
    print('Failed to create post: $
{response.statusCode}');
  }
}
```

This example demonstrates how to send a POST request to an API with JSON-encoded data. The response is logged for debugging.

15.3 Managing Async Calls

Asynchronous programming is essential for API integration to ensure smooth user experiences. Both JavaScript and Flutter provide robust solutions.

JavaScript: Promises and Async/Await

Promises in JavaScript handle asynchronous tasks:

```
//javascript
async function fetchPosts() {
  try {
    const response = await fetch('https://
jsonplaceholder.typicode.com/posts');
    const data = await response.json();
    console.log(data);
  } catch (error) {
    console.error('Error fetching posts:', error);
  }
}
fetchPosts();
```

The `async/await` syntax makes asynchronous code easier to read and maintain.

Flutter: Async/Await

In Flutter, asynchronous calls are managed using the `async` and `await` keywords:

```
//dart
Future<void> fetchData() async {
  try {
    final response =
        await http.get(Uri.parse('https://
jsonplaceholder.typicode.com/posts'));
    if (response.statusCode == 200) {
      print(response.body);
    } else {
      print('Failed to load data');
    }
  } catch (e) {
    print('Error: $e');
  }
}
```

Flutter's approach closely mirrors JavaScript, making it intuitive for developers transitioning between the two.

15.4 Displaying Fetched Data in Lists

Presenting API data in lists is a common requirement. Below are implementations for web and Flutter:

Web: Dynamically Populating Lists

```
<!-- html -->
<ul id="postList"></ul>
<script>
  fetch('https://jsonplaceholder.typicode.com/posts')
    .then((response) => response.json())
    .then((data) => {
      const list = document.getElementById('postList');
      data.slice(0, 10).forEach((post) => {
        const li = document.createElement('li');
        li.textContent = post.title;
```

```
            list.appendChild(li);
        });
    });
</script>
```

This code dynamically creates list items for each post fetched from the API.

Flutter: Displaying Data in a ListView

```
//dart
ListView.builder(
  itemCount: posts.length,
  itemBuilder: (context, index) {
    final post = posts[index];
    return ListTile(
      title: Text(post.title),
      subtitle: Text(post.body),
    );
  },
);
```

Flutter's `ListView.builder` efficiently renders large datasets, creating widgets only for items visible on the screen.

Tips

- **Cache API Responses**: Use caching to reduce unnecessary API calls and enhance performance.
- **Graceful Error Handling**: Always provide user-friendly error messages for failed network requests.
- **Optimize for Offline Use**: Implement features like data persistence to improve the offline experience.

Actionable Strategies

- **Use Retry Logic for API Calls**: Implement retry mechanisms to handle intermittent network failures.
- **Implement Loading Indicators**: Use widgets like `CircularProgressIndicator` in Flutter or CSS animations in web to provide visual feedback during data loading.
- **Secure API Communication**: Use HTTPS and secure authentication methods like OAuth or API keys.

- **Paginate Large Datasets**: Fetch and display data in chunks using pagination techniques to improve performance.
- **Monitor and Log API Performance**: Track API call durations and errors to identify bottlenecks.

15.5 Posting Data to APIs

Posting data to APIs is a critical aspect of developing interactive applications. It allows your app to send data, such as user inputs or form details, to a server. In Flutter, the `http` package provides robust tools for making POST requests. Understanding how to post data effectively while maintaining security and efficiency is vital for a seamless user experience.

Understanding the Structure of POST Requests

In a POST request, the app sends data to a server in the body of the request. Unlike GET requests, where parameters are appended to the URL, POST requests encapsulate data within the HTTP body. Here's the basic structure of a POST request:

1. **URL**: The endpoint of the server.
2. **Headers**: Metadata about the request (e.g., content type).
3. **Body**: The actual data being sent.

Example in JavaScript (AJAX)

```
//javascript
const data = { name: 'John Doe', age: 30 };

fetch('https://api.example.com/users', {
  method: 'POST',
  headers: {
    'Content-Type': 'application/json',
  },
  body: JSON.stringify(data),
})
  .then(response => response.json())
  .then(data => console.log('Success:', data))
  .catch(error => console.error('Error:', error));
```

Equivalent in Flutter

Flutter uses the `http` package for similar functionality:

```
//dart
import 'dart:convert';
import 'package:http/http.dart' as http;

Future<void> postData() async {
  const url = 'https://api.example.com/users';
  final response = await http.post(
    Uri.parse(url),
    headers: {'Content-Type': 'application/json'},
    body: json.encode({'name': 'John Doe', 'age': 30}),
  );

  if (response.statusCode == 200) {
    print('Success: ${response.body}');
  } else {
    print('Error: ${response.reasonPhrase}');
  }
}
```

Key Differences Between JavaScript and Flutter

- **Structure**: JavaScript relies on the `fetch` API, whereas Flutter uses the `http` package.
- **JSON Encoding**: In JavaScript, `JSON.stringify` converts an object to a string. Flutter uses `json.encode`.
- **Error Handling**: Both use `try-catch` patterns or equivalent methods for managing errors.

Tips for POST Requests

- Always validate user inputs before sending data.
- Use HTTPS for secure data transmission.
- Include appropriate headers like `Authorization` for protected APIs.
- Serialize complex objects into JSON using Dart's `jsonEncode`.

15.6 Handling Network Errors Gracefully

Network errors are inevitable in any app relying on APIs. Factors such as poor connectivity, server downtime, or invalid requests can disrupt the flow. Handling these errors gracefully ensures the app remains user-friendly.

Common Types of Network Errors

1. **Connection Timeout**: When the server takes too long to respond.
2. **HTTP Errors**: Status codes like `404` (Not Found) or `500` (Server Error).
3. **No Internet**: When the device has no active network connection.
4. **Invalid Data**: If the server returns malformed or unexpected data.

Error Handling in JavaScript

```
//javascript
fetch('https://api.example.com/data')
  .then(response => {
    if (!response.ok) {
      throw new Error(`HTTP error! status: $
{response.status}`);
    }
    return response.json();
  })
  .catch(error => {
    console.error('Network error:', error.message);
  });
```

Error Handling in Flutter

```
//dart
import 'dart:io';
import 'package:http/http.dart' as http;

Future<void> fetchData() async {
  try {
    final response = await http.get(Uri.parse('https://
api.example.com/data'));

    if (response.statusCode == 200) {
```

```
      print('Data: ${response.body}');
    } else {
      print('Error: ${response.statusCode}');
    }
  } on SocketException {
    print('No Internet connection');
  } catch (e) {
    print('Unexpected error: $e');
  }
}
```

Strategies for Graceful Error Handling

- **Show Informative Messages**: Replace generic error messages with user-friendly text like "Unable to fetch data. Please try again."
- **Retry Mechanism**: Allow users to retry failed actions.
- **Offline Mode**: Cache data locally for offline access.

15.7 Debugging Network Calls in Flutter

Debugging network calls is essential for resolving issues like incorrect responses, failed requests, or performance bottlenecks. Flutter provides several tools and best practices for effective debugging.

Using `dart:developer` for Logging

The `dart:developer` package includes utilities for logging requests and responses:

```
//dart
import 'dart:developer' as developer;
import 'package:http/http.dart' as http;

Future<void> debugNetworkCall() async {
  const url = 'https://api.example.com/debug';
  developer.log('Sending request to $url');

  final response = await http.get(Uri.parse(url));
  developer.log('Response: ${response.body}');
}
```

Advanced Debugging Tools

1. **Flutter DevTools**: Offers a network inspector for tracking API calls.
2. **Charles Proxy or Postman**: External tools for monitoring HTTP traffic.
3. **Custom Interceptors**: Middleware in libraries like `Dio` for logging requests and responses.

Best Practices for Debugging

- Use verbose logging during development but disable it in production.
- Capture and analyze full stack traces for errors.
- Validate API endpoints and payloads during debugging.

15.8 Sample Code: AJAX Requests vs Flutter HTTP

Comparing AJAX in JavaScript to HTTP requests in Flutter highlights differences in syntax, approach, and capabilities. Below are side-by-side examples of common operations.

1. Fetching Data

JavaScript (AJAX):

```
//javascript
fetch('https://api.example.com/data')
  .then(response => response.json())
  .then(data => console.log(data))
  .catch(error => console.error('Error:', error));
```

Flutter:

```
//dart
import 'package:http/http.dart' as http;

Future<void> fetchData() async {
  final response = await http.get(Uri.parse('https://
api.example.com/data'));
  print('Data: ${response.body}');
}
```

2. Posting Data

JavaScript (AJAX):

```
//javascript
fetch('https://api.example.com/add', {
  method: 'POST',
  headers: { 'Content-Type': 'application/json' },
  body: JSON.stringify({ name: 'Sample' }),
});
```

Flutter:

```
//dart
final response = await http.post(
  Uri.parse('https://api.example.com/add'),
  headers: {'Content-Type': 'application/json'},
  body: jsonEncode({'name': 'Sample'}),
);
```

3. Handling Errors

JavaScript:

```
//javascript
fetch('https://api.example.com/fail')
  .catch(error => console.error('Network error:', error));
```

Flutter:

```
//dart
try {
  final response = await http.get(Uri.parse('https://
api.example.com/fail'));
} catch (e) {
  print('Network error: $e');
}
```

Key Takeaways

- **Asynchronous Patterns**: Both use promises or futures for handling asynchronous operations.
- **Error Handling**: Flutter's Dart language uses `try-catch`, whereas JavaScript uses `.catch()`.
- **Logging**: Debugging tools vary; Flutter benefits from Dart-specific logging and debugging utilities.

By mastering these techniques, developers can build robust and user-friendly apps that interact effectively with APIs.

Examples

1. Fetching Data with Async Requests
HTML and JavaScript:
HTML provides a simple structure for rendering fetched data, while JavaScript handles the asynchronous call:

```
<!-- html -->
<!DOCTYPE html>
<html>
<head>
  <title>Async Fetch Example</title>
</head>
<body>
  <div id="data-container"></div>
  <script>
    async function fetchData() {
      try {
        const response = await fetch('https://
api.example.com/data');
        const data = await response.json();
        document.getElementById('data-
container').innerText = JSON.stringify(data, null, 2);
      } catch (error) {
        console.error('Error fetching data:', error);
      }
    }
    fetchData();
  </script>
</body>
</html>
```

Flutter:

The `http` package in Flutter provides similar functionality to fetch and render data dynamically.

```
//dart
import 'package:flutter/material.dart';
import 'package:http/http.dart' as http;
import 'dart:convert';

void main() => runApp(MyApp());

class MyApp extends StatelessWidget {
  @override
  Widget build(BuildContext context) {
    return MaterialApp(
      home: Scaffold(
        appBar: AppBar(title: Text('Async Fetch
Example')),
        body: DataScreen(),
      ),
    );
  }
}

class DataScreen extends StatefulWidget {
  @override
  _DataScreenState createState() => _DataScreenState();
}

class _DataScreenState extends State<DataScreen> {
  String _data = 'Loading...';

  Future<void> fetchData() async {
    try {
      final response = await http.get(Uri.parse('https://
api.example.com/data'));
      setState(() {
        _data = jsonDecode(response.body).toString();
      });
    } catch (error) {
```

```
      setState(() {
        _data = 'Error fetching data';
      });
    }
  }

  @override
  void initState() {
    super.initState();
    fetchData();
  }

  @override
  Widget build(BuildContext context) {
    return Center(child: Text(_data));
  }
}
```

2. Styling API Responses with CSS

HTML and JavaScript:

To format API responses into a styled UI, CSS can be applied to enhance visual presentation:

```
<!-- html -->
<!DOCTYPE html>
<html>
<head>
  <style>
    #data-container {
      font-family: Arial, sans-serif;
      color: #333;
      padding: 20px;
      background-color: #f9f9f9;
      border: 1px solid #ddd;
    }
  </style>
</head>
<body>
  <div id="data-container"></div>
  <script>
    async function fetchData() {
      const response = await fetch('https://
```

```
api.example.com/data');
      const data = await response.json();
      document.getElementById('data-container').innerText
= JSON.stringify(data, null, 2);
    }
    fetchData();
  </script>
</body>
</html>
```

Flutter:

Flutter uses widgets and `TextStyle` to style data dynamically:

```
//dart
import 'package:flutter/material.dart';
import 'package:http/http.dart' as http;
import 'dart:convert';

class StyledDataScreen extends StatefulWidget {
  @override
  _StyledDataScreenState createState() =>
_StyledDataScreenState();
}

class _StyledDataScreenState extends
State<StyledDataScreen> {
  String _data = 'Fetching data...';

  Future<void> fetchData() async {
    try {
      final response = await http.get(Uri.parse('https://
api.example.com/data'));
      setState(() {
        _data = jsonDecode(response.body).toString();
      });
    } catch (e) {
      setState(() {
        _data = 'Failed to load data';
      });
    }
  }
```

```
  @override
  void initState() {
    super.initState();
    fetchData();
  }

  @override
  Widget build(BuildContext context) {
    return Scaffold(
      appBar: AppBar(title: Text('Styled Data Example')),
      body: Container(
        padding: EdgeInsets.all(20),
        color: Colors.grey[200],
        child: Text(
          _data,
          style: TextStyle(fontSize: 16, color:
Colors.black87),
        ),
      ),
    );
  }
}
```

3. POST Request with Form Data

HTML and JavaScript:

Handling user inputs via forms and sending them to an API in JavaScript:

```
<!-- html -->
<form id="user-form">
  <input type="text" id="name" placeholder="Name">
  <input type="number" id="age" placeholder="Age">
  <button type="submit">Submit</button>
</form>
<script>
  document.getElementById('user-
form').addEventListener('submit', async (e) => {
    e.preventDefault();
    const name = document.getElementById('name').value;
    const age = document.getElementById('age').value;

    try {
```

```
      const response = await fetch('https://
api.example.com/users', {
        method: 'POST',
        headers: { 'Content-Type': 'application/json' },
        body: JSON.stringify({ name, age }),
      });
      console.log(await response.json());
    } catch (error) {
      console.error('Error:', error);
    }
  });
</script>
```

Flutter:
Flutter uses `TextEditingController` to manage form inputs for a POST request:

```
//dart
import 'package:flutter/material.dart';
import 'package:http/http.dart' as http;
import 'dart:convert';

class PostDataScreen extends StatelessWidget {
  final TextEditingController nameController =
TextEditingController();
  final TextEditingController ageController =
TextEditingController();

  Future<void> postData(String name, String age) async {
    try {
      final response = await http.post(
        Uri.parse('https://api.example.com/users'),
        headers: {'Content-Type': 'application/json'},
        body: json.encode({'name': name, 'age':
int.parse(age)}),
      );
      print('Response: ${response.body}');
    } catch (e) {
      print('Error: $e');
    }
  }
```

```
  @override
  Widget build(BuildContext context) {
    return Scaffold(
      appBar: AppBar(title: Text('Post Data Example')),
      body: Padding(
        padding: EdgeInsets.all(20),
        child: Column(
          children: [
            TextField(controller: nameController,
decoration: InputDecoration(labelText: 'Name')),
            TextField(controller: ageController,
decoration: InputDecoration(labelText: 'Age')),
            ElevatedButton(
              onPressed: () =>
postData(nameController.text, ageController.text),
              child: Text('Submit'),
            ),
          ],
        ),
      ),
    );
  }
}
```

4. Handling Loading States
HTML and JavaScript:
Displaying a loading spinner during network requests:

```
<!-- html -->
<div id="loading">Loading...</div>
<div id="data"></div>
<script>
  async function fetchData() {
    document.getElementById('loading').style.display =
'block';
    try {
      const response = await fetch('https://
api.example.com/data');
      const data = await response.json();
      document.getElementById('data').innerText =
JSON.stringify(data, null, 2);
    } finally {
```

```
      document.getElementById('loading').style.display =
'none';
    }
  }
  fetchData();
</script>
```

Flutter:

Using `FutureBuilder` to handle async states:

```
//dart
import 'package:flutter/material.dart';
import 'package:http/http.dart' as http;
import 'dart:convert';

class LoadingScreen extends StatelessWidget {
  Future<String> fetchData() async {
    final response = await http.get(Uri.parse('https://
api.example.com/data'));
    return jsonDecode(response.body).toString();
  }

  @override
  Widget build(BuildContext context) {
    return Scaffold(
      appBar: AppBar(title: Text('Loading Example')),
      body: FutureBuilder<String>(
        future: fetchData(),
        builder: (context, snapshot) {
          if (snapshot.connectionState ==
ConnectionState.waiting) {
            return Center(child:
CircularProgressIndicator());
          } else if (snapshot.hasError) {
            return Center(child: Text('Error: $
{snapshot.error}'));
          } else {
            return Center(child: Text(snapshot.data ?? 'No
Data'));
          }
        },
```

```
        ),
      );
    }
}
```

Tips

- Always use asynchronous patterns like `async-await` or `FutureBuilder` for network calls to prevent UI blocking.
- Cache frequent API responses locally using tools like `shared_preferences` or `Hive` in Flutter.
- Log errors systematically to ensure effective debugging and monitoring.

Actionable Strategies

- Ensure APIs are accessed over HTTPS for secure communication and to protect sensitive user data.
- Use environment-specific configurations for API URLs to separate development and production environments.
- Implement retry logic with exponential backoff for failed network requests to improve reliability.
- Optimize payload sizes by compressing data sent to and from the API to reduce latency.
- Test API integrations thoroughly using tools like Postman or integration test suites in Flutter.

Chapter 16: Working with Local Data

16.1 Persistent Storage Options in Flutter

Working with local data is an essential part of application development, enabling users to interact with applications offline and maintain state across sessions. Flutter provides a variety of persistent storage options tailored to different use cases. Whether you need a robust database system, lightweight key-value storage, or file-based storage, Flutter's ecosystem has tools to address these requirements effectively.

Persistent Storage in Flutter vs HTML/JavaScript

In traditional web development with HTML and JavaScript, local data storage often involves methods like:

1. **LocalStorage and SessionStorage**: Key-value storage provided by the browser.
2. **IndexedDB**: A more robust database-like storage.
3. **Cookies**: Lightweight storage primarily used for server communication.

These options are accessible via browser APIs, enabling asynchronous access and manipulation of stored data. In comparison, Flutter offers libraries and plugins for handling persistent data, such as `SharedPreferences` for key-value storage, `sqflite` for databases, and `path_provider` for file management.

Key Persistent Storage Solutions in Flutter

1. **SharedPreferences**
   SharedPreferences provides lightweight key-value storage for simple needs, like saving user preferences or settings.

2. **SQLite (sqflite plugin)**
   SQLite is a relational database system used for managing structured data with advanced querying capabilities.

3. **Hive**
   Hive is a lightweight and fast NoSQL database for handling structured and unstructured data.

4. **File-Based Storage**
   File-based storage is suitable for scenarios where data doesn't fit into structured

formats, such as storing configuration files or logs.

16.2 Using SQLite for Local Databases

Why SQLite?

SQLite is a popular database choice for mobile applications due to its light footprint, relational structure, and lack of a separate server process. In Flutter, the `sqflite` plugin simplifies the integration and management of SQLite databases.

Comparison with IndexedDB in JavaScript

While SQLite in Flutter provides an SQL interface, JavaScript developers often rely on IndexedDB for relational-like storage in web apps. IndexedDB uses key-value pairs but supports complex objects and transactions, whereas SQLite relies on traditional SQL.

Setting Up SQLite in Flutter

Add Dependencies
Begin by adding the `sqflite` and `path_provider` plugins to your `pubspec.yaml` file:

```
#yaml
dependencies:

  sqflite: ^2.0.0+4
  path_provider: ^2.0.13
```

Database Initialization
Use `getDatabasesPath()` from `path_provider` to define the database location:

```
//dart
import 'package:sqflite/sqflite.dart';

import 'package:path/path.dart';

Future<Database> initializeDB() async {
  String path = await getDatabasesPath();
  return openDatabase(
```

```
    join(path, 'example.db'),
    onCreate: (database, version) async {
      await database.execute(
        "CREATE TABLE items(id INTEGER PRIMARY KEY
AUTOINCREMENT, name TEXT NOT NULL, quantity INTEGER)",
      );
    },
    version: 1,
  );
}
```

Performing CRUD Operations

Insert Data:

```
//dart
Future<void> insertItem(Database db, String name, int
quantity) async {
  await db.insert(
    'items',
    {'name': name, 'quantity': quantity},
    conflictAlgorithm: ConflictAlgorithm.replace,
  );
}
```

Retrieve Data:

```
//dart
Future<List<Map<String, dynamic>>> fetchItems(Database db)
async {
  return await db.query('items');
}
```

Structured Query vs JavaScript JSON Storage

SQLite: Structured and normalized data storage with schema definitions.

```
#sql
SELECT * FROM items WHERE quantity > 10;
```

JavaScript IndexedDB: Relies on JSON storage and key-value pairing.
Example:

```
//javascript
const transaction = db.transaction('items', 'readonly');
const store = transaction.objectStore('items');
const items = store.getAll();
```

16.3 Key-Value Storage with SharedPreferences

SharedPreferences offers a simple API for storing small amounts of persistent data, such as user preferences and configuration.

How SharedPreferences Works

1. **Key-Value Mapping**
   SharedPreferences stores data as key-value pairs, making it an ideal choice for lightweight data storage.
2. **Async Access**
   The API is asynchronous, ensuring non-blocking operations.

Using SharedPreferences in Flutter

Install Plugin
Add the `shared_preferences` package to your `pubspec.yaml`:

```
#yaml
dependencies:

  shared_preferences: ^2.0.15
```

Store and Retrieve Data

Save Data:

```
//dart
import 'package:shared_preferences/
shared_preferences.dart';

Future<void> savePreference(String key, String value)
```

```
async {
  final prefs = await SharedPreferences.getInstance();
  await prefs.setString(key, value);
}
```

Retrieve Data:

```
//dart
Future<String?> getPreference(String key) async {
  final prefs = await SharedPreferences.getInstance();
  return prefs.getString(key);
}
```

Comparison with HTML's LocalStorage

SharedPreferences:

- Asynchronous API.
- Persistent across app sessions.

LocalStorage (HTML):

- Synchronous API.
- Used for similar purposes in web applications.

```
//javascript
localStorage.setItem('key', 'value');
const value = localStorage.getItem('key');
```

16.4 Reading and Writing Files

File storage is a versatile way to manage unstructured data, such as logs, configuration files, or user-generated content.

Setting Up File Operations in Flutter

Add Dependencies
Use the `path_provider` package for accessing device directories.

```
#yaml
```

```
dependencies:

  path_provider: ^2.0.13
```

Read and Write Files

Write to a File:

```
//dart
import 'dart:io';
import 'package:path_provider/path_provider.dart';

Future<File> writeFile(String content) async {
  final directory = await
getApplicationDocumentsDirectory();
  final file = File('${directory.path}/example.txt');
  return file.writeAsString(content);
}
```

Read from a File:

```
//dart
Future<String> readFile() async {
  try {
    final directory = await
getApplicationDocumentsDirectory();
    final file = File('${directory.path}/example.txt');
    return await file.readAsString();
  } catch (e) {
    return 'Error reading file: $e';
  }
}
```

Comparison with File Handling in JavaScript

In JavaScript, the File System API (available in Node.js) provides similar functionality:

Write to a File:

```
//javascript
const fs = require('fs');
fs.writeFileSync('example.txt', 'Hello, world!');
```

Read from a File:

```
//javascript
const content = fs.readFileSync('example.txt', 'utf8');
```

Key Takeaways and Tips

- **Choose the Right Tool**: Use SharedPreferences for lightweight data, SQLite for structured data, and file storage for unstructured or large files.
- **Optimize Asynchronous Operations**: Ensure all storage operations in Flutter are performed asynchronously to avoid blocking the UI thread.
- **Organize Data Storage**: Separate concerns by grouping related data into logical storage systems, such as using SharedPreferences for settings and SQLite for user data.

16.5 Caching Data for Offline Use

Caching is an essential technique for improving app performance and enabling offline functionality. It allows applications to store frequently accessed or critical data locally, reducing network calls and ensuring data availability when the device is offline. Flutter provides various tools and libraries to implement efficient caching mechanisms tailored to different use cases.

The Purpose of Caching in Mobile Applications

- **Improved Performance**: By reducing the need for repetitive API calls, caching minimizes latency and enhances app responsiveness.
- **Offline Access**: Cached data ensures that users can interact with the app even when disconnected from the internet.
- **Reduced Bandwidth Usage**: Caching prevents unnecessary data transmission, conserving bandwidth, especially on metered connections.

Caching Approaches in Flutter

Key-Value Caching with SharedPreferences

SharedPreferences is suitable for lightweight caching, such as storing app settings, user preferences, or small datasets.

```
//dart
Future<void> cacheUserData(String key, String value) async
{
  final prefs = await SharedPreferences.getInstance();
  await prefs.setString(key, value);
}

Future<String?> getCachedUserData(String key) async {
  final prefs = await SharedPreferences.getInstance();
  return prefs.getString(key);
}
```

Caching API Responses with Hive

Hive is a NoSQL database known for its speed and simplicity. It is ideal for caching API responses or storing session data.

Example:

```
//dart
import 'package:hive/hive.dart';

Future<void> cacheApiResponse(String key, String data)
async {
  var box = await Hive.openBox('cacheBox');
  box.put(key, data);
}

Future<String?> getCachedApiResponse(String key) async {
  var box = await Hive.openBox('cacheBox');
  return box.get(key);
}
```

Custom Caching Using Files

File-based caching is suitable for large data or binary content, such as images or media files.

Example:

```
//dart
Future<File> cacheFile(String filename, List<int> data)
async {
  final directory = await
getApplicationDocumentsDirectory();
  final file = File('${directory.path}/$filename');
  return file.writeAsBytes(data);
}

Future<List<int>> readCachedFile(String filename) async {
  final directory = await
getApplicationDocumentsDirectory();
  final file = File('${directory.path}/$filename');
  return file.readAsBytes();
}
```

Comparison with Browser Caching

Browser Cache: Browsers cache resources like images, scripts, and stylesheets automatically to optimize page load speeds. Developers can configure caching behavior through HTTP headers.

```
//javascript
fetch('/api/data', {
  cache: 'force-cache' // Ensures data is cached
});
```

Flutter Cache: Requires explicit implementation using libraries like `SharedPreferences`, `Hive`, or file storage for fine-grained control.

16.6 Debugging Data Storage Issues

Reliable data storage is critical for app stability and functionality. Debugging storage issues involves identifying and resolving problems that arise during read/write operations or while managing stored data.

Common Data Storage Issues

1. **Data Inconsistency**: Occurs when the stored data becomes corrupt or out of sync with the source.
2. **Storage Limits**: Some storage mechanisms, such as SharedPreferences or localStorage, have size constraints.
3. **Permission Errors**: Apps may fail to access certain directories due to missing permissions.
4. **Concurrency Conflicts**: Simultaneous read/write operations can cause race conditions or data corruption.

Tools and Techniques for Debugging in Flutter

Logs and Debug Console

Use `print()` or logging libraries to inspect data at runtime.

Example:

```
//dart
final prefs = await SharedPreferences.getInstance();
print('Cached Data: ${prefs.getString('user_data')}');
```

Error Handling

Always handle exceptions gracefully to prevent app crashes.

Example://dart

```
try {
  final prefs = await SharedPreferences.getInstance();
  final data = prefs.getString('key');
  if (data == null) throw Exception('Data not found');
} catch (e) {
  print('Error: $e');
}
```

Testing Storage Paths

Use the `path_provider` plugin to verify directory paths.

```
//dart
Future<void> testStoragePath() async {

  final directory = await
```

```
getApplicationDocumentsDirectory();
  print('Documents Directory: ${directory.path}');
}
```

Debugging Storage Issues in JavaScript

JavaScript provides tools like browser developer tools for debugging localStorage, IndexedDB, and cookies. For example:

Inspect `localStorage` values:

```
//javascript
console.log(localStorage.getItem('key'));
```

Debug IndexedDB transactions:

```
//javascript


const request = indexedDB.open('myDatabase');
request.onerror = function(event) {
  console.error('Error opening database:',
event.target.errorCode);
};
```

16.7 Sample Code: Local Storage in Web and Flutter

Flutter Code: Local Data Storage Example

SharedPreferences Example:

```
//dart
import 'package:shared_preferences/
shared_preferences.dart';


Future<void> saveUserPreference(String key, String value)
async {
  final prefs = await SharedPreferences.getInstance();
  await prefs.setString(key, value);
}
```

```
Future<String?> getUserPreference(String key) async {
  final prefs = await SharedPreferences.getInstance();
  return prefs.getString(key);
}
```

SQLite Example:

```
//dart
Future<void> saveToDatabase(Database db, String name, int
age) async {

  await db.insert('users', {'name': name, 'age': age});
}

Future<List<Map<String, dynamic>>>
readFromDatabase(Database db) async {
  return await db.query('users');
}
```

Web Code: Local Data Storage Example

localStorage Example:

```
//javascript
localStorage.setItem('user', JSON.stringify({ name:
'John', age: 30 }));

const user = JSON.parse(localStorage.getItem('user'));
console.log(user.name, user.age);
```

IndexedDB Example:

```
//javascript
const dbRequest = indexedDB.open('myDatabase', 1);

dbRequest.onsuccess = function(event) {
  const db = event.target.result;
  const transaction = db.transaction('users',
'readwrite');
  const store = transaction.objectStore('users');
```

```
  store.add({ id: 1, name: 'John', age: 30 });
};
```

16.8 Comparing Browser Storage with Flutter Storage

Key Differences

Feature	Browser Storage	Flutter Storage
Mechanism	localStorage, IndexedDB, cookies	SharedPreferences, sqflite, Hive
Size Limit	Typically 5–10 MB	Varies by storage type
Data Format	JSON or key-value	JSON, relational (SQLite), binary
Offline Access	Supported	Supported

Similarities and Best Practices

1. **Asynchronous Access**:
   Both platforms provide async APIs to avoid blocking operations.
2. **Structured Data**:
   IndexedDB in the browser and SQLite in Flutter allow storing structured data with querying capabilities.
3. **Persistence**:
   Data persists across sessions unless explicitly cleared by the user.

Tips for Managing Local Data Across Platforms

- **Optimize Storage Usage**: Use compression techniques to minimize data size.
- **Implement Expiration Policies**: Clear old or unused data periodically to free up space.
- **Secure Sensitive Data**: Encrypt sensitive information before storing.

Examples

HTML and JavaScript for Local Storage

In a web application, `localStorage` is a key-value store directly accessible via

JavaScript. Here's an example of storing and retrieving user preferences:

```
<!-- html -->
<script>
  // Save data to localStorage
  localStorage.setItem('theme', 'dark');

  // Retrieve and apply the theme
  const theme = localStorage.getItem('theme');
  if (theme === 'dark') {
    document.body.style.backgroundColor = '#333';
    document.body.style.color = '#fff';
  }
</script>
```

CSS Styling Persistence via JavaScript Storage
Use JavaScript and `localStorage` to persist user-selected styles dynamically:

```
<!-- html -->
<style>
  .dark-theme {
    background-color: #333;
    color: #fff;
  }
  .light-theme {
    background-color: #fff;
    color: #000;
  }
</style>
<script>
  const theme = localStorage.getItem('theme') || 'light';
  document.body.classList.add(`${theme}-theme`);

  function toggleTheme() {
    const newTheme = theme === 'light' ? 'dark' : 'light';
    localStorage.setItem('theme', newTheme);
    location.reload();
  }
</script>
```

Flutter Using SharedPreferences for Persistent Data

Flutter's `SharedPreferences` is used to store simple key-value data like user preferences:

```
//dart
import 'package:shared_preferences/
shared_preferences.dart';

Future<void> saveThemePreference(String theme) async {
  final prefs = await SharedPreferences.getInstance();
  await prefs.setString('theme', theme);
}

Future<String?> getThemePreference() async {
  final prefs = await SharedPreferences.getInstance();
  return prefs.getString('theme');
}
```

Comparison: IndexedDB for Web vs Hive in Flutter

IndexedDB is a robust database for the browser, while Hive provides a similar experience in Flutter.

IndexedDB (JavaScript)

```
//javascript
const request = indexedDB.open('myDatabase', 1);
request.onsuccess = function(event) {
  const db = event.target.result;
  const transaction = db.transaction('preferences',
'readwrite');
  const store = transaction.objectStore('preferences');
  store.add({ key: 'theme', value: 'dark' });
};
```

Hive (Flutter)

```
//dart
import 'package:hive/hive.dart';

Future<void> saveTheme(String theme) async {
```

```
  var box = await Hive.openBox('preferences');
  box.put('theme', theme);
}

Future<String?> getTheme() async {
  var box = await Hive.openBox('preferences');
  return box.get('theme');
}
```

Tips

- For secure data storage, always encrypt sensitive information before saving it, whether in the browser or in a Flutter app. Use libraries like CryptoJS for JavaScript or encrypt packages in Flutter.
- Optimize storage performance by minimizing the frequency of writes. Batch updates when possible to reduce overhead and potential performance issues.
- Regularly clean up stale or unnecessary data to prevent storage bloat. Implement expiration policies for temporary or cache data.

Actionable Strategies

- **Implement Cross-Platform Consistency**: Use a unified data model across web and Flutter applications. For instance, adopt a JSON structure for data persistence to make it easier to share and interpret data on both platforms.

- Web Example:

```
//javascript
localStorage.setItem('user', JSON.stringify({ name:
'John', age: 30 }));
const user = JSON.parse(localStorage.getItem('user'));
```

- Flutter Example:

```
//dart
import 'dart:convert';

final user = jsonEncode({'name': 'John', 'age': 30});
await prefs.setString('user', user);
final storedUser = jsonDecode(await
prefs.getString('user')!);
```

- **Integrate Error Logging for Storage**: Develop a centralized error logging mechanism for storage-related issues. For web applications, use `console.error()` alongside error-handling libraries. For Flutter, use a logger like `Logger`.
- Example for Flutter:

```
//dart
import 'package:logger/logger.dart';

final logger = Logger();

try {
  final prefs = await SharedPreferences.getInstance();
  final theme = prefs.getString('theme');
  if (theme == null) throw Exception('Theme not found');
} catch (e) {
  logger.e('Error fetching theme', e);
}
```

- **Build Interactive UIs for Managing Data**: Allow users to manage their stored data directly within your application. Provide options for viewing, updating, or clearing preferences.
- Web Example:

```
<!-- html -->
<button onclick="clearData()">Clear Preferences</button>
<script>
  function clearData() {
    localStorage.clear();
    alert('Preferences cleared!');
  }
</script>
```

- Flutter Example:

```
//dart


ElevatedButton(
```

```
  onPressed: () async {
    final prefs = await SharedPreferences.getInstance();
    await prefs.clear();
    print('Preferences cleared');
  },
  child: Text('Clear Preferences'),
);
```

- **Adopt Indexed Data for Scalability**: Use indexed storage mechanisms like IndexedDB or Hive for large-scale, structured data. These allow efficient querying and scalability for user-driven applications like e-commerce or analytics.
- **Create Fallback Mechanisms for Storage Failures**: In case of a storage failure (e.g., quota exceeded), build a fallback mechanism to notify users or switch to an alternative storage method.
- JavaScript Example:

```
//javascript
try {
  localStorage.setItem('key', 'value');
} catch (e) {
  console.error('Storage quota exceeded', e);
  alert('Unable to save data. Consider clearing storage
space.');
}
```

Chapter 17: Theming and Custom Styles

Theming and custom styles are fundamental to creating visually cohesive and interactive user interfaces. In this chapter, we dive deeply into how Flutter allows developers to define and manage themes, customize colors and fonts, implement light and dark modes, and strike a balance between using Material Design and creating custom styles. By leveraging Flutter's flexible theming options, you can create dynamic and visually consistent applications.

17.1 Defining Themes in Flutter

Themes in Flutter are managed using the `ThemeData` class. This class allows you to centralize your application's visual styles, ensuring consistency across all widgets. Flutter provides a `Theme` widget, which acts as a wrapper for the entire application or specific sections, allowing you to define global and local themes.

Example: Global Theme Definition

```
//dart
import 'package:flutter/material.dart';

void main() {
  runApp(MyApp());
}

class MyApp extends StatelessWidget {
  @override
  Widget build(BuildContext context) {
    return MaterialApp(
      theme: ThemeData(
        primarySwatch: Colors.blue,
        accentColor: Colors.orange,
        textTheme: TextTheme(
          headline1: TextStyle(fontSize: 24, fontWeight:
FontWeight.bold),
          bodyText1: TextStyle(fontSize: 16, color:
Colors.grey[700]),
        ),
      ),
```

```
      home: HomeScreen(),
    );
  }
}

class HomeScreen extends StatelessWidget {
  @override
  Widget build(BuildContext context) {
    return Scaffold(
      appBar: AppBar(
        title: Text('Theming Example'),
      ),
      body: Center(
        child: Text(
          'Hello, Flutter!',
          style: Theme.of(context).textTheme.headline1,
        ),
      ),
    );
  }
}
```

The `ThemeData` object in the `MaterialApp` widget defines global styles, such as primary colors and typography. Widgets like `Text` and `AppBar` automatically inherit these styles when `Theme.of(context)` is used.

Comparison with HTML and CSS

In web development, themes are defined using CSS stylesheets. Unlike Flutter, where `ThemeData` is strongly typed, CSS uses selectors and rules:

```
<!-- html -->
<!DOCTYPE html>
<html lang="en">
<head>
  <style>
    body {
      font-family: Arial, sans-serif;
      background-color: #f0f0f0;
    }
    h1 {
      font-size: 24px;
```

```
      font-weight: bold;
    }
    p {
      color: #555;
      font-size: 16px;
    }
  </style>
</head>
<body>
  <h1>Hello, Web!</h1>
  <p>This is a theming example in HTML and CSS.</p>
</body>
</html>
```

In both examples, the structure for applying themes is centralized, promoting consistency.

17.2 Customizing Colors and Fonts

Customizing colors and fonts allows you to match the application's style to a specific brand identity or user preference. Flutter makes this easy with the `Color` and `TextStyle` classes.

Using Custom Colors

Colors in Flutter are defined using the `Color` class, which supports both predefined colors and custom shades using hexadecimal values.

```
//dart
ThemeData customTheme = ThemeData(
  primaryColor: Color(0xFF6200EA), // Custom Purple
  accentColor: Color(0xFFFF5722), // Deep Orange
  scaffoldBackgroundColor: Color(0xFFF5F5F5), // Light
Gray
);
```

Custom Fonts

Custom fonts can be added by including font files in your project and referencing them in the `pubspec.yaml` file.

```
//yaml
flutter:
```

```
  fonts:
    - family: Roboto
      fonts:
        - asset: fonts/Roboto-Regular.ttf
        - asset: fonts/Roboto-Bold.ttf
          weight: 700
```

Use the font family in your theme or directly in widgets:

```
//dart
ThemeData customTheme = ThemeData(
  textTheme: TextTheme(
    headline1: TextStyle(
      fontFamily: 'Roboto',
      fontSize: 32,
      fontWeight: FontWeight.bold,
      color: Colors.black,
    ),
  ),
);
```

CSS Equivalent

In CSS, colors and fonts are similarly customized using selectors:

```
/* css */
body {
  font-family: 'Roboto', sans-serif;
  background-color: #f5f5f5;
}
h1 {
  color: #6200ea;
  font-size: 32px;
  font-weight: bold;
}
```

17.3 Light and Dark Mode Implementation

Light and dark modes improve accessibility and enhance the user experience in low-light environments. Flutter's `ThemeData` supports both modes with separate configurations.

Dynamic Theme Switching

Using the `ThemeMode` property, you can toggle between light and dark themes dynamically.

```
//dart
class MyApp extends StatefulWidget {
  @override
  _MyAppState createState() => _MyAppState();
}

class _MyAppState extends State<MyApp> {
  bool isDarkMode = false;

  @override
  Widget build(BuildContext context) {
    return MaterialApp(
      theme: ThemeData.light(),
      darkTheme: ThemeData.dark(),
      themeMode: isDarkMode ? ThemeMode.dark :
ThemeMode.light,
      home: Scaffold(
        appBar: AppBar(
          title: Text('Light/Dark Mode'),
        ),
        body: Center(
          child: Switch(
            value: isDarkMode,
            onChanged: (value) {
              setState(() {
                isDarkMode = value;
              });
            },
          ),
        ),
      ),
    );
  }
}
```

CSS for Light/Dark Modes

In web development, media queries are used to define light and dark themes:

```
/* css */
body {
  color: black;
  background-color: white;
}
@media (prefers-color-scheme: dark) {
  body {
    color: white;
    background-color: black;
  }
}
```

17.4 Material Design vs Custom Styles

Material Design is Google's design system, offering predefined components and styles. While it simplifies development, custom styles can offer unique branding.

Material Design in Flutter

Flutter's Material Design widgets come with built-in theming. For example:

```
//dart
AppBar(
  title: Text('Material Design'),
  backgroundColor: Theme.of(context).primaryColor,
);
```

Custom Styles

For a completely custom UI, bypass Material Design components and use `Container`, `Text`, and other basic widgets with custom styles:

```
//dart
Container(
  padding: EdgeInsets.all(16),
  decoration: BoxDecoration(
    color: Colors.white,
    borderRadius: BorderRadius.circular(8),
    boxShadow: [
```

```
      BoxShadow(
        color: Colors.black12,
        blurRadius: 4,
        offset: Offset(2, 2),
      ),
    ],
  ),
  child: Text(
    'Custom Style',
    style: TextStyle(fontSize: 18, fontWeight:
FontWeight.bold),
  ),
);
```

CSS Comparison

Material Design principles can also be applied in web frameworks like Angular Material, while custom styles rely on CSS:

```
/* css */
.card {
  padding: 16px;
  background-color: white;
  border-radius: 8px;
  box-shadow: 2px 2px 4px rgba(0, 0, 0, 0.1);
}
```

Tips

- Use a color palette generator to define a consistent color scheme across light and dark themes. Tools like Material Design's Color Tool are helpful.
- Leverage custom fonts sparingly to ensure accessibility and readability. Test font sizes on different screen sizes.
- Apply custom styles with reusable components to minimize code duplication and improve maintainability.

17.5 Using ThemeData Effectively

The `ThemeData` class is the backbone of theming in Flutter. A well-defined `ThemeData` improves the consistency and maintainability of your app's design. Effective use of `ThemeData` involves centralizing design decisions and leveraging properties to their fullest potential.

Core Components of `ThemeData`

ColorScheme

The `ColorScheme` property provides a structured way to define primary, secondary, and other key colors.

```
//dart
ThemeData theme = ThemeData(

  colorScheme: ColorScheme.fromSwatch(
    primarySwatch: Colors.blue,
    accentColor: Colors.orange,
  ),
);
```

Typography

Custom typography can be applied through `textTheme`.

```
//dart
textTheme: TextTheme(

  headline1: TextStyle(fontSize: 32, fontWeight:
FontWeight.bold, color: Colors.black),
  bodyText1: TextStyle(fontSize: 16, color: Colors.grey),
)
```

Custom Widgets Styling

Use the `buttonTheme`, `inputDecorationTheme`, and other specific properties to style widgets globally.

```
//dart
ThemeData theme = ThemeData(

  buttonTheme: ButtonThemeData(
    shape: RoundedRectangleBorder(borderRadius:
BorderRadius.circular(8)),
    buttonColor: Colors.blue,
  ),
```

```
);
```

Tips for Effective `ThemeData` Usage

- **Centralize Themes**: Define themes in a dedicated file for reusability.
- **Utilize `Theme.of(context)`**: Access and override themes dynamically.
- **Build Contrast**: Use complementary colors for light and dark modes.

17.6 Styling Buttons, Cards, and AppBars

Flutter provides a variety of customizable widgets, each of which can be styled globally through `ThemeData` or locally using their respective properties.

Styling Buttons

Buttons, a primary form of user interaction, include `ElevatedButton`, `TextButton`, and `OutlinedButton`. All can be customized via `ButtonStyle`.

```
//dart
ElevatedButton(
  style: ElevatedButton.styleFrom(
    primary: Colors.blue, // Background color
    onPrimary: Colors.white, // Text color
    shape: RoundedRectangleBorder(
      borderRadius: BorderRadius.circular(12),
    ),
  ),
  onPressed: () => print('Button Pressed'),
  child: Text('Click Me'),
);
```

Global Button Styling

```
//dart
ThemeData theme = ThemeData(
  elevatedButtonTheme: ElevatedButtonThemeData(
    style: ElevatedButton.styleFrom(
      primary: Colors.green,
      textStyle: TextStyle(fontSize: 18),
    ),
  ),
);
```

Web Comparison

In web development, button styling relies on CSS:

```
<!-- html -->
<button class="custom-button">Click Me</button>
<style>
  .custom-button {
    background-color: blue;
    color: white;
    border-radius: 12px;
    padding: 10px 20px;
    font-size: 16px;
  }
</style>
```

Styling Cards

Cards encapsulate content with elevation and padding.

```
//dart
Card(
  elevation: 4,
  shape: RoundedRectangleBorder(borderRadius:
BorderRadius.circular(8)),
  child: Padding(
    padding: EdgeInsets.all(16),
    child: Text('This is a styled card.'),
  ),
);
```

Web Comparison

```
<!-- html -->
<div class="card">
  <p>This is a styled card.</p>
</div>
<style>
  .card {
    box-shadow: 0 2px 4px rgba(0, 0, 0, 0.1);
    padding: 16px;
    border-radius: 8px;
```

```
    background-color: #fff;
  }
</style>
```

Styling AppBars

The `AppBar` widget can be styled using `ThemeData` or directly within its properties.

```
//dart
AppBar(
  title: Text('Styled AppBar'),
  backgroundColor: Colors.teal,
  elevation: 4,
  actions: [
    IconButton(
      icon: Icon(Icons.settings),
      onPressed: () {},
    ),
  ],
);
```

CSS Equivalent

```
<!-- html -->
<div class="appbar">
  <h1>Styled AppBar</h1>
</div>
<style>
  .appbar {
    background-color: teal;
    color: white;
    padding: 10px;
    display: flex;
    justify-content: space-between;
  }
</style>
```

17.7 Debugging Theming Issues

Debugging theming issues often involves identifying conflicts between global and local styles or understanding widget behavior.

Common Issues

- **Theme Not Applied** Widgets sometimes ignore the `ThemeData` configuration. Ensure `Theme.of(context)` is used properly.

```
//dart
Text(

  'Themed Text',
  style: Theme.of(context).textTheme.bodyText1,
);
```

- **Color Contrast** Inadequate contrast between text and background colors impacts readability. Use contrast testing tools to ensure accessibility.
- **Unintended Overrides** Custom widget styles can inadvertently override global themes. Review widget properties for conflicts.

Debugging Tips

- **Use Flutter Inspector**: Identify theme properties applied to a widget.
- **Log Theme Properties**: Print `ThemeData` values to check configurations.

17.8 Sample Code: Theming in Web and Flutter

Theming in Flutter and web technologies can be compared through an example of a complete layout.

Flutter Sample

```
//dart
import 'package:flutter/material.dart';

void main() {
  runApp(MyApp());
}

class MyApp extends StatelessWidget {
  @override
  Widget build(BuildContext context) {
```

```
    return MaterialApp(
      theme: ThemeData(
        primaryColor: Colors.blue,
        textTheme: TextTheme(
          headline1: TextStyle(fontSize: 24, fontWeight:
FontWeight.bold),
        ),
      ),
      home: HomePage(),
    );
  }
}

class HomePage extends StatelessWidget {
  @override
  Widget build(BuildContext context) {
    return Scaffold(
      appBar: AppBar(
        title: Text('Theming Example', style:
Theme.of(context).textTheme.headline1),
      ),
      body: Center(
        child: ElevatedButton(
          onPressed: () {},
          child: Text('Themed Button'),
        ),
      ),
    );
  }
}
```

Web Sample

```
<!-- html -->
<!DOCTYPE html>
<html lang="en">
<head>
  <style>
    body {
      font-family: Arial, sans-serif;
      background-color: #f5f5f5;
    }
```

```
    .appbar {
      background-color: blue;
      color: white;
      padding: 10px;
    }
    .button {
      background-color: blue;
      color: white;
      border: none;
      border-radius: 5px;
      padding: 10px 20px;
    }
  </style>
</head>
<body>
  <div class="appbar">
    <h1>Theming Example</h1>
  </div>
  <div>
    <button class="button">Themed Button</button>
  </div>
</body>
</html>
```

Comparison

- **Flutter**: Styles are applied programmatically using `ThemeData`, offering type safety.
- **Web**: Styles are defined using CSS, providing flexibility but requiring manual management.

Key Tips for Theming

- Maintain a consistent color palette across components.
- Use `Theme.of(context)` to dynamically adapt styles.
- Avoid hardcoding styles; rely on `ThemeData` wherever possible.
- Test themes under different conditions (e.g., light/dark modes).

With these advanced theming strategies, your Flutter applications can achieve a professional and cohesive look.

Examples

Styling Text in Flutter and Web

Flutter:

```
//dart
Text(
  'Styled Text',
  style: TextStyle(
    fontSize: 20,
    fontWeight: FontWeight.bold,
    color: Colors.blue,
  ),
);
```

HTML/CSS:

```
<!-- html -->
<p class="styled-text">Styled Text</p>
<style>
  .styled-text {
    font-size: 20px;
    font-weight: bold;
    color: blue;
  }
</style>
```

In Flutter, text styles are encapsulated in the `TextStyle` class, applied directly to the `Text` widget, while the web uses class-based CSS for text styling.

Button Styling Comparison

Flutter:

```
//dart
ElevatedButton(
  style: ElevatedButton.styleFrom(
    backgroundColor: Colors.green,
    foregroundColor: Colors.white,
    shape: RoundedRectangleBorder(borderRadius:
BorderRadius.circular(8)),
  ),
```

```
  onPressed: () {},
  child: Text('Click Me'),
);
```

HTML/CSS:

```
<!-- html -->
<button class="custom-button">Click Me</button>
<style>
  .custom-button {
    background-color: green;
    color: white;
    border-radius: 8px;
    padding: 10px 20px;
    border: none;
  }
</style>
```

Flutter's `ElevatedButton` uses the `ButtonStyle` API for customization, while web development leverages inline or external CSS for button design.

Container vs. Div Box Shadow

Flutter:

```
//dart
Container(
  decoration: BoxDecoration(
    color: Colors.white,
    boxShadow: [
      BoxShadow(
        color: Colors.grey.withOpacity(0.5),
        spreadRadius: 5,
        blurRadius: 7,
        offset: Offset(0, 3),
      ),
    ],
  ),
  child: Text('Shadowed Box'),
);
```

HTML/CSS:

```
<!-- html -->
<div class="shadowed-box">Shadowed Box</div>
<style>
  .shadowed-box {
    background-color: white;
    box-shadow: 0 3px 7px rgba(128, 128, 128, 0.5);
    padding: 10px;
  }
</style>
```

The `BoxDecoration` class in Flutter is analogous to CSS's `box-shadow` property but requires manual configuration of each aspect of the shadow.

Gradient Background

Flutter:

```
//dart
Container(
  decoration: BoxDecoration(
    gradient: LinearGradient(
      colors: [Colors.blue, Colors.purple],
      begin: Alignment.topLeft,
      end: Alignment.bottomRight,
    ),
  ),
);
```

HTML/CSS:

```
<!-- html -->
<div class="gradient-bg"></div>
<style>
  .gradient-bg {
    background: linear-gradient(to bottom right, blue,
purple);
    width: 100%;
```

```
    height: 100vh;
  }
</style>
```

Flutter and CSS both support gradient backgrounds, but Flutter's approach uses `LinearGradient` and aligns it to the layout direction.

Tips

- **Use Global Themes for Consistency**
  Centralize styling in Flutter using `ThemeData` and in the web through CSS variables. This reduces redundancy and ensures consistent updates.
- **Test in Light and Dark Modes**
  Create adaptable designs by testing light and dark themes early. Flutter's `ThemeMode` and CSS media queries (e.g., `@media (prefers-color-scheme: dark)`) enable seamless transitions.
- **Optimize for Accessibility**
  Ensure sufficient contrast between text and backgrounds using tools like `WCAG` for web and Flutter's `HighContrastTheme`.

Actionable Strategies

- **Build Reusable Theme Components**
  Create reusable `ThemeData` configurations in Flutter, similar to defining reusable CSS classes for multiple elements in web development. For example, define a `ButtonThemeData` globally for all buttons.
- **Leverage Platform-Specific Features**
  Use platform-specific theming, such as Material Design for Flutter and frameworks like Tailwind CSS for web styling. Tailor designs based on user expectations and platform standards.
- **Combine Dynamic and Static Styling**
  Blend static styles with runtime configurations. Flutter allows widget-specific themes (e.g., `Theme.of(context)`) while CSS supports inline styles alongside global stylesheets.
- **Adopt Component-Based Architecture**
  Flutter widgets inherently follow this pattern. In web development, use

frameworks like React with CSS Modules or Styled Components to encapsulate styles.

- **Debug Styling with Visual Tools**
  In Flutter, use the Widget Inspector to analyze themes. On the web, use browser developer tools to inspect and modify styles in real-time.

Chapter 18: Deploying Flutter Apps

18.1 Building for Mobile, Web, and Desktop

Flutter offers the flexibility to deploy applications across mobile, web, and desktop platforms using a unified codebase. This reduces development time and ensures consistent user experiences. Each platform has specific build requirements and configurations to optimize performance and usability.

Building for Mobile (Android and iOS)

When building for mobile, Flutter compiles the Dart code into native ARM machine code. This ensures high performance, as the application runs directly on the device without any intermediary interpretation.

Steps for Android Builds

Prepare the Android Manifest
Update the `AndroidManifest.xml` file to ensure proper permissions and configurations for your app. For example:

```
<!-- xml -->
<manifest xmlns:android="http://schemas.android.com/apk/
res/android"

    package="com.example.flutter_app">
    <uses-permission
android:name="android.permission.INTERNET" />
    <application
        android:label="Flutter App"
        android:icon="@mipmap/ic_launcher">
        <activity
            android:name=".MainActivity"
            android:exported="true"
            android:launchMode="singleTop">
            <intent-filter>
                <action
android:name="android.intent.action.MAIN" />
                <category
android:name="android.intent.category.LAUNCHER" />
```

```
            </intent-filter>
        </activity>
    </application>
</manifest>
```

Generate a Release Keystore

A keystore is required for signing the APK. Use the following command to create one:

```
# bash
keytool -genkey -v -keystore release-key.jks -keyalg RSA
-keysize 2048 -validity 10000 -alias release-key
```

Add the Keystore to the Gradle Configuration

Update the `android/app/build.gradle` file with the keystore details:

```
// gradle
android {

    signingConfigs {
        release {
            keyAlias 'release-key'
            keyPassword 'your-key-password'
            storeFile file('release-key.jks')
            storePassword 'your-store-password'
        }
    }
    buildTypes {
        release {
            signingConfig signingConfigs.release
        }
    }
}
```

Build the APK

Run the following command to generate a release APK:

```
# bash
flutter build apk --release
```

Steps for iOS Builds

Building for iOS requires a macOS environment with Xcode installed.

Update the Info.plist
Configure the `Info.plist` file for app settings such as permissions and metadata:

```
<!-- xml -->
<key>NSAppTransportSecurity</key>

<dict>
    <key>NSAllowsArbitraryLoads</key>
    <true/>
</dict>
```

Configure Signing and Capabilities
Use Xcode to set the development team, bundle identifier, and signing certificates.

Build the iOS App
Run the following command:

```
# bash
flutter build ios --release
```

Building for Web

Flutter's web support compiles Dart code into HTML, CSS, and JavaScript.

Enable Web Support
Ensure web support is enabled in your Flutter installation:

```
# bash
flutter channel stable

flutter upgrade
flutter config --enable-web
```

Generate the Web Build

Use the command:

```
# bash
flutter build web
```

The output is placed in the `build/web` directory.

Optimize for Production

1. Use `--release` to minimize the build size.
2. Ensure your app uses tree-shaking to remove unused code.

Building for Desktop

Flutter supports desktop builds for Windows, macOS, and Linux.

Enable Desktop Support
Run:

```
# bash
flutter config --enable-windows-desktop --enable-macos-
desktop --enable-linux-desktop
```

Build for Specific Platforms
For Windows:

```
# bash
flutter build windows
```

For macOS:

```
# bash
flutter build macos
```

For Linux:

```
# bash
flutter build linux
```

18.2 Creating APKs and Web Builds

Generating APKs and web builds involves creating distributable files for Android and web platforms. APKs are Android application packages, while web builds are optimized for browser deployment.

APK Variants

Flutter supports two APK types:

Fat APK: Contains binaries for all architectures but is larger in size.

```
# bash
flutter build apk --release
```

Split APK: Generates separate APKs for different architectures.

```
# bash
flutter build apk --split-per-abi
```

Web Deployment Steps

1. Generate the web build.
2. Upload the contents of `build/web` to a web hosting service like Firebase Hosting or AWS S3.

Example Firebase Hosting Configuration

```
# bash
firebase init
firebase deploy
```

18.3 Setting Up CI/CD Pipelines

CI/CD automates building, testing, and deploying Flutter applications. Tools like GitHub Actions, GitLab CI, and Jenkins are popular choices.

Sample GitHub Actions Workflow for Flutter

```
//yaml
```

```yaml
name: Flutter CI/CD

on:
  push:
    branches:
      - main

jobs:
  build:
    runs-on: ubuntu-latest

    steps:
      - uses: actions/checkout@v3
      - uses: subosito/flutter-action@v2
        with:
          flutter-version: 'stable'

      - name: Install Dependencies
        run: flutter pub get

      - name: Run Tests
        run: flutter test

      - name: Build APK
        run: flutter build apk --release
```

Benefits of CI/CD

- Reduces manual intervention.
- Ensures code quality with automated testing.
- Speeds up deployment cycles.

18.4 Hosting Web Apps on Firebase or AWS

Web apps built with Flutter can be hosted on Firebase Hosting or AWS S3.

Firebase Hosting

Install Firebase CLI

```
# bash
```

```
npm install -g firebase-tools
```

Initialize Firebase Hosting

```
# bash
firebase init hosting
```

Deploy the Web Build

```
# bash
firebase deploy
```

AWS S3 Hosting

Upload to an S3 Bucket
Use the AWS CLI:

```
# bash
aws s3 sync build/web s3://your-bucket-name --acl public-
read
```

Configure the S3 Bucket for Static Hosting
Enable static website hosting in the S3 settings.

Highlighted Code Tips

- Use `flutter build` commands with appropriate flags (`--release`, `--split-per-abi`) to generate optimized builds.
- Maintain separate build configurations for development and production environments.
- Use `.env` files to manage sensitive keys and configuration variables across environments.

18.5 Debugging Build Errors

Debugging build errors in Flutter requires a structured approach to identify, diagnose, and resolve issues. Build errors can occur during development, testing, or deployment. Common causes include misconfigured files, outdated dependencies, platform-specific issues, or code incompatibilities.

1. Understanding Build Error Messages

Build error messages provide key insights into what went wrong. A typical error includes:

- A **description** of the problem.
- The **file path** where the error occurred.
- **Stack traces** pointing to the source of the issue.

Example Error Message

```
# bash
FAILURE: Build failed with an exception.

* What went wrong:
Execution failed for task
':app:compileFlutterBuildRelease'.
> A problem occurred configuring project ':app'.
```

This error indicates a problem during the build configuration process.

2. Common Build Errors and Fixes

Dependency Version Conflicts

This occurs when libraries have incompatible versions. Fix this by resolving dependencies in the `pubspec.yaml` file:

```
//yaml
dependencies:
  flutter:
    sdk: flutter
  http: ^0.15.0
```

Run `flutter pub get` to fetch compatible versions.

Android Build Issues

Errors in the Gradle configuration often arise when upgrading Flutter or Android SDK versions. Check `android/build.gradle` and ensure compatibility:

```
// gradle
buildscript {
    ext.kotlin_version = '1.8.0'
```

```
    repositories {
        google()
        mavenCentral()
    }
}
```

iOS Build Errors
Issues can occur due to mismatched provisioning profiles or CocoaPods errors. Update CocoaPods and ensure all dependencies are installed:

```
# bash
pod install --repo-update
```

3. Debugging Tools and Techniques

- **Flutter Doctor**: Run `flutter doctor` to identify and fix environment setup issues.
- **Verbose Logs**: Use `flutter build apk --verbose` for detailed logs.
- **Testing on Multiple Platforms**: Ensure the app builds successfully on both Android and iOS simulators.

18.6 Optimizing Apps for Performance

Optimizing Flutter apps ensures smooth and responsive user experiences. Performance bottlenecks can stem from inefficient code, heavy assets, or unoptimized widgets.

1. Reducing Widget Rebuilds

Flutter's widget tree structure can cause unnecessary rebuilds. Use `const` widgets to reduce rebuild overhead:

```
//dart
class MyApp extends StatelessWidget {
  @override
  Widget build(BuildContext context) {
    return const Text('Optimized Widget');
  }
}
```

2. Leveraging Lazy Loading

Lazy loading minimizes memory usage by loading assets or data only when required.

For example, use `ListView.builder` for large lists:

```
//dart
ListView.builder(
  itemCount: 1000,
  itemBuilder: (context, index) {
    return ListTile(title: Text('Item $index'));
  },
);
```

3. Compressing Images

Large images slow down performance. Use plugins like `flutter_image_compress` to optimize image sizes:

```
//dart
import 'package:flutter_image_compress/
flutter_image_compress.dart';

Future<Uint8List?> compressImage(File file) async {
  return await FlutterImageCompress.compressWithFile(
    file.absolute.path,
    quality: 80,
  );
}
```

4. Optimizing Animations

Use Flutter's built-in `ImplicitlyAnimatedWidgets` to simplify animation rendering:

```
//dart
AnimatedOpacity(
  opacity: _visible ? 1.0 : 0.0,
  duration: const Duration(seconds: 2),
  child: const Text("Hello, World!"),
);
```

18.7 Sample Deployment Process Comparison

Flutter's deployment capabilities span multiple platforms, each with unique steps and requirements. Comparing these processes helps in understanding platform-specific nuances.

Mobile Deployment (Android and iOS)

Step	Android	iOS
Build Command	`flutter build apk`	`flutter build ios`
Signing	Keystore	Provisioning Profile
Store Upload	Google Play Console	App Store Connect
Testing Environment	Android Emulator	iOS Simulator

Web Deployment

Process for Firebase Hosting

Build the web app:

```
# bash
flutter build web
```

Deploy using Firebase CLI:

```
# bash
firebase deploy
```

Process for AWS S3 Hosting

Configure S3 bucket for static hosting.
Upload `build/web` contents:

```
# bash
aws s3 sync build/web s3://your-bucket
```

18.8 Tips for Seamless Flutter Deployments

Ensuring a smooth deployment process involves following best practices and anticipating potential pitfalls.

- **Test Thoroughly**: Use emulators and real devices to test your app across platforms.
- **Monitor Dependencies**: Keep libraries updated and ensure compatibility with your Flutter version.
- **Configure Properly**: Double-check build configurations in `pubspec.yaml`, Gradle, and Xcode settings.
- **Automate Deployments**: Use CI/CD pipelines to automate building and deployment processes.
- **Minimize Asset Size**: Compress images and assets to reduce app size and improve loading times.

Highlighted Tips

- Use `flutter clean` before builds to remove cached files and prevent conflicts.
- Always sign APKs and iOS builds to avoid deployment rejections.
- Regularly backup your `keystore` and `provisioning profile` files to avoid loss.

Examples

Building an Android APK
Open your terminal and run the command below to build a release APK:

```
# bash
flutter build apk --release
```

Once the process completes, locate the APK file in the `build/app/outputs/flutter-apk/` directory. This file can be installed on Android devices or uploaded to the Google Play Store.

Deploying a Web App to Firebase Hosting
First, build the web project:

```
# bash
flutter build web
```

Initialize Firebase Hosting:

```
# bash
firebase init hosting
```

Then deploy the app:

```
# bash
firebase deploy
```

Creating a CI/CD Pipeline with GitHub Actions

Use the `.github/workflows/flutter.yml` configuration file:

```
#yaml

name: Flutter CI/CD


on:
  push:
    branches:
      - main

jobs:
  build:
    runs-on: ubuntu-latest

    steps:
    - uses: actions/checkout@v2
    - uses: subosito/flutter-action@v2
      with:
        flutter-version: 'stable'
    - run: flutter build apk --release
```

This setup builds your app on every push to the `main` branch.

Deploying an iOS App

Ensure that you've set up your signing certificates and provisioning profiles in Xcode.

Build the iOS app with the following command:

```
# bash
flutter build ios --release
```

Open the project in Xcode, archive the build, and upload it to App Store Connect for distribution.

Tips

- Always test your app on real devices for both Android and iOS to identify platform-specific issues that might not appear on simulators or emulators.
- Optimize your app size by removing unused assets, libraries, and dependencies. Tools like `flutter analyze` can help identify unnecessary elements.
- Ensure you have proper environment variables set for your CI/CD pipelines to manage sensitive information like API keys and signing credentials securely.

Actionable Strategies

Integrate Automated Testing in CI/CD
Add test execution to your pipeline to ensure that code changes don't introduce bugs. For instance, include a step in your CI configuration:

```
#yaml
- run: flutter test
```

Use Platform-Specific Features
Customize your app for each platform by using conditional imports or directives to provide a better user experience. For example:

```
//dart
if (Platform.isAndroid) {

  // Android-specific code
} else if (Platform.isIOS) {
  // iOS-specific code
}
```

Leverage Lazy Loading for Assets
Reduce initial load times by loading assets only when needed. For instance, use:

```
//dart
AssetImage('assets/images/example.jpg')
```

Set Up Firebase Crashlytics for Debugging
Add the `firebase_crashlytics` plugin to monitor and debug issues in real-time:

```
#yaml
dependencies:

  firebase_crashlytics: ^3.0.0
```

Document Your Deployment Process
Create comprehensive documentation for your deployment workflow, including commands, configurations, and troubleshooting steps. This helps onboard new team members and reduces errors.

Chapter 19: Debugging and Testing

19.1 Debugging Widgets and Layouts

Debugging widgets and layouts is an essential part of Flutter development. Flutter provides powerful tools and techniques to identify and resolve layout or widget issues efficiently. Developers can use features like `debugPrint`, the `debugPaintSizeEnabled` flag, and layout inspection tools to refine their UI and resolve issues effectively.

Common Issues in Widgets and Layouts:

Overflow Errors: These occur when the widget's size exceeds its parent container.

Example: A `Text` widget with too much content may throw an overflow error.

```
//dart
Container(

  width: 100,
  child: Text('This is a very long text that will
overflow.'),
);
```

Solution: Use the `overflow` property or wrap the text with `Flexible` or `Expanded`:

```
//dart
Container(

  width: 100,
  child: Text(
    'This is a very long text that will overflow.',
    overflow: TextOverflow.ellipsis,
  ),
);
```

Misaligned Widgets: These occur when child widgets are not positioned as intended.

- Solution: Wrap widgets with alignment containers like `Center` or `Align`.

Performance Bottlenecks: Caused by excessive widget rebuilds.

- Solution: Use `const` constructors where possible and `RepaintBoundary` to isolate rebuilds.

Using Debug Flags and Tools:

`debugPaintSizeEnabled`: Highlights the layout boundaries of widgets.

```
//dart
debugPaintSizeEnabled = true;
```

`debugPrint`: Logs custom debug information to the console for identifying issues in widget trees.

```
//dart
debugPrint('Widget State: ${widget.key}');
```

Comparison to HTML/CSS/JavaScript Debugging:

- In **HTML**, debugging layout issues typically involves inspecting elements in the browser's developer tools, adjusting CSS properties, and observing changes live.
- In **Flutter**, the equivalent is the `Flutter Inspector` in DevTools, which provides a visual representation of the widget tree.

Example: HTML Code:

```
<!-- html -->
<div style="width: 100px; overflow: hidden;">
  <p>This is a long paragraph that will overflow.</p>
</div>
```

Flutter Equivalent:

```
//dart
Container(
  width: 100,
  child: Text(
    'This is a long paragraph that will overflow.',
    overflow: TextOverflow.clip,
  ),
);
```

19.2 Using Flutter DevTools

Flutter DevTools is a robust suite designed to inspect and debug Flutter applications. It offers tools to monitor app performance, analyze layout structure, and track runtime issues.

Key Features of DevTools:

Widget Inspector:

- Visualizes the widget tree, allowing developers to inspect widget properties and layout constraints.
- Interactive: Clicking on a widget highlights its corresponding area in the app.

Performance View:

- Tracks app performance metrics like frame rendering times and identifies slow frames.
- Developers can enable the `performance overlay` to debug rendering bottlenecks:

```
//dart
debugShowPerformanceOverlay = true;
```

Memory View:

Monitors memory usage, garbage collection, and potential leaks.

Network View:

Displays HTTP requests made by the app, including headers and payloads.

Using DevTools in Practice:

Inspect a Widget:

- Run your app in debug mode.
- Open DevTools by typing `flutter pub global run devtools` in the terminal.
- Navigate to the `Widget Inspector` tab and interact with widgets.

Analyze Performance: Use the timeline view to monitor rendering performance and optimize animations or large widget trees.

Comparison with Browser DevTools:

In **HTML/CSS/JavaScript**, browser DevTools allows direct editing of CSS styles and DOM structures. Flutter DevTools, while similar in purpose, focuses more on widget tree hierarchy and state management.

19.3 Writing Unit Tests in Flutter

Unit testing ensures individual components of an application function correctly. In Flutter, the `test` package provides tools to write comprehensive unit tests for various features.

Creating a Simple Unit Test:

Add the `test` dependency:

```
#yaml
dev_dependencies:

  test: ^1.20.1
```

Write a test for a simple Dart function:

```
//dart
```

```
int add(int a, int b) => a + b;


void main() {
  test('Addition test', () {
    expect(add(2, 3), 5);
  });
}
```

Run tests using:

```
# bash
flutter test
```

Advanced Testing: Mocking and Dependency Injection

Mocking allows developers to isolate units of code by simulating external dependencies. For example:

```
//dart
class MockService extends Mock implements RealService {}

void main() {
  final service = MockService();

  when(service.fetchData()).thenReturn('Mocked Data');

  test('Fetch Data Test', () {
    expect(service.fetchData(), 'Mocked Data');
  });
}
```

Comparison with JavaScript Testing:

- In **JavaScript**, frameworks like Jest or Mocha are used for unit testing, often paired with libraries like Sinon for mocking.
- A similar unit test in Jest:

```
//javascript
function add(a, b) {
```

```
  return a + b;
}

test('Addition test', () => {
  expect(add(2, 3)).toBe(5);
});
```

19.4 Testing UI Interactions

Testing user interfaces ensures the app behaves correctly during user interactions. Flutter uses the `flutter_test` package to simulate and validate UI behavior.

Writing a Basic Widget Test:

Add `flutter_test` dependency:

```
#yaml
dev_dependencies:

  flutter_test:
    sdk: flutter
```

Test a button interaction:

```
//dart
void main() {

  testWidgets('Button interaction test', (WidgetTester
tester) async {
    await tester.pumpWidget(MyApp());

    expect(find.text('Click Me'), findsOneWidget);

    await tester.tap(find.text('Click Me'));
    await tester.pump();

    expect(find.text('Clicked!'), findsOneWidget);
  });
}
```

Tips for Effective UI Testing:

- Use `pumpAndSettle` to handle animations or delayed interactions.
- Test accessibility features by verifying `Semantics` widgets.

Comparison with Web Testing:

In web development, libraries like Selenium or Puppeteer simulate user interactions:

```
//javascript
await page.click('button#submit');
const text = await page.$eval('h1', el => el.textContent);
expect(text).toBe('Clicked!');
```

Flutter achieves similar results through the `WidgetTester` class, which simplifies simulating user actions like taps or scrolls.

19.5 Mocking Network Calls for Testing

Mocking network calls is an integral part of testing applications, as it allows developers to simulate external API responses without making actual network requests. This ensures tests are predictable, fast, and isolated from external systems.

Why Mocking is Essential:

1. **Isolation of Logic:** Allows developers to test the app's behavior without relying on live API endpoints.
2. **Consistency in Testing:** Mocked responses eliminate issues caused by API downtime or network fluctuations.
3. **Performance Gains:** Mocked APIs execute faster than real network requests.

Mocking Network Calls in Flutter:

The `http` package is widely used for handling network requests in Flutter. Mocking network calls in Flutter typically involves using the `mockito` or `http_mock_adapter` packages.

Example Using `http_mock_adapter`:

```
//dart
import 'package:http/http.dart' as http;
```

```
import 'package:http_mock_adapter/http_mock_adapter.dart';

void main() {
  final dio = Dio();
  final dioAdapter = DioAdapter(dio: dio);

  dioAdapter.onGet('/users', (request) {
    return request.reply(200, [
      {'id': 1, 'name': 'John Doe'},
    ]);
  });

  test('Fetch users mock API test', () async {
    final response = await dio.get('/users');
    expect(response.statusCode, 200);
    expect(response.data, isNotEmpty);
  });
}
```

Comparison with JavaScript:

In JavaScript, libraries like Jest and Axios-mock-adapter are used for mocking network calls.

Mocking in Jest with Axios:

```
//javascript
const axios = require('axios');
jest.mock('axios');

test('Fetch users mock API test', async () => {
  axios.get.mockResolvedValue({ data: [{ id: 1, name:
'John Doe' }] });

  const response = await axios.get('/users');
  expect(response.data).toHaveLength(1);
});
```

Flutter achieves similar functionality using mock libraries to intercept and return predefined responses.

Tips for Mocking:

- Use dependency injection to pass mock clients into your app.
- Always test edge cases, such as network errors or timeouts.
- Separate mock data into reusable files for better maintainability.

19.6 Debugging State Management Issues

State management is central to Flutter applications, and debugging state-related problems ensures smooth app behavior. Common issues include unexpected state changes, improper updates, and performance bottlenecks.

Identifying State Management Issues:

1. **Overlapping States:** This occurs when multiple widgets share a state and cause conflicts.
2. **State Not Updating:** Widgets fail to rebuild even when state changes.
3. **Performance Degradation:** Caused by unnecessary rebuilds of widgets.

Debugging Strategies:

Logging State Transitions: Use `print` or logging libraries to track state changes:

```
//dart
print('Current state: $currentState');
```

Using Flutter DevTools:

- Monitor state variables in real-time.
- Inspect widget rebuilds and optimize.

Breakpoints: Set breakpoints in the state management logic to observe runtime values.

Common State Management Approaches:

- **Provider:** Tracks state changes efficiently with `ChangeNotifier`.

Debug with `notifyListeners` to observe updates:`//dart`

```
class Counter with ChangeNotifier {
  int _count = 0;

  int get count => _count;

  void increment() {
    _count++;
    notifyListeners();
  }
}
```

- **Riverpod:** Simplifies debugging with scoped providers.
- **Bloc/Cubit:** Provides well-defined state transitions.

Comparison to JavaScript State Management:

In React, state management debugging often involves using Redux DevTools or logging state in React components:

```
//javascript
const [count, setCount] = useState(0);

console.log('Current count:', count);
```

Flutter offers similar debugging capabilities through DevTools and state inspection methods.

19.7 Sample Code: Testing in React Native vs Flutter

Testing frameworks differ between Flutter and React Native, yet both focus on ensuring reliability and performance. Below are examples comparing the two platforms.

Unit Testing:

Flutter Example:

```
//dart
int add(int a, int b) => a + b;

void main() {
  test('Addition Test', () {
    expect(add(2, 3), 5);
  });
}
```

React Native Example (Jest):

```
//javascript
function add(a, b) {

  return a + b;
}

test('Addition Test', () => {
  expect(add(2, 3)).toBe(5);
});
```

Widget Testing:

Flutter:

```
//dart
testWidgets('Button tap test', (WidgetTester tester) async
{

  await tester.pumpWidget(MaterialApp(home: MyWidget()));

  expect(find.text('Tap Me'), findsOneWidget);

  await tester.tap(find.text('Tap Me'));
  await tester.pump();

  expect(find.text('Tapped!'), findsOneWidget);
});
```

- **React Native:**

```
//javascript
import { render, fireEvent } from '@testing-library/react-native';

import MyComponent from './MyComponent';

test('Button tap test', () => {
  const { getByText } = render(<MyComponent />);
  const button = getByText('Tap Me');

  fireEvent.press(button);
  expect(getByText('Tapped!')).toBeTruthy();
});
```

Both examples validate UI interactions, demonstrating similar workflows.

19.8 Automating Tests for Continuous Integration

Automation is key to maintaining code quality during continuous integration (CI). CI pipelines execute tests automatically on every code commit, ensuring the application remains robust.

Setting Up CI for Flutter Apps:

Choose a CI Tool: Popular options include GitHub Actions, Travis CI, and Jenkins.
Create a Workflow File: Define steps to install Flutter, fetch dependencies, and run tests.
GitHub Actions Example:

```
#yaml
name: Flutter CI

on:
  push:
    branches:
      - main
```

```yaml
jobs:
  build:
    runs-on: ubuntu-latest

    steps:
      - uses: actions/checkout@v2
      - name: Set up Flutter
        uses: subosito/flutter-action@v2
        with:
          flutter-version: '3.3.0'
      - run: flutter pub get
      - run: flutter test
```

Best Practices:

- Configure code coverage tools to track test effectiveness.
- Set up parallel testing for faster execution.
- Use CI notifications to alert teams about failures.

Comparison to React Native CI:

React Native CI with GitHub Actions:

```yaml
#yaml
name: React Native CI

on:
  push:
    branches:
      - main

jobs:
  build:
    runs-on: ubuntu-latest

    steps:
      - uses: actions/checkout@v2
      - name: Install Node.js
        uses: actions/setup-node@v2
        with:
          node-version: '16.x'
```

```
    - run: npm install
    - run: npm test
```

Both workflows automate test execution and provide reports to developers.

Benefits of Test Automation in CI:

- Reduces manual effort in testing.
- Speeds up deployment cycles.
- Improves code reliability and reduces bugs in production.

Flutter's powerful testing capabilities, combined with automation tools, ensure seamless development workflows, making apps more reliable and maintainable across their lifecycle.

Chapter 20: Advanced Flutter Concepts

20.1 Dependency Injection in Flutter

Dependency Injection (DI) is a design pattern that helps manage dependencies and make the application more modular, scalable, and testable. In Flutter, DI is often used to manage and provide objects like repositories, services, and controllers to the parts of the app that need them.

Why Dependency Injection is Important:

1. **Modularity:** Encourages separation of concerns by decoupling object creation from the business logic.
2. **Testability:** Makes it easier to mock dependencies during testing.
3. **Reusability:** Reduces redundancy and allows multiple parts of the app to use the same instance of a service or repository.

Implementing Dependency Injection:

One common way to implement DI in Flutter is through the `provider` package. Below is an example of setting up DI for a simple app:

Example with `Provider`:

```
//dart
import 'package:flutter/material.dart';
import 'package:provider/provider.dart';

class CounterService {
  int _count = 0;

  int get count => _count;

  void increment() {
    _count++;
  }
}

void main() {
  runApp(
```

```
    MultiProvider(
      providers: [
        Provider(create: (_) => CounterService()),
      ],
      child: MyApp(),
    ),
  );
}

class MyApp extends StatelessWidget {
  @override
  Widget build(BuildContext context) {
    return MaterialApp(
      home: CounterScreen(),
    );
  }
}

class CounterScreen extends StatelessWidget {
  @override
  Widget build(BuildContext context) {
    final counterService =
Provider.of<CounterService>(context);

    return Scaffold(
      appBar: AppBar(title: Text('Dependency Injection
Example')),
      body: Center(
        child: Column(
          mainAxisAlignment: MainAxisAlignment.center,
          children: [
            Text('Count: ${counterService.count}'),
            ElevatedButton(
              onPressed: counterService.increment,
              child: Text('Increment'),
            ),
          ],
        ),
      ),
    );
  }
}
```

Comparison with JavaScript:

In JavaScript, DI is often implemented using services or context providers in frameworks like React:

- **React Example:**

```
//javascript
import React, { createContext, useContext, useState } from
'react';

const CounterContext = createContext();

function CounterProvider({ children }) {
  const [count, setCount] = useState(0);

  const increment = () => setCount((prev) => prev + 1);

  return (
    <CounterContext.Provider value={{ count, increment }}>
      {children}
    </CounterContext.Provider>
  );
}

function CounterDisplay() {
  const { count, increment } = useContext(CounterContext);

  return (
    <div>
      <p>Count: {count}</p>
      <button onClick={increment}>Increment</button>
    </div>
  );
}

export default function App() {
  return (
    <CounterProvider>
      <CounterDisplay />
    </CounterProvider>
```

```
  );
}
```

Both approaches use providers to inject and manage dependencies efficiently across the app.

20.2 Understanding Isolates and Background Tasks

In Flutter, Isolates provide a way to run expensive computations or tasks in parallel without blocking the main thread. Unlike threads, isolates do not share memory, ensuring safe concurrent execution.

How Isolates Work:

- **Independent Memory:** Each isolate has its memory, so data sharing requires explicit message passing.
- **Communication via Ports:** Isolates use `ReceivePort` and `SendPort` for communication.

Creating and Managing Isolates:

Basic Isolate Example:

```
//dart
import 'dart:isolate';

void isolateTask(SendPort sendPort) {
  int result = 0;
  for (int i = 0; i < 1000000; i++) {
    result += i;
  }
  sendPort.send(result);
}

void main() async {
  final receivePort = ReceivePort();

  await Isolate.spawn(isolateTask, receivePort.sendPort);

  receivePort.listen((message) {
```

```
    print('Result from isolate: $message');
  });
}
```

Using Flutter's Compute Function:

For simpler use cases, Flutter provides the `compute` function as a wrapper around Isolates:

Example Using Compute:

```
//dart
import 'package:flutter/foundation.dart';

int sumUpTo(int limit) {
  int sum = 0;
  for (int i = 0; i < limit; i++) {
    sum += i;
  }
  return sum;
}

void main() async {
  final result = await compute(sumUpTo, 1000000);
  print('Result: $result');
}
```

Comparison with JavaScript Web Workers:

In JavaScript, Web Workers provide similar functionality to Isolates for running background tasks:

- **Web Worker Example:**

```
//javascript

// worker.js
self.onmessage = function (e) {
  let sum = 0;
  for (let i = 0; i < e.data; i++) {
    sum += i;
  }
```

```
  postMessage(sum);
};

// main.js
const worker = new Worker('worker.js');
worker.postMessage(1000000);
worker.onmessage = (e) => console.log(`Result: ${e.data}
`);
```

Both use message-passing mechanisms for communication and avoid blocking the main thread.

20.3 Advanced Animations with CustomPainters

Animations in Flutter become highly customizable with the `CustomPainter` class, which allows developers to draw complex shapes and implement custom animation logic.

Creating a CustomPainter:

The `CustomPainter` class is used to define how a widget should paint on the canvas:

Basic CustomPainter Example:

```
//dart
import 'package:flutter/material.dart';

class CirclePainter extends CustomPainter {
  @override
  void paint(Canvas canvas, Size size) {
    final paint = Paint()
      ..color = Colors.blue
      ..style = PaintingStyle.fill;

    canvas.drawCircle(Offset(size.width / 2, size.height /
2), 50, paint);
  }
```

```
  @override
  bool shouldRepaint(covariant CustomPainter oldDelegate)
=> false;
}

void main() {
  runApp(MaterialApp(
    home: Scaffold(
      body: CustomPaint(
        size: Size(200, 200),
        painter: CirclePainter(),
      ),
    ),
  ));
}
```

Animating with CustomPainter:

Animations can be added to `CustomPainter` by combining it with `AnimationController` and `StatefulWidget`:

Example of Animated Circle:

```
//dart
class AnimatedCircle extends StatefulWidget {
  @override
  _AnimatedCircleState createState() =>
_AnimatedCircleState();
}

class _AnimatedCircleState extends State<AnimatedCircle>
    with SingleTickerProviderStateMixin {
  late AnimationController _controller;

  @override
  void initState() {
    super.initState();
    _controller =
        AnimationController(vsync: this, duration:
Duration(seconds: 2))
          ..repeat();
  }
```

```
  @override
  Widget build(BuildContext context) {
    return CustomPaint(
      painter: CirclePainter(progress: _controller.value),
    );
  }

  @override
  void dispose() {
    _controller.dispose();
    super.dispose();
  }
}

class CirclePainter extends CustomPainter {
  final double progress;

  CirclePainter({required this.progress});

  @override
  void paint(Canvas canvas, Size size) {
    final paint = Paint()
      ..color = Colors.blue
      ..style = PaintingStyle.fill;

    final radius = 50 + (50 * progress);

    canvas.drawCircle(Offset(size.width / 2, size.height /
2), radius, paint);
  }

  @override
  bool shouldRepaint(covariant CustomPainter oldDelegate)
=> true;
}
```

Comparison with CSS and JavaScript:

Animating shapes in CSS often uses SVG or Canvas:

CSS Example:

```
/* css */
@keyframes pulse {
  0% { r: 50; }
  100% { r: 100; }
}

circle {
  animation: pulse 2s infinite;
}
```

CustomPainter in Flutter provides more control than CSS or JavaScript Canvas, making it suitable for complex animations.

20.4 Building Plugins and Packages

Flutter plugins extend the app's functionality by providing access to platform-specific features. Packages, on the other hand, are reusable libraries for sharing functionality across apps.

Creating a Flutter Plugin:

- **Setup:** Use `flutter create --template=plugin` to create a plugin template.
- **Implement Native Code:** Add platform-specific logic in `android` and `ios` folders.
- **Expose APIs to Flutter:** Use platform channels for communication.

Example Platform Channel:

```
//dart
const platform = MethodChannel('example.com/native');

Future<String> getNativeMessage() async {
  try {
    final String result = await
platform.invokeMethod('getMessage');
    return result;
  } on PlatformException catch (e) {
    return 'Failed to get message: ${e.message}';
  }
```

```
}
```

20.5 Platform Channels for Native Features

Flutter apps often need to interact with native platform APIs or hardware that isn't supported directly out of the box. **Platform Channels** serve as the bridge for Flutter to communicate with native code written in **Kotlin/Java** (for Android) or **Swift/Objective-C** (for iOS). This section breaks down how this mechanism works and provides structured examples.

How Platform Channels Work

The communication happens via three main components:

- **MethodChannel**: Used to call native functions from Dart code.
- **BasicMessageChannel**: For sending and receiving raw data as strings.
- **EventChannel**: For streams or continuous data, such as sensor updates.

Here's an example structure to illustrate the communication:

1. **Dart Side**: Use `MethodChannel` to invoke platform-specific code.
2. **Native Side**: Implement the corresponding logic in Android (Kotlin/Java) or iOS (Swift/Objective-C).
3. **Message Flow**: Data flows from Dart to native code and back, enabling complex interactions.

Example: Accessing Battery Level

This example demonstrates a Flutter app fetching the device's battery level.

Dart Code:

```
//dart
import 'package:flutter/services.dart';


class BatteryLevel {
  static const platform =
MethodChannel('battery_channel');
```

```
  Future<int?> getBatteryLevel() async {
    try {
      final int batteryLevel = await
platform.invokeMethod('getBatteryLevel');
      return batteryLevel;
    } on PlatformException catch (e) {
      print("Failed to get battery level: '$
{e.message}'.");
      return null;
    }
  }
}
```

Kotlin Code (Android):

```
// kotlin
import io.flutter.embedding.engine.FlutterEngine

import io.flutter.plugin.common.MethodChannel

class MainActivity : FlutterActivity() {
    private val CHANNEL = "battery_channel"

    override fun configureFlutterEngine(flutterEngine:
FlutterEngine) {
        super.configureFlutterEngine(flutterEngine)


MethodChannel(flutterEngine.dartExecutor.binaryMessenger,
CHANNEL).setMethodCallHandler { call, result ->
            if (call.method == "getBatteryLevel") {
                val batteryLevel = getBatteryLevel()
                if (batteryLevel != -1) {
                    result.success(batteryLevel)
                } else {
                    result.error("UNAVAILABLE", "Battery
level not available.", null)
                }
            } else {
                result.notImplemented()
            }
```

```
        }
    }

    private fun getBatteryLevel(): Int {
        val batteryManager =
getSystemService(BATTERY_SERVICE) as BatteryManager
        return
batteryManager.getIntProperty(BatteryManager.BATTERY_PROPE
RTY_CAPACITY)
    }
}
```

This setup enables seamless interaction between Flutter and native code, bridging gaps that might otherwise limit your app's functionality.

Comparison with Web (HTML/JS/CSS):

In web development, accessing native hardware requires **JavaScript APIs** like:

Battery Status API:

```
//javascript
navigator.getBattery().then(battery => {
  console.log(`Battery Level: ${battery.level * 100}%`);
});
```

Flutter's **Platform Channels** achieve a similar goal but with cross-platform native code integration.

20.6 Debugging Advanced Features

Debugging is a cornerstone of software development. For advanced features in Flutter, robust debugging practices ensure the reliability and stability of applications.

Techniques for Debugging

Logging with DebugPrint: Use `debugPrint` for verbose output in debug mode.

```
//dart
debugPrint("Fetching user data...");
```

Flutter DevTools: A suite of tools for inspecting UI, performance, and network activity.

Error Handling: Encapsulate code in `try-catch` blocks for better error diagnostics.

```
//dart
try {

  var result = await fetchData();
} catch (e) {
  debugPrint("Error: $e");
}
```

Widget Inspector: Helps identify layout issues. Activate it in the **Flutter DevTools** UI.

Debugging Asynchronous Code

Handling `Future` and `Stream` can introduce subtle bugs. Use these tips:

- Always await asynchronous calls.
- Use the `Future.error` and `Future.timeout` methods to simulate scenarios.

```
//dart
Future<int> fetchUserData() async {
  await Future.delayed(Duration(seconds: 3)); //
Simulating delay
  return 42; // Sample data
}
```

Debugging Platform Channel Errors

Verify these areas:

1. Channel name mismatch between Dart and native code.
2. Platform-side logic errors (e.g., missing permissions).

20.7 Optimizing App Performance

Performance optimization is critical, especially for complex Flutter apps. This section highlights key strategies.

Reduce Widget Rebuilds

Use efficient state management techniques:

- Prefer `Provider` or `Riverpod` for scalability.
- Wrap widgets with `const` to prevent unnecessary rebuilds.

Lazy Loading

Defer the creation of expensive resources until necessary:

Example:

```
//dart
final items = List.generate(1000, (index) => "Item
$index");
ListView.builder(
  itemCount: items.length,
  itemBuilder: (context, index) {
    return ListTile(title: Text(items[index]));
  },
);
```

Optimize Animations

Use `ImplicitlyAnimatedWidgets` or the `flutter_rive` package for smooth animations.

20.8 Final Project: A Complete Web-to-Flutter App

In this final project, the goal is to transform a **web-based app** into a fully functional Flutter app. This demonstrates advanced concepts covered in this chapter.

Project Overview

Web App Features:

- User authentication.
- Interactive dashboard.

- Dynamic data visualization.

Flutter Equivalent:

- `firebase_auth` for authentication.
- `fl_chart` for visualizations.

Step-by-Step Workflow

Authentication: Migrate web-based OAuth2 to Flutter using `google_sign_in` or `flutter_facebook_auth`.

Responsive UI: Replace CSS media queries with Flutter's `LayoutBuilder` and `MediaQuery`.

```
//dart
LayoutBuilder(

  builder: (context, constraints) {
    if (constraints.maxWidth > 600) {
      return TabletLayout();
    } else {
      return MobileLayout();
    }
  },
);
```

Interactive Charts: Compare web's Chart.js to Flutter's `fl_chart`:

```
//dart
LineChart(

  LineChartData(
    lineBarsData: [
      LineChartBarData(
        spots: [
          FlSpot(0, 1),
```

```
          FlSpot(1, 3),
          FlSpot(2, 2),
        ],
      ),
    ],
  ),
);
```

- **Backend Integration**: Use `http` or `dio` packages for API calls.
- **Deployment**: Deploy the final app using tools like Firebase Hosting or custom CI/CD pipelines.

Key Tips for the Final Project:

- Modularize your code for scalability.
- Use analytics tools like Firebase to track user behavior.
- Test thoroughly across devices.

Examples

Implementing Dependency Injection with Provider

```
//dart
import 'package:flutter/material.dart';

import 'package:provider/provider.dart';

class ApiService {
  String fetchData() => 'Fetched Data';
}

void main() {
  runApp(
    MultiProvider(
      providers: [
        Provider(create: (_) => ApiService()),
      ],
      child: MyApp(),
    ),
  );
```

```
}

class MyApp extends StatelessWidget {
  @override
  Widget build(BuildContext context) {
    final apiService = Provider.of<ApiService>(context);
    return MaterialApp(
      home: Scaffold(
        appBar: AppBar(title: Text('DI in Flutter')),
        body: Center(child: Text(apiService.fetchData())),
      ),
    );
  }
}
```

Using Isolates for Background Task in Flutter

```
//dart
import 'dart:async';

import 'dart:isolate';

Future<void> fetchData() async {
  final receivePort = ReceivePort();
  await Isolate.spawn(computeExpensiveTask,
receivePort.sendPort);
  receivePort.listen((data) {
    print('Received data: $data');
  });
}

void computeExpensiveTask(SendPort sendPort) {
  // Simulating an expensive task
  Future.delayed(Duration(seconds: 3), () {
    sendPort.send('Task Completed');
  });
}
```

Advanced Animation with CustomPainter

```
//dart
import 'package:flutter/material.dart';


void main() {
  runApp(MaterialApp(home: CustomPaintDemo()));
}

class CustomPaintDemo extends StatelessWidget {
  @override
  Widget build(BuildContext context) {
    return Scaffold(
      appBar: AppBar(title: Text('Custom Painter
Example')),
      body: Center(
        child: CustomPaint(
          size: Size(300, 300),
          painter: CirclePainter(),
        ),
      ),
    );
  }
}

class CirclePainter extends CustomPainter {
  @override
  void paint(Canvas canvas, Size size) {
    final paint = Paint()
      ..color = Colors.blue
      ..style = PaintingStyle.fill;
    canvas.drawCircle(Offset(size.width / 2, size.height /
2), 100, paint);
  }

  @override
  bool shouldRepaint(covariant CustomPainter oldDelegate)
{
    return false;
  }
}
```

Building a Plugin to Access Device Features (Platform Channels)

Dart Side:

```
//dart
import 'package:flutter/services.dart';

class DeviceInfo {
  static const platform =
MethodChannel('device_info_channel');

  Future<String> getDeviceInfo() async {
    try {
      final String deviceInfo = await
platform.invokeMethod('getDeviceInfo');
      return deviceInfo;
    } on PlatformException catch (e) {
      return "Failed to get device info: ${e.message}";
    }
  }
}
```

Kotlin Side:

```
// kotlin
class MainActivity: FlutterActivity() {
  private val CHANNEL = "device_info_channel"

  override fun configureFlutterEngine(flutterEngine:
FlutterEngine) {
    super.configureFlutterEngine(flutterEngine)

MethodChannel(flutterEngine.dartExecutor.binaryMessenger,
CHANNEL).setMethodCallHandler { call, result ->
      if (call.method == "getDeviceInfo") {
        val deviceInfo = getDeviceInfo()
        result.success(deviceInfo)
      } else {
        result.notImplemented()
      }
    }
  }
```

```
  private fun getDeviceInfo(): String {
    return "Device: ${Build.MODEL}, Version: $
{Build.VERSION.RELEASE}"
  }
}
```

Tips

- **Use `const` Constructors for Better Performance**: Where possible, use `const` constructors for widgets. This avoids unnecessary widget rebuilding, enhancing the app's performance.
- **Leverage `Riverpod` or `Provider` for Effective State Management**: These libraries are optimized for scalability and help in managing complex states and dependencies in larger apps.
- **Prioritize `ListView.builder` for Large Lists**: When dealing with large sets of data in lists, always use `ListView.builder` over `ListView`. The builder approach lazily loads items, reducing memory usage and improving performance.

Actionable Strategies

- **Optimize Asynchronous Operations**: Whenever possible, minimize blocking the main thread in Flutter by utilizing isolates and asynchronous operations. Isolates help offload intensive tasks from the main thread, ensuring the UI remains smooth even during heavy computations.
- **Efficient Widget Rebuilding**: Ensure widgets are only rebuilt when absolutely necessary. Use the `shouldRebuild` method or `const` widgets to optimize performance. In cases where widget rebuilding becomes an issue, consider using `Provider` or `Riverpod` for better state management, which minimizes unnecessary rebuilds.
- **Leverage Flutter's Rendering Pipeline for Custom Animations**: For custom animations, Flutter's rendering pipeline can be fully controlled through `CustomPainter`. This allows for complex animations that are drawn directly on the canvas, offering great flexibility and performance.
- **Use Dependency Injection for Modular Code**: Organizing your app using

Dependency Injection (DI) promotes scalability and testability. Implement DI patterns with libraries like `Provider` or `get_it` for better separation of concerns in your Flutter code.

- **Optimize Image Loading**: Use `CachedNetworkImage` or similar packages to cache images when possible, reducing loading times and preventing unnecessary network requests. This can significantly improve the user experience, especially in apps where images are frequently loaded from the internet.

This detailed explanation includes **examples, tips,** and **actionable strategies** to deepen the understanding of **Advanced Flutter Concepts**. These suggestions provide practical guidance and coding implementations for developers looking to master Flutter's advanced features.

List of Recommended Books to Read:

Checkout All My Books
https://www.amazon.com/stores/author/B0BHF5T1V7/allbooks

ChatGPT for Authors and Writers Books
ChatGPT Secret Weapon: 5 Steps to Start Writing and Selling Books within 24 Hours
https://amazon.com/dp/B0BV6TQL55

The Future of Writing and Selling Books: A Guide to ChatGPT-3 AI Technology
https://www.amazon.com/dp/B0BTWVXFFS

How to Get Rich with ChatGPT and Amazon KDP: Unlocking the Power of AI and Self-Publishing to Grow Your Wealth
https://www.amazon.com/gp/product/B0C398P8RW

ChatGPT's 2000+ Low-Content Book Ideas: Designing, Marketing Tactics and Proven Strategies to Sell Fast
https://amazon.com/dp/B0BYXVQY7Q

Unleashing the Power of Amazon Kindle: How to Sellur First 1000 Copies &Get Reviews Without Breaking a Sweat Earn $1k-$20k/Mon -ChatGPT
https://www.amazon.com/dp/B0BX6K1TJN

$100 Million Ideas Books
Build a $100 Million Empire: The Power of Intellectual Property: Leveraging Patents, Copyrights, and Trademarks
https://www.amazon.com/gp/product/B0C4LH5L1L

From Side Hustle to $100 Million: Building a Successful Business While Keeping Your Day Job
https://www.amazon.com/dp/B0C4PWPWFS

Freelancing Books
ChatGPT with Fiverr and Upwork: 30 Freelancing Job you can Start Immediately using ChatGPT to Generate Ideas and Content for your Clients
https://www.amazon.com/dp/B0C42JXBRC

GumRoad and Social Media Marketing Books
GumRoad Mastery Self-Publishing: Boosting Sales and Building Audience for Your Book Ultimate Guide
https://www.amazon.com/dp/B0C1QWZL5B

ChatGPT, YouTube &GumRoad: Beginner's Guide to Monetizing, Building an Engaged Audience and Sell Products
https://www.amazon.com/dp/B0C1ZXDGS2

ChatGPT, Facebook &GumRoad: Beginner's Guide to Monetizing, Building an Engaged Audience and Sell Products
https://www.amazon.com/dp/B0C1MC4JBH

AI Video Creators Books
Get Started with Pictory AI Video Creation: The Beginner Cookbook
https://amazon.com/dp/B0BYB6QFY1

App Ideas and Development Books
App Ideas for the Future; The Next Big Thing: Ultimate Thousands of App Ideas Handbook
https://www.amazon.com/dp/B0BT8NKYNQ

Social Media Books
ChatGPT + YouTube Channel or Real Estate: How to Make $10,000-$50,000 Monthly with Your YouTube Channel and ChatGPT
https://amazon.com/dp/B0BVCQBBXY

Still Dismissing TikTok as Something for the kids? : Short-form video content created by ChatGPT is exploding right now!
https://amazon.com/dp/B0BWQZ92BH

ChatGPT Millionaire's Books
ChatGPT Millionaire's Ideas: 230+ Ways to Use ChatGPT and Other Hidden Secret Information
https://www.amazon.com/dp/B0BW85S76R

Zero to Millionaire Online: ChatGPT + Facebook: Making Millions on Social Media - Step-by-Step Guide, How to Make Money Online
https://www.amazon.com/gp/product/B0BXYBWJW8

Zero to Millionaire Online: ChatGPT + Blogging: Build your own (WordPress) Website within 24 Hours - Step-by-Step Guide, How to Make Money Online
https://www.amazon.com/gp/product/B0BXY9W6P8

Zero to Millionaire Online: ChatGPT + eCommerce: Create & set up your own Online Store: Generate Product Descriptions, SEO Ranking, Making Money Online
https://www.amazon.com/gp/product/B0BXY6NX3J

Zero to Millionaire Online: ChatGPT + Affiliate Marketing: How to Make Money Online without any Products or Service
https://www.amazon.com/dp/B0BY38K3WV

Personal Development, Success and Financial Mindset Books
The 4 Pillars of Wealth Creation
https://www.amazon.com/dp/B0BKYH7ZTG

REPEAT AFTER ME; I AM A MILLIONAIRE: THE SECRET OF THE MILLIONAIRES
https://www.amazon.com/dp/B0BNLXGYYV

The Mindset of Financial Planning: Make it, Manage it, and Invest it - the Beginner Guide to Financial Freedom
https://www.amazon.com/dp/B0BWLWXD3S

Time Management Books
The Power of Planning: Achieving Your Goals Through Strategic Action
https://www.amazon.com/dp/B0BTGT58F2

Conquering Distraction: Mastering Time Management for Success
https://www.amazon.com/dp/B0BTGT7MHB

From Chaos to Control: Strategic Planner for Busy Professionals/CEO: A Guide for Planning and Productivity
https://www.amazon.com/dp/B0C83W7MSC

Psychologies Books
The Psychology of Writing: Overcoming Writer's Block and Finding Your Voice
https://www.amazon.com/dp/B0C1X83FWX

The Psychology of Leadership: Mastering the Art of Influence
https://www.amazon.com/dp/B0C3SL4ZXR

The Psychology of Greatness: How to Unlock Your Full Potential
https://www.amazon.com/dp/B0C5JRH894

The Psychology of Sales: Mastering the Art of Persuasion
https://www.amazon.com/dp/B0C3Y13RHR

The Power of Positive Thinking: Harnessing the Psychology of Success
https://www.amazon.com/dp/B0C692B11F

The Psychology of Reading: How to Read More and Retain More
https://www.amazon.com/dp/B0C3829WZX

Notebooks & Journals
Lined Journal Notebook: Writing Note Book 8.5inched x 11inches
https://www.amazon.com/dp/B0BQ99KTT5

Planner 2024 Yearly Monthly Weekly Organizer for Students, Men and Women's Planning, Time Management Notebook with Goals, To-Do List, and Notes | 8.5" x 11" | 154 Pages | Blue
https://www.amazon.com/dp/B0CHCWPPSR

Blank 12 Months Calendar, Yearly, Monthly and Weekly Planner for men and women, Monthly and Weekly Goals, To Do List and Notes
https://www.amazon.com/dp/B0BR9J8QXW

www.ingramcontent.com/pod-product-compliance
Lightning Source LLC
LaVergne TN
LVHW072121210926
848482LV00028B/711